AF621088

ALSO BY SEAN FEAST

Gestapo Hunter, 9781911714118 (2024) *
Halton Boys, 9781911621942 (2020)

Available in eBook format only
An Alien Sky, 9781910690840 (2015)
Churchill's Navigator, 9781908117946 (2010)
The Last of the 39-ers, 9781909808553 (2013)
Master Bombers, 9781909166981 (2010)
A Pathfinder's War, 9781909166714 (2009)
The Pathfinder Companion, 9781909808829 (2012)

* Audiobook available

AIRMAN, PRISONER, SAVIOUR, SPY

AIRMAN, PRISONER, SAVIOUR, SPY

The Remarkable Story of Squadron Leader Stanley Booker MBE,

Buchenwald Survivor and Cold War Spy

SEAN FEAST

Foreword by John Nichol

GRUB STREET • LONDON

Published by Grub Street
4 Rainham Close
London SW11 6SS

Copyright © Grub Street 2026
Copyright text © Sean Feast 2026

A CIP record for this title is available from the British Library.

ISBN 978-1-911714-37-8

All rights reserved. No part of this publication may be reproduced, stored in a retrieval system, or transmitted in any form or by any means electronic, mechanical, photocopying, recording or otherwise, without the prior permission of the copyright owner. No part of this book may be used or reproduced in any manner for the purpose of training artificial intelligence technologies or systems.

Design by Myriam Bell Design, UK

Printed and bound by Finidr, Czechia

DEDICATION

This book is dedicated to the memory of the countless numbers of innocent civilians of the occupied countries, who took such great risks and personal sacrifices to protect and support the Allied forces in their time of great need. Also, to the individuals who helped me personally throughout my own journey – you risked so very much, and without your courage and bravery I may never have returned.

My thanks go to Sean Feast, whose writing has brought my story to a younger generation and to my grandchildren and great-grandchildren, who brought light and love into my world of shadows: Emma, Claire, Kieran, Ava and Isla, Chris, Jo and Sennen.

Stanley Booker, January 2025.

Stanley before being shot down

CONTENTS

ACKNOWLEDGEMENTS

WHILE I AM THE AUTHOR of this book, none of it would have been possible without the tireless help and support of Stanley's daughter, Pat.

As the custodian of her father's memory, and of his quest for justice, peace and reconciliation that spanned more than eight decades, Pat has curated an immense archive of material from which I have been able to tell Stanley's story and place his life and achievements in the context of the times in which he lived. It is to Pat, her splendid husband Keith and their lovely family that I owe an enormous debt of gratitude for introducing me to Stan, and for the two years of writing and additional research that has finally led us to this moment. I have enjoyed every minute and hope between us we have done Stanley proud.

Pat's passion and commitment enabled me to meet or engage with an amazing cast of characters including, but not limited to, Jean-Pierre Curato, Paul McCue, Martin Phelps, Graham Booker, Gary Clarke, and Rob Culverhouse, all of whom have contributed to Stanley's story. I am also most grateful once again to Nick Dexter for helping me navigate my way around the National Archives on this, our second sortie, and to John Nichol, retired RAF navigator and prolific author, who graciously agreed to write the foreword. I could not imagine anyone better placed in the modern age to have at least some understanding of Stanley's experience.

My personal thanks go to that remarkable man John Davies and his splendid team at Grub Street Publishing for this, our ninth book together. It was John who more than twenty years ago published my first ever title in hardback, and he continues to be the 'William Kimber' of his generation, publishing outstanding books that will grace the shelves of discerning aviation enthusiasts for many decades to come.

I beat John to retirement from 'the day job' but would still like to publicly thank my now former work friends at Gravity Global – Iona Yadallee, Imogen K. Hart and Rob Howard – for just being who they are and three of the loveliest people on the planet. Hopefully that also guarantees three more sales, and a fourth if I mention the incomparable Vicky Hendry, my PA extraordinaire who made the last ten years at work such fun. How I already miss them all more than they realise. As well as the Thursday drinks trolley.

Finally, last but never least, my thanks and love to the genius that is my wife, Elaine, who is thrilled to have me at home full-time (!). With the two boys Matt and James now all grown up and fledged, we're spending their inheritance just as fast as we can, while keeping a little back to invest in more research and travel for future book-writing projects. There are still plenty more stories waiting to be told...

Sean Feast
Sarratt, December 2025.

FOREWORD

Stanley Booker volunteered for aircrew at the age of 18 and qualified as an observer, flying operations with 10 Squadron in the summer of 1944. Shot down just before D-Day, and after several weeks on the run, he was betrayed to the Gestapo and imprisoned in Fresnes, the notorious gaol on the outskirts of Paris, where he was subjected to a brutal interrogation and torture at the hands of the SS. His experiences troubled him for the rest of his life.

Rather than being treated as a prisoner of war, Stanley was one of 168 airmen transported to Buchenwald concentration camp to await execution as 'terror flyers', only to be saved at the eleventh hour by the intervention of the Luftwaffe. On his ultimate return to England, no one wanted to believe where he had been or what he had seen. So began an 80-year battle with the authorities to prove what had happened, and to receive the recognition he and his fellow prisoners were due, as well as ensuring those servicemen who had died or were murdered in the camp were properly commemorated.

After the war, Stanley flew more than two hundred operations during the Berlin airlift, aiding a nation which only a few years earlier had been intent on his elimination. He was later recruited by intelligence agencies in Berlin at the height of the Cold War, and suffered another betrayal, this time at the hands of the traitor George Blake.

Stanley Booker's extraordinary story is painstakingly researched and sympathetically written, providing a remarkable account of individual service and sacrifice. Even though I was shot down myself during the Gulf War in 1991, held as a prisoner of war by hostile captors, I can only begin to imagine the terrible suffering Stanley had to endure, and I marvel at his fortitude as a survivor who died in January 2025, still fighting for justice, at the remarkable age of 102.

John Nichol, former RAF navigator
and author of *TORNADO: In the Eye of the Storm*
(Simon & Schuster, 2021)

CHAPTER ONE

BOMBER BOY

"IF YOU ARE SHOT DOWN – bury your parachute; move away from the area and contact the local Resistance. Find a Catholic priest or a madame of a brothel, who should be able to help you."

Twenty-one-year-old Stanley Booker listened to the words in companionable silence with a group of other young men who formed part of his bomber crew. It was the early autumn of 1943 at an operational training unit (OTU) in Oxfordshire. They were paying close attention to an intelligence lecture on escape and evasion given by a fellow officer who had learned the hard way what it was like to be shot down, on the run, and captured by the Germans. Remarkably he had escaped and made it home and had now been pressed into service by MI9, the British government's intelligence agency tasked with aiding escape and evasion, to talk about his adventures so others could benefit from his experience.

The officer in question, Flight Lieutenant Eric Williams, deserved the respect of the men in the room. A navigator by trade, he'd been shot down in December 1942 and evaded capture for three days before his luck finally gave out. Imprisoned first at Oflag XXI-B in Poland, he escaped, was recaptured and sent to Stalag Luft III in Sagan from where he escaped again, one of the three participants in the famous episode later recounted as the 'Wooden Horse'.[1]

Stanley looked around at his companions and wondered how they would fare if faced with the ultimate challenge. He also considered how little he really knew about the four other men with whom he was now entrusting his life.

Aside from Stanley, the pilot, Alexander 'Sandy' Murray, was the only other officer in the crew. The rest were non-commissioned officers (NCOs). Sandy was only a year older but had significantly more experience, having logged more than one thousand hours flying Blenheim twin-engine bombers earlier in the war, as a staff pilot at a bombing and gunnery school. He was Stanley's closest friend and had a girlfriend on the base. John 'Taffy' Williams, the wireless operator, was also a thing of wonder, for he already had a tour of operations under his belt. Bomber Command crews at that time, all volunteers, flew a first tour of 30 operations and a second of 20, with a six-month 'rest' in between.[2] Taffy's 'rest' had been spent instructing at a signals training school. Now he was going back through the loop of aircrew training to prepare for a second turn in the ring.

Sergeants Ernest 'Snooky' Stokes and Terry Gould completed the crew as air bomber and rear gunner respectively. Snooky had been an optician on 'civvy street' and had recently been interviewed for a commission. Terry was another Welshman, from Caerphilly, who'd trained as a master butcher before enlisting in the RAF as far back as the summer of 1940. Terry was considered the 'lucky' man of the crew. Stanley hoped he had enough luck to go around.

As the navigator, Stanley had gone through the usual aircrew selection and training, albeit he had something of an advantage over his friends. Born on 25 April 1922 in Gillingham to Bert and Lilian, and a proud Kentish man, Stanley had joined the RAF before the war as an apprentice clerk (part of the 55th Entry[3]) and despite investing five shillings of his own money to buy a Pitman's shorthand pen, noted that he never got to use the pen in anger:

> *"We never took a final shorthand exam and never once in the years that followed, when I was in the orderly room before going off to aircrew training, was I ever called upon to do any shorthand. Days were filled with drill, service tradecraft, lots of PT and professional typing – all very useful later."*

The military had always been something of a passion of his, and as an adventure-seeking child, he'd grown up exploring the seaplane and flying-boat bases along the River Medway with four of his friends, watching the comings and goings of Royal Navy warships into and out of Chatham dockyards. Stanley's father was a senior musician in the Royal Engineers' staff band, and Chatham was home to the RE's main depot, with its school of engineering, a magnificent museum and vast exercise grounds upon which bridges were both built and demolished in accordance with every schoolboy's dream. Saturdays, in Stanley's opinion, could never come quickly enough, and when he wasn't outside playing his head could often be found inside a book. His heroes from the First World War were the tunnellers of Holzminden – a famous tale of 29 officers who made a bid for freedom from a prisoner-of-war camp in Germany. One day, perhaps, he meant to emulate their daring:

> "We had *little money, but we had a tremendous sense of freedom and of adventure. On our precious bicycles, with a few pennies in our pockets, a packet of wholesome but unexciting sandwiches in our packs, almost every weekend was something special, a whole world out there to explore, secrets to unfold.*"

Being so close to the Shorts aircraft factory, it was little wonder that aircraft would feature prominently in Stanley's life. He distinctly recalls seeing the half-scale version of the Short Stirling, the RAF's first four-engined bomber, long before news of the aircraft's existence was ever officially released. He remembers also the thrill of seeing the mighty Short Sunderland, with its distinctive retractable gun turret and depth charges that would be rolled out on racks from beneath its wing roots.

Each morning at exactly 0745 hrs a Lufthansa Junkers 52 would pass over his head on its scheduled flight, and Stanley and his friends would imagine its real purpose of intelligence gathering, for since the Munich crisis the old town's fortifications had found a modern purpose with new searchlight and anti-aircraft batteries in preparation for the anticipated war with Germany. The boys would regularly scout the new defensive line, checking, noting, recording:

> "We *knew exactly where every single AA and coastal gun was emplaced, its calibre and where its ammunition was stored. Our treasured Ordnance Survey map was earmarked with every conceivable military establishment, gun pit, searchlight site and practice landing grounds in a 30-mile radius of home. We had no fear of the Official Secrets Act because we never knew it existed!*"[4]

A bright, inquisitive boy, he'd won a scholarship to the fee-paying Gillingham Grammar School for Boys and passed every examination with ease. Among the many subjects he studied, he left with a passable knowledge of German. He also breezed through his apprenticeship exams and was justifiably proud of the apprentice's 'wheel' that he wore on his sleeve. When his apprenticeship had started, they were held in comparatively low regard by their peers, certainly compared to the 'real' apprentices at RAF Halton with whom they enjoyed an ongoing rivalry. Now, with the country at war, the whole concept of apprentices changed overnight:

> *"With Records Office suddenly too overstretched to cope, we became accepted, appreciated members of a new office routine. Whole new sections were opened with specific functions such as casualty records, overseas drafting, training cadres etc. and a sprinkling of old warrant officers was recalled to take charge."*

When given a 'preference of posting' chit, Stanley put RAF Detling or HQ 16 Group, near his home town. The Air Ministry, however, had other ideas. Posted initially to RAF Worksop, only to be told there was no such place (the station was still in development and on the secret list), he arrived at Netherthorpe in Yorkshire, previously home to the Sheffield Aero Club and now occupied by 613 City of Manchester Auxiliary Squadron. It was 29 June 1940.

Sometimes unfairly overlooked as mere 'weekend flyers', characterised by the hotchpotch assembly of aircraft – Westland Lysanders, Hawker Hectors and a single Miles Magister – 613 had only recently been fighting in France where they had shown immense courage, dive-bombing enemy gun positions.[5] Neither the Lysander, a high-winged monoplane, nor the Hector, a biplane, were especially suited to a modern war, but nonetheless played their part in holding the German onslaught at bay and buying British ground troops precious time to withdraw.[6]

With its fair share of eccentrics, Stanley immediately fitted in with the squadron's carefree existence and impressed the squadron commander with his organisational abilities in setting up the orderly room, so much so that when the squadron received orders to move, he was asked to go with them. It seemed that the recently appointed wing commander, John Stephenson,[7] and Stanley, an aircraftman first class (AC1), were the only two 'regulars'. Stephenson had also started out as an apprentice; in the wingco's mind, therefore, they were the only two who could be trusted.

"It was the ideal working community; relaxed. Fixed day/night working hours didn't come into the question, the weather was delightful, the countryside also tranquil and peaceful. The war seemed to have passed us by."

Since returning from France, the squadron had moved north to re-equip with Lysander IIs which had a more powerful Bristol Perseus XII engine. They were away from the action and relegated to long and usually uneventful reconnaissance patrols along the east coast, from Donna Nook on the north Lincolnshire coast down to the Wash. They also practised spraying gas on 'enemy' troops; desperate times call for desperate measures, and 613 Squadron's responsibilities, come the invasion, included protecting the beaches with mustard gas.[8]

Stanley's first impressions of Netherthorpe, the squadron and its aircrew were that they were friendly and relaxed:

"When I arrived, the little airfield was completely unguarded, with a small tent at the entrance with a duty airman being the only obvious occupant. In no time, however, he had summoned the duty sergeant who escorted me across the open airfield to a cluster of bell tents which apparently was where the new main domestic site was to be. There were no electric lights to be seen, just the odd airman carrying a hurricane lamp, and I was left at a small marquee that served as the mess hall where a very cheerful cook soon turned up and made me a massive pan of delicious bacon, eggs and fried bread.

"The duty NCO soon returned and allocated me to an empty tent which had but a groundsheet, a heap of rough blankets and a straw-filled palliasse. There were no coat hangers and not even a hook on the tent pole to hang my best uniform. We had austerity at Ruislip but it was three-star compared with this new-found home. After a restless night I found an ablution site in a hedge with a water bowser and a row of bowls and a couple of mirrors. Cold water was never a problem as our barrack huts never had the luxury of hot water. Somehow I was able to present myself in best blue and a pair of highly polished boots at the flying club building where there was a welcome RAF ensign being flown. Clearly this was the station headquarters (SHQ) and orderly room. I had arrived."

Stanley enjoyed his time with 613 so much that he followed the squadron to Firbeck, 15 miles further north, when it moved on 7 September 1940.

"It soon became obvious that when the weather broke the small airfield site would be unsuitable. The lack of hard surface or even tracks soon became obvious from the air when the ground was churned up with the rain and the overall landing strip was too small. This was soon appreciated when one of the pilots made a low approach and overturned when the huge fixed undercarriage of his Lysander hit the top of the solid hedge, and a very distressing fatality occurred which shook us all rather badly, especially given the absence of any crash crane to lift the heavy radial engine and free the occupants."

The accident Stanley refers to didn't quite happen as he remembers, although the outcome was just the same. It occurred the day before they were due to leave, as one of the squadron's most experienced pilots, Flying Officer Grosvenor Edwards, was coming in to land. Somehow Edwards failed to see a lorry which was not where it should have been, and his undercarriage clipped the top of the vehicle, cartwheeled and burst into flames. The gunner crawled out, but his pilot was trapped inside and had to be dragged free by two airmen. He was admitted to hospital but later died, the squadron's first fatal casualty of the war. His two rescuers, who as well as the flames had to overcome the risk of exploding ammunition, were awarded the George Medal.[9]

Firbeck, though small, was a step-up from Netherthorpe:

"Firbeck had a proper smallish hangar and workshop, and a comfortable clubhouse that was taken over as the orderly room. The main attraction was the nearby country house, and we were allotted the huge stone stable block with wooden bunks and warm water of sorts."

Juggling service life with his love life, meanwhile, proved something of a challenge, for Stanley was now very much besotted with a nurse, Marjorie Champney, three years his senior, who would shortly become his wife. They'd met at Rotherham General Hospital when Stanley was being treated for a skin condition brought on by a combination of rough serge uniforms and a life lived under canvas.

Marjorie's job at the hospital was all-consuming. She was a diligent student, and their paths rarely crossed. It led to petty jealousies and squabbles, typically illustrated in a letter from Stanley to Marjorie on 19 January 1941 and written in great haste:

> "You've no idea what trouble I have to go through up here to get the same day off as you. It's not just a matter of asking the other chaps to swap but there's the flight sergeant and the adjutant to approach who, believe me, are not very understanding as to why I should have to alter my day. Every day is the same to them and they have no personal feelings for us. I mustn't forget that if it hadn't been for the hospital we should never have come together should we dear? So we must be thankful for that if nothing else."[10]

Stanley and the squadron were constantly on the move, working in conjunction with their army colleagues, often billeted at opposite ends of the country.

> "Our first year had been one of gradual improvement and practice. Local exercises gradually expanded to major national movements, involving maximum deployment of the entire squadron in its full mobile role, often as far away as Dartmoor or Salisbury Plain. It's no easy matter to assemble a complex convoy of thirty to forty specialist vehicles of various types, with complete self-sufficiency in fuel, essential aircraft spares, rations, complex signals etc. It was an extremely interesting and variable role, so completely at variance to normal routine station administration for which we had been trained in the pre-war pattern."

The weekend flyers and their airmen were not always greeted with enthusiasm by their 'regular' colleagues:

> "We arrived at Andover after a tedious two-day journey in convoy. After establishing ourselves in our allotted muddy perimeter site, and camouflaging our vehicles, we made our way over to the station mess hall only to be advised by a rather officious senior NCO that it was shut and that we were improperly dressed. Muddy wellies were not acceptable."

It took the intervention of their fatherly warrant officer (discipline) for the situation to be resolved. They were admitted, and a suitable meal provided, albeit grudgingly:

> "It was an experience that stayed in our memories long after we returned back to Firbeck. We began to count our blessings and grew to accept that we really weren't in the 'real' air force!"

In the summer of 1941, orders were received for a further planned move to Doncaster, to commence on 7 July 1941. The role of the squadron was evolving again with the promised arrival of P40 Tomahawks to replace the ageing Lysanders – but still in an army co-operation/tactical reconnaissance role. The squadron also had a new CO, Wing Commander Viscount Acheson, the 6th Earl of Gosford, who officially took command on 16 June.

Doncaster had the advantage of being a permanent airfield adjoining the racecourse. The former Imperial Airways control tower was immediately requisitioned by the CO for his HQ and orderly room, while the racecourse buildings were occupied by the airmen and aircrew, all delighted with the abundance of lavatories and washroom facilities.

It was in Doncaster, while the squadron pilots were getting to grips with the first of their new aircraft,[11] that instructions finally arrived for Stanley to attend an aircrew selection board interview. It meant travelling to London to assemble with hundreds of others at the aircrew receiving centre (ACRC) at Lord's cricket ground:

> *"I had the tremendous advantage of having been a pre-war regular serviceman and having complete confidence at interview from the experience of serving with 613 Squadron whose very understanding wing commander, aware of my ambitions to become a pilot, had given me every opportunity to fly in the back of his Lysander – from which I gained valuable practical air experience of map reading, meteorology and the essential practical handling and firing of the Vickers K machine gun."*[12]

Stanley's ambition to become a pilot was cut short owing to a minor eye defect. Being a bright boy, however, the authorities believed he would be wasted as an air gunner, and he was instead recommended for training as an air observer/navigator. Rather than being sent overseas, where an entire training infrastructure had been created as part of the British Commonwealth Air Training Plan, Stanley had other ideas. Having successfully completed his elementary navigation training at RAF Bridgnorth in Shropshire (at 1 EANS – elementary air navigation school), he wangled himself a place at one of the RAF's few remaining air observer schools (AOS) still operating in the UK. He perfected his craft in north Wales at 9 AOS at RAF Penrhos and 9 (Observer) Advanced Flying Unit at RAF Llandwrog, and remembers it mainly for the cold:

"The winter in north Wales was cruel and challenging, the weather often overcast and wet. The surrounding mountain ranges made me very conscious of the dangers of low flying, and the safety of our aircraft was foremost in our minds. To survive we learned the hard way, we had no navigation aids; there were permanent blackouts over the entire UK; barrage balloons and air raids presented the trainee navigators with numerous challenges, and joint exercises with the Royal Navy over the turbulent Irish Sea enhanced our training."

From north Wales Stanley progressed to RAF Cranage near Middlewich in Cheshire, for a three-month staff navigation and instructors' course. Having been rated 'above average' and commended for his 'neat work', Stanley had clearly impressed his peers. Flying with a number of different British and Polish NCOs, it was here that he was introduced to 'Gee', a primitive navigational aid that he nonetheless described as "a navigator's dream tool". Simple to use, this magic box of tricks could give an accurate fix on an aircraft's position. While it never quite achieved the accuracy its inventors envisaged, it was still a godsend for navigators who had previously relied on a compass and the stars, but little else. It was also at Cranage, having graduated top of the class, that Stanley was commissioned as a pilot officer, without ever once attending any kind of officer-training establishment. He left at the end of August 1943, on a posting to 10 OTU at Abingdon.

Stanley had joined a crew at the OTU in the way that everyone formed a crew in those days. Men were assembled in a hangar and told to sort themselves out over tea and sandwiches. Pilots might typically start by finding a navigator and then look for an air bomber and so forth. Occasionally, men might have already served with one another or simply had the same accent or came from the same town. They may have just been fellow smokers who hung out together. It was random, but it worked:

"You all had your flying logbook with everything recorded. If you'd been flying since the beginning of the war, your logbook might be fairly thick. If you had just started, then it might only have a few pages. So if you saw someone with a thicker logbook, like our wireless operator who had already completed a tour in Wellingtons, you knew he was an 'oldie' and were immediately drawn to him."

At the OTU crews were divided into flights, one flight remaining at Abingdon with its comfortable, well-laid-out accommodation and the other at Stanton Harcourt which was a little more primitive. At both airfields they flew the Armstrong Whitworth Whitley, a sturdy warhorse with two engines and a distinctive nose-down gait which one contemporary described as looking like it was "sniffing the ground".[13] The Whitley had been the mainstay of Bomber Command in the early stages of the war but was now being steadily removed from front-line service, other than for Coastal Command and certain theatres of war where any working aircraft were welcome.

Stanley first flew with Sandy on 19 October 1943, and aside from a cross-country with a Flying Officer Chinnell halfway through the course, flew with no other captains. The crew were instructed together, both on the ground and in the air, with long-distance cross-countries and practice bombing exercises in preparation for the real thing. They were not without their dangers. On one night, a fellow crew was lost when its aircraft exploded for no apparent reason. Accidents were common, and though not always fatal, inexperienced crews flying aircraft well past their sell-by dates were often dangerous concoctions.

Negotiating their way through the course had not been without its challenges. They qualified, however, after successfully completing a six-hour sortie to Paris (known as a 'nickel') where they dropped propaganda leaflets, rather than bombs, on 5 December 1943. Ten days later, Stanley's logbook was signed by the officer commanding C Flight, and endorsed by the chief instructor, Wing Commander Alfred Ogilvie, at the start of the New Year.[14]

Their final test before progressing to a heavy conversion unit (HCU) was an exercise at the dreaded aircrew survival and escape school at Driffield in Yorkshire. Unlike at Abingdon – with its comfortable officers' and sergeants' messes – Stanley and his crew were to spend two weeks living in a vast, windswept airmen's barrack block. They were each issued with a set of shapeless rough denim overalls, a pair of gumboots and an elderly Ross rifle, a relic from the First World War that didn't work especially well even then!

> *"We were put through our paces under the most atrocious cold east coast Yorkshire winter weather, enduring the commando-style obstacle courses, route marches, tactical field assault training, concealment and unarmed combat. We, as rather cosseted airmen, did not appreciate being shouted at and having to spend hours concealed in frozen muddy ditches. After*

each day's torments we had to take our mud-encrusted rifles back to the barrack block and clean our guns ready for inspection by our eagle-eyed NCO trainer."

The ultimate challenge was the 48-hour escape-and-evasion exercise, which restored the crew's sense of humour and ability to beat the system:

"Each crew was loaded into a closed lorry and driven to various isolated places near the east coast; it was a dark and drizzly night, and the wild terrain was devoid of signposts. We assessed the landscape and calculated that we had been dropped near the inhospitable Hornsey Marshes. Officially we had no money, no maps nor any special protective clothing; we had been instructed to make our way back to our base at RAF Driffield – undetected by the police, Home Guard or members of the RAF regiment (whom we called rather rudely 'the Rock Apes') who patrolled the perimeter of the airfield."

This well-planned exercise had not taken into account the hospitality and good nature of the local Yorkshire people:

"Across the county there were numerous special auxiliary fire service units; these self-contained and remote outposts provided a cheery welcome to visitors seeking refuge from the cold. As we explored our route back to base, we spotted one of these isolated units and to our delight we were invited by a friendly fireman to dry off in the warmth of the building. In exchange for a few NAAFI cigarettes (gold dust in those heavily rationed days) we were given a welcome mug of tea and a plate of delicious eggs and bacon. To our delight we were offered the warm beds vacated by the next shift of part-time fire officers. There was no urgency for us to leave this safe haven and we were able to hide for 24 hours in this comfortable retreat! Eventually, we were driven incognito back to base in a fire service vehicle and dropped at a secluded area on the perimeter of RAF Driffield; our undercover return had been undetected by the opposition."

Stanley was rather pleased with their achievement. Wartime rules were made to be broken, and the crew had proven to be resourceful and resilient. It had helped create a close bond of friendship and mutual respect.

At HCU, the final leg of their training, the five became seven, and two engines became four. The Driffield experience was one they were pleased to forget, but at their new posting, RAF Riccall, home to 1658 HCU, there were no such reservations.[15] The Halifax IIs with which the unit was equipped demanded an additional air gunner and a flight engineer, the latter to provide direct support to the pilot and undertake many of the duties that would have previously befallen a second pilot which had long since been dispensed with. The new gunner was Clifford Hallett, from Yeovil, and the flight engineer was John 'Jack' Osselton, who was living in Staines. Both were NCOs and took the crew's average age up to 23. Jack, whose family came from Middlesbrough, was particularly well educated and classically minded and, although very young, proved unflappable in the air. He was still a student when he volunteered for aircrew.[16] Clifford, a publishing clerk in peacetime, had actually started out training as a pilot at an air school in Rhodesia[17] but had somehow fallen foul of the authorities, even to the point of being considered 'lacking in moral fibre' (LMF) – RAF parlance for being a coward. Rather than being given the chance like Stanley to remuster as a navigator or air bomber, he was returned to the UK and told he could either become an air gunner or join the army. He was given 24 hours to decide; it took him 24 seconds.[18]

Stanley took his first flight in a Halifax on 25 February 1944 and, after a brief hiatus, flew almost every day (and sometimes twice a day) in the first two weeks of March.

HCUs experienced the same challenges as other flying training establishments, notably the quality and reliability of the aircraft with which they were equipped. As one instructor at the time attests: "Seldom did we get hands on anything new; more usually they were second-hand, tired old crates whose airframes and engines had been flogged beyond endurance. Serviceability was an issue, despite the heroic efforts of the ground crews who, it seems, were fighting a daily battle they could rarely win."[19]

As part of D Flight, their course comprised 20 hours of flying as a crew, after which time they were rated by the chief flying instructor (CFI). He was impressed, and Stanley was delighted to be told that they would be posted to 10 Squadron at RAF Melbourne, just a few miles down the road. The squadron was just in the throes of re-equipping with the new Halifax III. With its four 1,675-hp Bristol Hercules XVI radial engines, the Halifax III was a worthy companion to the more famous Merlin-engined Avro Lancaster and much loved by its crews. It cruised at 225 mph and could top almost 280 mph flat out.

The crew left Riccall at the end of the second week in March for a spot of short leave prior to reassembling and reporting to 10 Squadron on 18 March 1944 – almost a full two years after Stanley's training had begun. It seemed a world away from his carefree days with the auxiliaries, and he often wondered how they were getting on. Five other crews were posted in at the same time to keep the squadron up to strength after a difficult few weeks. The Battle of Berlin, an all-out assault on the German capital throughout the winter of 1943/1944, had taken its toll.

While many crews at the time, if expressing a preference, would prefer the Avro Lancaster, Stanley was more inclined towards the Halifax. Lancasters were more refined in every sense; Halifaxes, on the other hand, had comparatively poor aerodynamics and didn't fly as well on three engines. "Part of the problem with the Halifax was that it was too fussy," one veteran recalls. "There were too many fuel tanks, the hydraulics had too many remedies, and too many other things that could go wrong. Choosing the right course of action in an emergency, when you are under real pressure, is the difference between life and death."[20] Stanley's preference, however, was based not so much on the aircraft itself, but rather on the fact that the Halifax squadrons were all based in the north, where he and Marjorie were now settled.

As part of 4 Group, which had bases all over Yorkshire, 10 Squadron had a proud tradition that stretched back to the very beginning of the war, having flown the first of its night operations within a week of war being declared. It had also been an early exponent of the first Pathfinder-style operations, finding ways of illuminating targets so that others could see and bomb them, a full 18 months before the actual Pathfinder Force was founded. Having originally been formed at the beginning of 1915, the squadron had always been special, taking part in the Battles of Loos, Arras and the Somme. Disbanded at the end of the First World War, it had reformed ten years later and become part of the newly formed 4 Group at the start of 1937, and under which it served for the duration.

Having been equipped with Whitleys at the start of the war, it converted to the Halifax at the end of 1941 as 4 Group evolved into an all-Halifax command. Sidney Bufton, who was instrumental in founding the Pathfinder Force while at the Air Ministry and Directorate of Bomber Operations, had commanded the squadron in the summer of 1940, as had Willie Tait, later known as 'Tirpitz' Tait for helping sink the German battleship, and Donald Bennett, the Australian who became the air officer commanding (AOC) Pathfinder Force on its formation in August 1942. Stanley and the crew arrived just as Wing Commander John

Sutton DSO, DFC, AFC was passing on the baton to Wing Commander Dudley Radford DFC, AFC – a short service commission officer who had won his first award for gallantry while officer commanding (OC) 8 Squadron in the Middle East and added a second for his time as a chief flying instructor (CFI).[21]

As was customary, the new crew was not immediately placed on the battle order, the list of those crews chosen for that night's operation. It was just as well, for it meant Stanley avoided the possibility of his first trip being the disastrous raid on Nuremberg on the night of 30/31 March 1944 in which Bomber Command suffered its highest number of casualties in a single raid.[22] Such were the losses that the Command was stood down, giving Stanley and his crew even more time to settle in, do some cross-country flying, and generally acclimatise to local conditions and characters. For Sandy, this was his first chance to get behind the controls of the Halifax III, and the first few flights were dual with an instructor, usually one of the squadron's more experienced pilots. After a series of circuits and landings and loaded climbs, Sandy was allowed to fly solo prior to joining another crew as a 'second dickie' – a flight over enemy territory with Sandy acting as an observer to get a feel for the real thing before taking his own crew on 'ops'.[23]

With just a handful of weeks to go before the invasion of Europe, and the long-awaited opening of a second front to ease the pressure on 'Uncle Joe' Stalin's troops in the east, the main weight of Bomber Command's forces was directed at transport targets, taking out the roads, bridges, railways, marshalling yards etc. in order to disrupt the Germans' ability to move their arms in response to an Allied threat. The Transportation Plan, as it was officially designated, was vital work, as were the additional raids that had to be made in and around Calais, part of the deception plan to convince the Germans that an invasion force was still heading that way, rather than to Normandy.

Stanley's first official operation with 10 Squadron was on a typical target of the time, the marshalling yards at Tergnier, between Saint-Quentin and Laon, once the scene of fierce fighting in the First World War. The air officer commanding-in-chief (AOC-in-C) of Bomber Command, Arthur Harris, had been obliged to abandon his attacks on major German cities in favour of multiple tactical raids comprising anything between one and two hundred aircraft on each. Tergnier was a critical transport hub, and for the night of 18/19 April Harris allocated 171 bombers to complete the task, most of them Halifaxes. General-purpose (GP) bombs were preferred to incendiaries, since the purpose was to destroy as much of the railway track as possible, along with any associated rolling stock and infrastructure (such as turntables). The Tergnier raid was only partially successful, although from Stanley's perspective they believed the bombs to have been well concentrated and had observed a number exploding in the yard itself. All 13 aircraft from 10 Squadron taking part returned safely.

A few nights later they were back out again, in larger squadron numbers, to attack the marshalling yards at Ottignies, to the south-east of Anderlecht in Walloon Brabant, Belgium. A maximum effort by the squadron meant that both flight commanders, Squadron Leader Michael Maw, a former first-class cricketer, and Squadron Leader Jack Trobe, a hugely experienced Australian, were leading by example. Unusually, not a single aircraft was lost from any of the squadrons taking part, and the southern half of the railway yards was severely damaged.[24]

Stanley's crew were not on the battle order for the next few trips, including attacks on Düsseldorf and Essen. Stanley was asked to fly as a 'spare bod' on the night of the 27th when the squadron was involved in an attack on the marshalling yards at Aulnoye. His captain for the trip was Martin Livesey, a flight sergeant, with an all-NCO crew.[25] Their regular navigator, Alfred Rhodes, wasn't available. While 18 aircraft were originally detailed, only 14 crews actually made it to the target. The Halifax of one of the pilots swung off the runway, breaking its back, and preventing two other aircraft from taking off. A fourth Halifax had trouble in retracting its undercarriage and flaps, obliging its pilot to abandon the mission and return to base having jettisoned its bombs. Of the remaining crews, most reported bombs being seen to explode in the target area, and Australian Warrant Officer James Murtha[26] had a tale to tell the intelligence officer – having got into a tangle with a Dornier 217 over the Channel and only escaping after an engagement that lasted almost ten minutes. In a most unusual incident, the German pilot made his attack by accelerating ahead and slightly below the Halifax and opening fire with his rear guns. It meant that neither of the two Halifax gunners could engage, rendering them virtually defenceless. Murtha's aircraft was hit several times and holed, and the wireless and special equipment were a total write-off.[27]

Livesey's aircraft, with Stanley navigating, was also attacked. Forty minutes into their return journey, having successfully dropped their bombs on the green target indicators (TIs) as instructed by the master bomber, their Aural Monica tail warning radar system alerted the gunners that a night fighter was approaching. Fishpond, a further aid, also warned of an impending attack, and then both gunners saw it within moments of one another and shouted a warning. Livesey immediately and instinctively threw the Halifax into a starboard corkscrew manoeuvre, a practiced evasion technique, as the rear and mid-upper gunners opened fire at a range of 600 yards. Both had the satisfaction of seeing the fiery glow of their tracer rounds strike the enemy aircraft, identified in the gloom as a single-engined Focke-Wulf Fw 190, as it broke away to port without firing, and very much with its tail between its legs.[28] A second enemy fighter, another single-engined aircraft, was spotted off the port beam by the air bomber and flight engineer but made no move to attack. The Halifax landed safely home without further incident as dawn was breaking on a new day, and the armourers later counted that the two gunners had fired off 250 rounds of ammunition between them.

Stanley was reunited with his regular crew (minus Snooky) as one of ten aircraft from the squadron selected for a bombing attack on the marshalling yards at Malines at the beginning of May. It was only partially successful, many of the bombs falling in civilian areas, with almost three hundred Belgians killed or injured by what was described as 'scattered' bombing. Opposition was described as very weak with only one gun in action in the target area. One crew, however, failed to return. They included a Canadian along as a 'second dickie'.[29]

They flew again on the night of 6/7 May to bomb the railway installations in the Gassicourt suburb of Mantes-la-Jolie in France, landing at RAF Carnaby due to a lack of brake pressure. The airfield had been specifically designed as an emergency landing ground with an unusually long and wide runway. It was a busy night, and several aircraft reported seeing fighter flares. Two were attacked on the flight home but both successfully evaded their assailants without sustaining any damage.[30] Bomber Command recorded significant damage in the target area as well as some collateral damage in the old part of the town where a church, town hall and a school were destroyed. Although only three aircraft in the attacking force were shot down, these included two very experienced Pathfinder crews.[31]

Hasselt in Belgium was their destination for the night of 12/13 May, a simple enough trip involving 100 Halifaxes as the 'main force', and seven Lancasters and four Mosquitoes from Pathfinder Force to mark the target and direct the bombing. For its part, 10 Squadron was to contribute 11 crews, led by the wing commander, and all equipped with more than ten thousand pounds of bombs.

Stan navigated his skipper to the target, in time to see the red and green TIs from the Pathfinders land plumb in the centre of the railway marshalling yards. The weather was clear, and while there was a thick haze on the ground it was not sufficient to obscure the flashes of light as the first bombs exploded spectacularly. So great was the concentration that the squadron commander's Halifax was visibly lifted by the shock waves as it flew over the target area.

Everything was fine in Stanley's aircraft until suddenly there was a sickening crash, and an immediate loss of power in the port inner engine. Sandy and Jack had only moments to register the whirling dials on their respective control panels before a second engine died and the aircraft veered violently to one side, the failing engines now a dead weight rather than producing any power. While Sandy trimmed the aircraft to fly on just two engines, pilot and flight engineer were able to take stock of what had happened. Somehow, the port inner had been struck, almost certainly by a bomb or incendiary dropped by a friendly aircraft above them. It did happen – and more than anyone liked to admit. The damage was such that the propeller had advanced from its mounting, fouling the port outer engine and slicing eight inches off the port outer's propeller tips. The crew, and the flight engineer especially, remained calm throughout as Stanley plotted them a course home. The Halifax could fly using only two of its four Bristol Hercules easily enough, but it would take longer, and they would need to take care not to place too much strain on the remaining engines. Fuel was also a potential difficulty, and Jack worked hard to manage the overly complicated fuel system to save what little he had left from draining away. It was an anxious flight home, but they made it, ultimately no worse for their experience.

The near miss made them redouble their drills for escaping the aircraft in an emergency. Crew positions in a Halifax determined the method and order of escape. The pilot was effectively elevated on a platform, with the wireless operator, navigator and air bomber sat underneath. The flight engineer sat with his back to the pilot, facing a panel housing a duplicate set of the aircraft's systems and controls. The air gunners occupied their respective turrets in the mid-upper and rear positions:

> *"All the four-engine aircraft used in Bomber Command like the Halifax had two means of escape in the event of an emergency. The first was the main door opposite the mid-upper gun turret which was used for the two gunners and the flight engineer. The second escape hatch was at the front of the aircraft below a six-foot folding navigation table. This was the designated escape hatch for the rest of the crew and the cumbersome four-foot-square door could not be accessed until the navigator's table and chair*

that obstructed it were removed. This unwieldy hatch was the only means of escape for the pilot, wireless operator, navigator and bomb aimer who were normally positioned in the nose of the aircraft.

"Regular exercises were carried out on the ground to practise our escape procedures, but we never used the huge, heavy doors. As a consequence, we had no idea of how these doors would operate during an emergency with the Halifax making steep spiral turns to avoid enemy attacks. In preparing for operations, duty crews were encouraged to utilise their aircraft for cross-country flying, bombing and photography practice. Sandy had an unofficial training arrangement with colleagues at RAF Leconfield – a pair of fighter pilots agreed to make a series of mock attacks which enabled Sandy to practise his highly effective 'corkscrew' manoeuvre. This evading skill required the pilot to immediately close the throttles, which shut the engines down and put the aircraft into a very steep dive. This resulted in the attacking fighters overshooting and completely missing their target. The steeper the descent, the more effective the manoeuvre became. When the inevitable attack by the enemy night fighters occurred during one of our operations over France, we were all thankful for Sandy's perseverance and dedication to training, which saved the lives of five of our crew."

For six nights in the middle of May, the squadron was stood down as the weather closed in, allowing for only a few hours of local flying. Stanley enjoyed two weeks' leave with his now-wife, Marjorie, which he described in a letter as "perfect heavenly bliss". The pain of separation was keenly felt: "I wish I could have held you in my arms and clung to you forever."[32]

Conditions over England improved sufficiently to allow an operation on the first night of June; 23 squadron aircraft took part in an attack on a German radio-listening and signals installation at Ferme d'Urville in Normandy. Cloud, however, prevented any form of accurate bombing, despite the very best efforts of the Pathfinder Mosquitoes. It was an unsatisfactory trip for Stanley and the crew, as they were forced to return early due to lack of air speed. It happened. Another of their number was obliged to abandon his trip when an engine caught fire, and the Canadian pilot was unable to maintain height. A further aircraft also lost its starboard outer engine but continued on to the target. A third couldn't release its bombs, and a fourth returned with one of its 500-pounders 'hung up' having been hit by heavy anti-aircraft fire ('flak') over the target area.

Stanley wrote to Marjorie on the afternoon of Friday 2 June, in which he recorded his frustration at having to make an early return: "Just our luck. We had engine trouble going down England and had to come back just when it was quite an easy target. We could have wept."[33]

That evening, the Murray crew sought to make up for their disappointment. They also got to put their escape drill to the ultimate test.

CHAPTER TWO

"BALE OUT, BALE OUT!"

ALL ALONG THE SOUTH COAST of England, a great army of soldiers, tanks, guns, equipment and other paraphernalia of war was being assembled to embark on the mighty armada that would transport them across the Channel to the beaches of Normandy. While the supreme commander, General Eisenhower, agonised over the timing of the invasion with his deputies, frustrated by the weather, the British and American bombers continued their relentless attacks on enemy positions. To the Transportation Plan had been added coastal batteries around Calais and the 'real' invasion area to keep the Germans guessing.

Trappes, an important rail junction to the west of Paris, had been successfully attacked on the last night of May 1944. The Germans were quick to make good some of the damage and on the night of 2/3 June it was to be attacked again, with a mixed bag of Lancasters and Halifaxes from 1 and 4 Group respectively, as well as a small number of aircraft from 8 Group PFF. Take-off was 2230 hrs, with a scheduled time on target (TOT) of 0050 hrs.

It should have been just another trip; it proved to be anything but.

Halifax MZ630 'S' Sugar, with Sandy at the controls, climbed steadily over the airfield and added power to make for the rendezvous point.[34] Stanley gave his pilot a course to steer that would take them south to the turning points at Basingstoke and Pevensey Bay, across the beaches where another invasion had taken place almost nine hundred years ago and reshaped the history of the British Isles. They continued to climb over the Channel and across into France, the gunners keeping a sharp lookout for other friendly aircraft as the risk of collision was always there, especially in a stream. A burst of flak appeared briefly from somewhere in a puff of ominous black smoke and then faded as the bombers continued to head south, making for the target on the outskirts of the French capital.

Behind the curtain at his navigator's station, his mind focused on his plot, Stanley continued giving his pilot course and speed until he estimated that they were now only a few minutes from the aiming point. Snooky Stokes, the air bomber, clambered through into the nose and prepared for the bombing run. The gunners, Terry in the rear turret and Clifford in the mid-upper, continued to scan the sky, traversing their turrets, peering into the dark and alive to the threat that still existed from enemy fighters. The much-vaunted Luftwaffe may have been down, but it was far from out, as it had demonstrated just two months earlier when it had hacked almost a hundred bombers from the skies over Nuremberg and reminded Harris that the bombers would not be having it all their own way.

The weather was almost perfect. No cloud, good visibility and a brilliant three-quarter moon to help the gunners in maintaining a good lookout and report aircraft of any persuasion coming too close. The marker Mosquitoes had done their jobs well, backed up by target indicators that burned brightly on the ground. The master bomber responsible for controlling the raid gave clear and precise instructions of where to bomb, Snooky helping to guide his pilot with a series of 'right, left and steady' commands until the target drifted into his bombsight. Snooky pressed the bomb release, calling "bombs gone" as he did so, and the aircraft palpably lifted as 18 500-pound bombs fell from its belly. They continued flying straight as the photoflash released and a photograph was taken of the target for analysis by the intelligence officers on their return. At the start of the war, some bombers were missing the target by 70 miles. By the summer of 1944, and with the advent of Oboe, a highly sophisticated blind-bombing device, and H2S, a ground-scanning radar, they could now determine the accuracy within yards, with the photographs to prove it.[35]

With the bomb doors closed, 'S' Sugar turned westwards and towards home, some members of the crew reporting a huge explosion just as they left the target area and a large fire breaking out that began to glow orange in the dark. Sandy advanced the throttles to increase the speed, the aircraft now lighter and more responsive to his touch. While flak over the target had been light, the gunners reported seeing tracer fire in the air, suggesting that night fighters were in the vicinity. Then they saw first one and then another Halifax in flames and out of control, crashing into the ground from 10,000 ft. The bomber stream had been left unmolested on its route into the target while the night fighters assembled, but now the German pilots were ready to be unleashed.[36]

Ever on the alert, the gunners still failed to see the Messerschmitt Bf 110 twin-engined night fighter that now had them in his sights. Oberleutnant Jakob Schaus of Stab II/NJG 4 had benefited from a running commentary from his colleagues in ground interception who had plotted the bombers' withdrawal until they reached the area of Évreux. Schaus was already an 'ace' having shot down a dozen or so of what the Germans called 'Viermots' (literally 'four motors'). Now he was about to add to his score.

His first burst shattered the port wing of Halifax MZ630, ripping great chunks out of the mainplane and the two engines – which also immediately burst into flames. Sandy, the pilot, was caught completely unawares but instinctively threw the damaged bomber into a violent corkscrew, placing intolerable strain on the aircraft's structure. For a few brief moments the Halifax still responded to the pilot's controls, but then the aircraft began to fall away, and the captain gave the order to bale out, realising the hopelessness of their situation. Despite their parlous state, and the night fighter still being in the vicinity, each of the crew members responded to the instruction in turn, before making his way to his respective escape route. Taffy, the wireless operator, jettisoned the trailing aerial of his set, mindful of injuries it could inflict on an escaping parachutist. Struggling from his seat in his bulky flying gear, his first thought was to help his pilot, and he clambered up to see what assistance he could provide. By now the noise was terrifying and the whole of the port wing was ablaze. Further evasive action, even if possible, was pointless – for their fiery form could be seen from dozens of miles away across the night sky.

Stan and Snooky, down in the nose, struggled with the navigator's plotting table and bench seat which were blocking the access to the main escape hatch in the floor. It had been difficult enough in training, but now in the real thing, with the aircraft mortally hit, they needed to redouble their efforts or else risk being trapped.

Now at 4,000 ft, pieces began falling from the aircraft as it started to disintegrate, its final moments hurried along by a second burst of cannon fire that shattered the starboard wing and carried on until it reached the cockpit – killing Sandy and Taffy, the pilot and wireless operator, outright. The pair had battled heroically to keep the aircraft sufficiently flying to enable the others to escape, and now paid the ultimate price.

Everything then happened in a rush. Snooky was the first to go from the front, with Stan only moments behind. Both left the aircraft at the very instant it began to spiral out of control. Stan, bareheaded (he had left his flying helmet in the aircraft), almost instantly pulled his ripcord as the chest pack flew over his head, painfully banging into his face and scalp as it did so before opening with a reassuring crack and arresting his descent. Despite all their training, they had never once practised a parachute jump, and it came as quite a shock. Stan had often wondered how the clip-on, chest-style parachute he and most of the crew wore differed from the seat-type chutes worn by pilots and some rear gunners, and now he knew and had the cuts and scratches to show for it:

> *"After the trauma and tension of the escape from the blazing bomber, it was suddenly quiet and completely unreal. I was suspended in space with just the soothing swish of the air being forced through the rigging of the parachute. It was like waking from a bad dream, but this was real, and quite unexpectedly I felt composed and completely in command of the situation."*

Thoughts began running through his head at a hundred miles per hour: "I'm alive, that's good. How soon will they tell my wife? How can I let her know I'm safe?"

Just a few miles to the north, he saw their aircraft crash into the ground and explode. The ground, that for some time seemed a little far off, now seemed to rise towards him in a rush, and with a terrific thud he landed heavily on one leg which immediately gave way beneath him. For the second time that night, he praised God that he was still alive.

For the briefest of moments, Stan sat to gather his thoughts and recover his senses. Above him, the sounds of battle continued, as well as the drone of aircraft that would make it home and crews who would soon be tucking into their post-op bacon and eggs. Stan sprang into action, unbuckling his parachute harness and gathering in the silken canopy that was billowing gently in a light breeze. The parachute that had just been his saviour could now prove his nemesis, so obviously visible in the brilliant moonlight. He began to make a scraping in the ground to bury it as best he could, hampered by soil hardened by the early summer:

> *"I sank to my knees and prayed as I had never prayed before. I had so much to be thankful for. I had been so very close to death and been spared to live another day."*

With his chute taken care of, Stan started to consciously think of his training, and in particular how to make contact with the local Resistance. This was easier said than done, like burying his chute. Villages with understanding pastors, or houses with conspicuous red lights to symbolise their purpose, were rather hard to come by. Then a cold fear began to set in. Rumours were that the Germans were reserving a special interrogation for navigators, keen to learn the secret of the new H2S ground-scanning radar now being widely used, and not just reserved for the Pathfinders. The question was therefore how to remove his observer's badge:

> *"Fortunately, the new-pattern flying boots brought into service, replacing the earlier floppy brown suede model that always fell off the feet when an airman took to his parachute, came to the rescue. Learning from the experience of helpers on the Continent, a specially designed flying boot was introduced consisting of a 'civilian'-pattern black shoe which could be detached from the warm sheepskin upper wrap-round, by means of using a concealed knife to cut along a special double seam. Using this knife, I cut away the uppers from the shoe and also removed the observer brevet. Additionally, I removed the flying officer insignia from my epaulettes thus making the jacket free of service badges."*

Within his escape kit were a few essentials to help him on his way. They included 2,000 French francs, all in brand-new 100-franc notes, a small carton holding an assortment of various tablets, a rubber-encased hacksaw blade, a razor, malted milk tablets and a rubber water container. The collar stud with its concealed compass proved to be a problem, as the glass face had been coated with a paint which was difficult to remove.

Stan started making a plan. Any moment now, he told himself, the Germans would be scouring the area with their *Kübelwagens* and dogs and mobilising the hated milice and other collaborationist forces to hunt him down, a most wanted man:

> *"Nothing could have been further from the truth, but naturally, there was no way I could have known this fact at the time. Fortunately, as a trained navigator, I was able to orientate myself, and taking a bearing from the pole star I set off in a southerly direction away from the blazing wreck of the bomber and the coastal belt which I considered, with the invasion of*

France so imminent, would be densely packed with enemy soldiers and establishments."

Once the bombers overhead had flown on, the night was very still, save for the noise of a bird disturbed from its slumber. Taking a trail into the undergrowth proved to be a mistake, for Stan soon found himself in the middle of a forest, seemingly with no way out. Even as an adult, being alone at night in a thick forest was a test of nerves, and he was somewhat relieved when dawn began to break and free him from the sinister blackness that had enveloped him.

The early adrenaline had now faded, and he became more conscious of pain in his knee, which had begun to swell. It was clear he would need help before going much further. Slowly, cautiously, he kept in the shadows of the hedgerows, giving a wide berth to the farmhouses with their barking dogs, until he came to a running stream. He drank from the cool, refreshing water and was momentarily revived. He also began cleaning himself up as best he could, shaving without a mirror and irritating the scratches already on his face. Mirror or no, he knew he must look a sight and one which would surely give the game away if he were caught out in the open.

Several hours passed and he began to feel hungry. He had already gobbled down the few edible items in his escape kit but now craved something more substantial. He had to settle for what he could stuff in his pockets and his mouth from a nearby cherry orchard, and with darkness approaching he buried himself within a haystack to conserve his strength and prepare for a longer journey the following day.

Stan passed an uncomfortable and largely sleepless night. His knee was now so inflamed that to put any weight on it caused him instant pain. He was still considering his options, and starting to lose heart, when he saw an elderly farmworker approaching in the distance. This was his chance to break cover and seek help:

"I hobbled up to him explaining that I was an English officer in the Royal Air Force who had been shot down the previous night. In my basic schoolboy French, I requested his assistance for shelter and food, for which I was prepared to pay, proffering one of my crisp 100-franc notes. To my complete relief and surprise, he explained, with emotion, that he was a friend and that he had a son in England serving with the Free French forces under General de Gaulle."

The old man pointed to a large chateau a mile or so across the valley where Stanley could find help.[37] He explained that the place was owned by an English woman who had somehow managed to avoid being interned. He said that she would be sure to help, but that Stanley should be careful, for the lady had a particularly fierce guard dog.[38]

The 'English woman' turned out to be a frail old lady who had married a French industrialist after the First World War. Her name was Madame Grace le Fèvre, and she lived with her spinster sister, Miss Forge, together with a personal maid-cum-companion, 'Lilly', who was a courier for the Resistance. They also had a gardener who lived in his own annex.

The completely self-contained estate had its own pigs, poultry, and goats, as well as a well-stocked stream and mill pool. The whole isolated complex was about two miles from the next occupied community, the village of Muzy, in Eure. In every way it was the desperate evader's dream of paradise, and Stan could hardly believe his good fortune.

With Stan in his somewhat bedraggled state, the old lady was at first hesitant about allowing the stranger into her house and began asking questions of him in French. Stan's command of the French language was rudimentary at best, but he somehow managed to persuade Madame le Fèvre that he was indeed RAF aircrew on the run, and he was ushered upstairs for a bath and his clothes taken away. Little did he know it would be his last hot bath for over a year.

His reverie was disturbed soon after when two strongly built men entered brandishing weapons and asked Stan to follow them into an adjoining room where the madame and her sister were waiting. One of the men, he was later to learn, was Francis Dablin – codename 'Mathurin' – a radio operator in the local Resistance which was a communist-run cell. The other was Monsieur Joseph Bergeron, a fellow Resistance fighter and a local plumber from Dreux.[39]

> *"Absurdly wrapped in the small towel provided, and with no attempt to return any of my clothing, I was subjected to very hostile questioning, in French, which Madame translated in her perfect English. The two men wanted details of the target we had attacked, the time, the type of bomber and the approximate crash time and place, relative to where we were (which I naturally did not know). They further wanted to know the names and localities in England where my crew came from and the name and place of my bank which they claimed they could check."*

Stan was at first suspicious and declined to answer. He soon appreciated, however, this was no time for 'name, rank and number' only. The hostile atmosphere only lifted after the sister began asking him whether he could tell her anything about Brighton and the south coast, which had been her home before the war. Stan reassured her that Brighton was very much on the south coast, next to the town of Hove, with two large hotels – the Grand and the Metropole – in one of which he had fortunately spent a whole month in 1942 when stationed at the aircrew holding unit based there. Thus satisfied, the two strangers produced the identity photographs, which they had taken from his battledress for just such an emergency, saying they would take them away and prepare a false identity card as soon as possible.[40] His clothes were returned to him, but instead of his uniform jacket he was given a rough and ill-fitting gardener's coat and was thus transformed into Pierre Lecomte, a gardener from the village of Saint-Vigor-le-Grand in the département of Calvados. Given the village would soon be in Allied hands, it was unlikely his identity would be checked.[41]

Dressed in his new 'disguise', Stan enjoyed a hearty meal of ham and eggs, with a ubiquitous fresh baguette, while the two old ladies began chattering nineteen to the dozen about life in England and when the invasion was likely to take place. None of them knew that the invasion fleet was, at that very moment, embarking on one of the truly great adventures of the war.

The peaceful scene was interrupted with the return of the Resistance chief who had good news. Not only had Stanley's story checked out, but he also had news of other members of Stanley's crew. Jack Osselton, the flight engineer, was safe and well, and sheltering at a nearby farm. Snooky Snokes was also alive but had been badly injured, and the French doctor who came to his aid had been obliged to hand him over to the authorities. Several bombers had been shot down that night, and there were many Germans in the area on the lookout for aircrew on the run. With Stanley's bad knee, it was decided he should sit tight for a few days and wait for the initial excitement to blow over.

On the morning of 6 June, Stanley's sleep was interrupted by the arrival of Madame (in a shapeless nightgown), Lilly (in something less shapeless), and a huge bottle of champagne with three glasses. The invasion had started, and later that morning the skies were filled with both German and Allied fighters skimming across the valley, and loud explosions coming from the vicinity of Dreux where Stanley was told there was a large enemy presence. More Germans began to appear in the neighbouring fields from a local flak battery, attracted by the drop tanks which had fallen from the wings of some marauding P-51 Mustangs. Working to a well-rehearsed plan, Lilly led Stanley from the chateau and into the woods and left him to hide in a woodcutter's hut. Only when they were sure the danger had passed was he taken to 'Le Verger', a small chalet-style residence across the valley. Here he was introduced to another grand old lady who Stanley learned was Madame Marie Orial. Her only son had been killed fighting the Germans in 1942, and she now lived with her 18-year-old maid and co-résistante Geneviève Desnos. As they opened the door to greet him, standing beside them, with a big grin on his face, was Jack Osselton.

Jack told Stanley his story. The second person to bale out of the burning Halifax, Jack had come down in a meadow near the hamlet of Boissy-en-Drouais. Frustratingly, his parachute lines and canopy became entangled in the branches of a tree, and he spent a worrying few minutes tearing it free, desperate not to make a sound. Treading the parachute into a deep ditch, and burying it under some leaves, he set off due south, determined to put some distance between himself and his burning aircraft. Travelling all night until well after dawn and the rising of the sun, he sought cover again in some long grass and lay there all day until the sun set and the moon rose. He spent another long and tiring night walking in the vague direction of Spain until morning came, and he hid in a convenient haystack. Later that evening he was alarmed to see a man approaching but relieved to find it was a young local farmer, Louis Godin, who offered to help. Only then did Jack realise that he was hurt; his wrist was aching, and he had twisted his ankle.

Louis helped Jack to hobble as far as a small farm owned by Monsieur Hervé, whose son, Henri, was a Resistance sympathiser. Jack remained hidden at the farm for three days until it was deemed too dangerous to stay any longer, and it was arranged that he should be taken back to 'Le Verger'. This involved a very risky eight-mile hike under the very noses of the Germans who were hunting him. The dangers were not only from the enemy, but also from the constant bombing and strafing of the main highways by their own side, which made for a somewhat perilous journey. With Louis as his guide, however, Jack was delivered safely into Madame Orial's care. His identity was verified by the same Resistance chief who had been so suspicious of Stanley, and he was given a false identity: René Bardin. Comparing the photograph of Jack to the photograph on Stanley's own fake identity card was something of a shock: they were wearing identical jackets and ties. The money they had been given to recompense any Good Samaritan was also in 100-franc notes which were sequentially numbered, and therefore an immediate giveaway as to their owner's identity.[42]

Stanley and Jack were delighted to be reunited and shared their experiences long into the night. They knew about Snooky, and steadily a more detailed picture of his capture emerged. Snooky had been so badly injured upon landing that his cries for help had been heard by Monsieur Yver, who farmed the nearby hamlet of Jersey. Yver was quick to appreciate the seriousness of Snooky's condition and, after carting him back to his home in a wheelbarrow, summoned the local doctor for help. The doctor patched Snooky up as best he could but said that he needed hospital treatment and probably surgery. There was nothing for it other than for the farmer to tell the Germans, for which he and his wife were beaten for their troubles, as well as for failing to inform them sooner. Snooky was treated at a hospital in Paris for six weeks before being transferred to a prison hospital in Germany.[43]

While pleased to know that Snooky was safe, they were saddened to learn from their Resistance friends that both Taffy and Sandy were dead, their remains having been retrieved from the wreckage of the crashed bomber and buried with full military honours by the Luftwaffe. Of the two other members of the crew, Terry Gould and Cliff Hallett, there was as yet no word. Only much later would their fate be discovered.[44]

While Stanley was in hiding, the RAF administrative process that followed the loss of any aircrew had swung into action.

The last aircraft had landed at Melbourne shortly after 0345 hrs, and since no further information was forthcoming to suggest the whereabouts of Stanley's Halifax, they were recorded as 'missing'. A second Halifax, flown by Flight Sergeant Vijendra Kumar, had also failed to return.[45] The debriefing of the crews by the intelligence officer suggested only fragments of information that may or may not have related to their loss. One crew had clearly observed two aircraft hitting the ground, while another was too busy fending off the attention of a Bf 109. Such was the case with any raid – some crews reported little or no opposition, while others had their hands full all the way in and out of the target area. Night fighters were certainly very active, and at least one Me 210 was seen shot down north of Évreux.

On the station, Stanley's logbook was brought up to date by the C Flight deputy commander, Flight Lieutenant Gordon Culverhouse, and dutifully signed with the word 'missing' after the final entry. Stanley had been a little behind in recording his trips, principally because of a shortage of red ink, and now the neatness of his writing (for which he had previously been commended) was somewhat disfigured with crossings out where his duty had been incorrectly recorded as 'rear gunner'. Gordon Culverhouse knew Stanley's crew well, for they were flying 'his' aeroplane; he had flown the last five trips of his first '30' in MZ630, his final operation being on 1 June. It was a sobering thought: Gordon had flown eight different aircraft during his tour, and all eight went missing when flown by other crews.[46] The committee of adjustment packed Stanley's belongings and personal effects to be forwarded to his next of kin, in doing so confusing one bundle with another which led to some of his effects – and specifically his dressing gown with the receipt still in its pocket – being sent to Sandy's parents, to the obvious distress of Mrs Murray.

At home in Yorkshire, Stanley's wife Marjorie was clinging to the hope that he might still be alive but had heard very little since receiving the dreaded telegram saying that he had failed to return. The telegram, dictated by the squadron adjutant and comprising the 'usual' language ("Deeply regret to inform you etc . . .") had been swiftly followed by a personal letter dated 3 June from the commanding officer, Dudley Radford. Radford went to great pains neither to raise her hopes nor to dash them, suggesting that Stanley might still be alive. "It is desired to explain that the request in the telegram notifying you of the casualty to your husband was included with the object of avoiding his chance of escape being prejudiced by undue publicity in case he was still at large," the letter ran. "This is not to say that any information about him is available but is a precaution adopted in the case of all personnel reported missing."

In Kent, Stanley's parents had also been notified. On hearing the news, Mrs Booker was described by a friend as being "heartbroken" while Stanley's little brother Leslie sobbed so much "he could hardly drink his tea".[47]

The station chaplain, Squadron Leader Leslie Perfect, also wrote to say that up to 50 per cent of personnel listed as missing were later found to be safe.[48] Marjorie did not question where his data came from. The chaplain also warned her not to be concerned if she heard nothing for the next few weeks, for if Stanley had been taken prisoner of war, it would take that time to process him and for the news to filter through via the International Red Cross.

Meantime, Marjorie began corresponding with other members of Stanley's crew, expressing her sympathy for their shared loss and concern, and praying for their safe return. All promised to keep one another informed should any news be forthcoming. Letters also began arriving from friends and family, including nurses with whom Marjorie had worked at Abingdon Hospital while Stanley was at the OTU. One came from the matron, Frances Macdonald: "We all are very much upset about him, for as you know we are all very fond of him," she wrote. "I most sincerely hope and trust he is a prisoner."[49]

'Le Verger' and its environs were considered safe for evading airmen. Both Madame Orial and Geneviève Desnos were key members of the 'Hunter' network headed by Pierre Juillet.[50] It was also a place of refuge for 'Mathurin' and his radio set, which he kept hidden in a chicken coop, along with a small cache of weapons.

The tactics of every evasion line were to limit the amount of contact with the airmen. It was also important that they should not be kept in any one place for longer than necessary, and to hide them as far away from the original crash sites as possible. Stanley and Jack thus found themselves constantly on the move and in the care of other members of the 'Hunter' network at various times.

Lilly was a frequent visitor but not, it seems, fully trusted by some of the other women, though Stanley put this down to the maternal nature of the older ladies, keen on protecting the younger men in their care.[51] Jean Gaspard also arranged for their injuries to be treated in secret, and further shelter and food provided, at a preventorium in the nearby village of Les Buissons. This was thanks to the kindness of the manager, Monsieur Mottier. The airmen were not allowed inside the facility, however. Instead, they were obliged to shelter in an adjoining stable block which was both uncomfortable and cold. It was also somewhat crowded, for Stanley and Jack had now been joined by two American airmen who were similarly on the run.

The size of the facility, and its location in a dense wood, made it comparatively safe, especially since the matron was prepared to turn a blind eye, but not so all of the nurses.[52] As such, it was decided to split the RAF and USAAF evaders into two separate groups, and hide the Americans elsewhere, much to Stanley's relief. At one point they had been given brandy and had become completely intoxicated; the behaviour of the US airmen, and their total lack of security, was becoming something of a concern. Stanley and Jack were pleased, therefore, with the brief respite afforded them by yet another of the network's helpers, Madame Duval.[53] She was a frail and somewhat vulnerable widow who was clearly in financial distress – to the point that Stanley determined that he would find a way of getting money to her through Madame Orial. Her house was empty of all but the essentials, almost as though she had packed up to move, and there was little in the way of food. She had a kind heart, however, and at least Stanley and Jack were away from the Americans and the fear of being compromised. They stayed with Madame Duval for two days before being taken back to 'Le Verger'.

In total, Stanley and Jack spent more than three weeks in hiding as the Allied advance from Normandy became bogged down:

"Our orders from the Resistance were to stay put, only rotating between various widows' houses until the Allied armies overran the area."

Being moved from safehouse to safehouse, sometimes at a moment's notice, or hiding in the woods, was not without its dangers. On one occasion, while Stanley was being led by Francis Dablin to the bridge at Muzy, they stumbled across two German soldiers standing by the edge of the River Avre. Being six feet tall, and conscious that he was wearing trousers that ended high above his ankles, Stanley was all for turning back, but Dablin created a diversion by asking the Germans for directions to Saint-Georges, and Stanley's strange attire went unnoticed. On another occasion, while Stanley was still in some discomfort from his leg, he was offered a piggyback by Jean Gaspard – but politely declined![54]

On the morning of 28 June, with Stanley now back at 'Le Verger', Monsieur Bergeron returned with news that Madame le Fèvre's home had been raided. Stanley feared the worst:

"As far as we could gather the Germans had spent over an hour searching the house and grounds after suspecting an arms drop had been made to the local Resistance group."

The Germans were now too close for comfort, and it was decided that Stanley and Jack should be moved out of the area. That evening they were to be taken to a farm near Maintenon, around 20 miles the other side of Dreux towards Paris, and await the arrival of an RAF aircraft bringing in fresh supplies of arms and munitions. The farm was owned by Raymond and Yvonne Vauvilliers. Bergeron handed Stan a bulky, wax-sealed brown envelope with instructions to hand it to the pilot, and only the pilot, on pain of death.[55]

The two men were taken though the village of Muzy to a church and, after a surprisingly emotional and tearful farewell with Madame Orial, stood quietly in the shadows awaiting their transport. After a nervous hour, by which time they had persuaded themselves the plan had gone to pot, a black front-wheel drive Citroën pulled up, and a young man in his late thirties along with a woman of similar age who they took to be his wife jumped out of the car. He was a doctor with the Resistance, he explained, and as such had access to petrol and a set of wheels. The two airmen clambered into the back, and the car drove off through the outskirts of the city until eventually they reached a desolate farm. Stanley was underwhelmed:

> *"The driver took us into the farm, a very run-down and evil-smelling place, such a complete contrast to the high-class establishments experienced during the previous three weeks. Leaving us with the farmer, he departed, and we were taken into a nearby barn where, to our surprise, there were two American aircrew. One of these, it transpired, was in the P-51 that had dropped its fuel tanks near Madame le Fèvre's and been shot down by the anti-aircraft battery. He had also been hiding out in the woods, near the sanatorium, where the matron had been bringing him nightly food baskets.*[56]
>
> *"Both were in a very dirty (and smelly) condition after their privations in the woods and had been taken to the farm, the previous day, again by the young couple in their black Citroën car. Later that evening the farmer's wife took us into the equally squalid kitchen where we were each given a plate with one very undercooked fried egg and a hunk of bread, most unappetising after being spoiled with such sumptuous fare by our previous hosts."*

Both Stanley and Jack felt uneasy about their new accommodation. Neither the farmer nor his wife made any conversation, and there was a pervading air of hostility. The contrast from their previous sanctuary was stark, and the heavy rain beating against the windowpanes did not augur well for a clandestine pickup that night.

> *"The evening wore on until, quite late, a stranger appeared and informed us that we would have to stay at the farm overnight as different plans had to be made for us. Afterwards we were taken back into the farm and given an untidy room, with just one very large bed, a few unclean blankets and a long bumpy bolster in lieu of the normal pillows."*

The four men made themselves as comfortable as possible, but sleep – even top to tail – proved virtually impossible. The next morning, a different black Citroën appeared, and the party of airmen prepared to set off for a destination as yet unknown. The Americans went first, and after the car returned a few hours later it was the Englishmen's turn.

Stanley was surprised that, despite being about the only civilian vehicle on the road, they weren't stopped, and nor did the driver show any apparent concern that they might be. He drove into the centre of Paris near the Arc de Triomphe and stopped outside a small and rather insignificant hotel incongruously called the Hotel Piccadilly. There was no concierge and no one on reception. The two Americans were already hiding upstairs, and Stanley and Jack were shown to a room with a bed, a basin and a bidet, and instructed that under no circumstances were they to leave the room except to use the toilet at the end of the corridor. It did not take Stanley long to realise that they were in fact being hidden in a brothel, the thin walls and open windows allowing the unmistakable sounds of couples in the heights of passion (feigned or otherwise) to escape into the warm night air. It did not take him long, either, to realise that Jack had not only never been in a brothel before but also had no idea what a bidet was!

For two days the men were effectively prisoners in their own room, their daily routine punctuated twice a day by the arrival of their driver with a baguette and a bottle of watery beer. In response to their constant badgering asking how soon it would be before they were on their way, he would only mutter "soon".

On the third day, Jack was taken away on the pretext of being moved to another safe house, because the Americans in a room above in the same 'maison de rendez-vous' had been indiscreet. It was the last Stanley would see of Jack for some time. A few hours later, Stanley was in the hands of the Gestapo.

CHAPTER THREE
BETRAYED

IT ALL HAPPENED IN A rush. The English-speaking driver burst into the room clutching a bloodstained wrist, stammering that he had been ambushed and had only managed to escape by the skin of his teeth. A traitor was in their midst, he cried, and said that "le chef" would be there presently and would know what to do.

Le chef duly arrived, waving a pistol and looking suitably dramatic, and Stanley was ushered out of the room and down the backstairs to a black-market restaurant behind the hotel. The man then disappeared out the back, claiming he had to talk to London, returning a few moments later with a form that he asked Stanley to complete. It was in English and asked for the name of the target he had attacked and when, the type of aircraft he'd flown, and the airfield at which he was based. It did not ask for his squadron, but it did ask where he drank, the price of beer and the name of the local landlady![57]

As part of their escape-and-evasion training, the importance of establishing their bona fides had been drummed into them from the start, and Stanley naturally assumed this was all part of the process. After a simple meal, and with no attempt on the part of the Frenchman to talk 'shop', Stanley was taken back to the hotel and put in a smaller room, nearer the roof. Again, he was told to keep out of sight and not leave his room, but expect to be collected.

A short while later, yet another Frenchman arrived to say Stanley was being taken to Orléans and led him downstairs into a waiting Citroën. In the back seat was an injured American pilot, Robert Hoffman. They stopped for a short while outside a post office, and a conspicuous plastic-coated card was placed in the windscreen behind the driver's wheel. It was not clear to Stanley what they were waiting for, but feigning impatience the driver once again sped off – only to drive straight into a German roadblock, complete with sinister-looking German military police with machine pistols slung over their shoulders and with their familiar metal gorget plates that gave inspiration to their 'chain dogs' nickname.

> *"Covered by another of the policemen I was dragged from the front seat and handcuffed behind my back; without a word being spoken or any attempt made to ask my identity, I was bundled into a small military van. No attempt was made to detain the Citroën driver, and with his departure the roadblock broke up. Two soldiers joined me in the rear of the vehicle which was driven away."*

The van sped along the city roads heading south, until it drew up outside the high-walled gateway of the vast Napoleonic prison of Fresnes near Orly, on the southern outskirts of Paris. Driven into the prison courtyard the van stopped, the doors opened, and Stanley was violently thrown out of the back and onto the ground, where the guards proceeded to beat him with rifle butts accompanied by insults and abuse and accusations of being a filthy "terrorist". Roughly manhandled into the guardroom, he was punched in the face and then subjected to a painful and humiliating strip-search and rectal examination by the senior NCO, who seemed convinced Stanley had managed to hide a blade inside his body.[58] No questions were asked of him, but everything in his possession was confiscated, including the sealed brown envelope he had been given to hand to the pilot.[59] Then he was hauled along an underground corridor past a series of locked cells to his own new accommodation, his nose bleeding profusely from where he had been struck.

The cell was tiny, measuring only ten feet by seven feet, and contained an iron bed with a badly stained and foul-smelling mattress, a small folding table beneath a frosted glass window set high in the wall, and some antiquated plumbing that served as both a toilet and a washbasin combined. Stanley – prisoner 14385 – was miserable, confused and scared. It was the first time he had ever been subjected to physical violence, and the thought of what might follow appalled him:

> *"The fantasy that being captured by the enemy consisted of just giving one's name, rank and number, and being immediately recognised as a protected prisoner of war had been rudely shattered. I was in a hopeless dilemma with the*

alternative of trying to maintain the pretence, as the false documents indicated, of being a French gardener, Pierre Lecomte, which my inadequate knowledge of the language could not support, or persevere with my genuine identity as an RAF officer. The question of where I obtained the false documents and who had been helping me was clearly going to be the problem."

Depression began setting in, not helped by the onset of fleas – one of the miseries of Fresnes remembered by all incarcerated there. They came out at night which made sleep impossible. Peter Phelps, shot down on the night of 7/8 July 1944 and betrayed to the Germans for the price of 20,000 francs, remembers that the most he caught in a day was 112.[60] Stanley recalls the gloom that had descended:

"The following day was to prove to be the one that I have long and desperately tried to forget. The one experience that gave me frequent and violent nightmares. After a thoroughly disturbed night, aggravated by the frequent cries from the depths of the vast prison and the occasional shot that struck fear within the heart, the cell door opened, and a bowl of weak coffee and a hunk of black bread were passed in. Hardly had the cell door closed when the German guard threw it open again, screeching out 'Tribunal – los, los!', and herded me out into the underground corridor, aiming a vicious kick as I passed. I was escorted back through the various locked gates out into a courtyard and, after being checked against a list, was pushed into a large black van, the inside of which was partitioned off into numerous locked compartments."

Following a lengthy journey across Paris, the van halted in the courtyard of a large building that Stanley believed later was the headquarters of security services in the avenue Foch. Today one of the most expensive addresses in the world and home to many grand palaces,[61] during the war it was known locally as the 'street of horrors'. It was specifically the main headquarters for the *Sicherheitsdienst* (SD), the Gestapo's brutal and unforgiving counter-intelligence branch. The sixth floor housed a series of rooms where prisoners were tortured, their screams often heard beyond the building's walls.[62]

The men were again pushed out of the van while the guards hurled threats and abuse in their direction. As they stood, waiting to see what happened next, a dozen or so dishevelled and badly beaten forms, men and women, shuffled out of the entrance and into the van that Stanley had only just vacated. They now knew what the Germans had in store for them, and it was the most demoralising spectacle possible. Many were unable to walk unaided, some were without shoes and their feet were bleeding. All had been beaten to some degree, the blood and bruising evident on their swollen faces.

> *"For a young, relatively innocent and sheltered former schoolboy of 22, the bloodshed that faced us and the brutality already experienced proved to be a shattering emotion."*

An SS-uniformed NCO appeared,[63] names were called out, and the prisoners were escorted singly inside and up various staircases into the heart of the building. When his name was called, Stanley was taken up several flights of stairs and into a large bare room with barred windows. Here his clothes were forcibly removed and his hands secured behind his back with thin wired handcuffs.

Naked, Stanley was pushed through an open door into a poorly lit room where an SS officer was seated behind a table with two SS soldiers standing nearby. Stanley was told that they knew all about him – that he was a British agent and that being in civilian clothes with forged papers pretending to be a British officer in the air force would do him no good. He was a terrorist and knew what fate he could expect. Stanley stuck to the truth, that he was indeed an RAF officer on the run, and that apart from his jacket he was still in the uniform he had worn when shot down. He also said that his official 'dog tags', which the guard at the prison had removed, would prove his identity.

His response displeased his interrogators. Almost before he had finished talking, he was struck a fierce blow with a rubber truncheon full in the mouth, breaking one of his front teeth. The officer told him that Stanley had forfeited any right to be treated as a prisoner of war, since he was disguised as a civilian and carrying false papers. He demanded to know the names of the people who had helped him. Stanley, still smarting with the pain from the blow to his face, refused to answer, and received an excruciating knee in the groin for his troubles, after which the officer rained blow upon blow on the defenceless man as he cried out in pain. Another tooth was broken and there was blood oozing from his mouth and nose, a small pool forming on the floor.

> *"I was in extreme pain and very frightened. It was a terrible situation having before my eyes the faces of the wonderful brave old ladies, Madame le*

Fèvre, Madame Orial, Madame Duval, the two maids and the old gardener, knowing that their very lives depended upon me somehow maintaining silence."

To his horror, the interrogator threw the brown envelope on the desk in front of him and demanded to know who had given it to him and who it was for. Stanley had no idea what the package contained; he hadn't asked and he hadn't looked. With no answer forthcoming, the SS men were now enraged:

"My silence provoked one of the SS soldiers to give my already swollen knee a severe blow with his club, causing me to fall, following it up with two severe blows to my genitals. With this I was immediately sick, unfortunately missing the interrogator and the contents of his table, and I mercifully went into a dead faint. When I came to, I was lying in an uncomfortable heap on the floor, in a pool of my own vomit, doubled with the agonies in my groin having fallen awkwardly and with my hands still secured behind my back."

Hauling him roughly back to his feet, Stanley's captors dragged him to a bathtub full of frozen water, forcing his head below the surface as he desperately fought for breath. He had vague recollections of women in the room, laughing and pointing, humiliating and degrading, a deliberate act of emasculation that then and now was nothing short of sexual abuse. Hauled out of the water, Stanley could only hear the questions now being fired at him in something of a fug, and his silence only brought further retribution. He was grabbed and held by two of the guards while the officer slowly began to grind a lighted cigar out on his chest. By some small mercy, Stanley once again fainted, the body's ultimate recourse to self-preservation.

Eventually, Stanley came to with the foul taste of blood and vomit in his mouth, bleeding profusely from the beating to his face and nose. He lay as still as possible, not wanting to attract further violence, in a state of terror as he listened to the screams of the man in the neighbouring cell undergoing unthinkable pain.

A guard re-entered, unlocked Stanley's handcuffs and threw him his bundle of clothes. He stood impatiently as Stanley got dressed, every movement causing him more pain and distress from the agonies in his groin. In the forecourt he waited for the van that would return him to Fresnes prison and comparative safety, at least for a few hours:

"I was in a sorry state – my scrotum was almost black, distorted and swollen to the size of a grapefruit. My already swollen knee would hardly bend, and my mouth and nose were still bleeding. There was no mirror in which to examine my wounds and only my shirt and singlet with which to try and staunch the flow of blood. The exposed nerve in one of my broken teeth was reacting violently after I sought relief with a draught of cold water. This was to make life even more depressing as it was to be November, some four months later, before I was able to receive any form of dental treatment."

For several days Stanley was consumed by fear, misery and pain, listening out for the shouts of "Aus! Aus! Tribunal! Los! Los!" which would mean another round of beatings and interrogation. He was in a nightmare from which it was impossible to wake up, with only the prospect of a quick death to look forward to.

Returned to his place of interrogation, Stanley noted that the number of prisoners now awaiting collection had dwindled. Some had undoubtedly died, others already despatched to a concentration camp or execution. Stanley was separated from the group and placed in a small windowless room with the graffiti of desperate souls scratched into the walls. The senior SS NCO drew his thumb across his throat, a clear sign that Stanley was now living on borrowed time. He was a shitty British 'terror flyer' (*Scheissene Britische Terrorflieger*) responsible for murdering innocent German women and children and would pay with his life. But nothing happened. Stanley returned to Fresnes without further punishment.

Stanley was relieved but still frightened. The inference from the SS NCO was clear, and while the Germans clearly now accepted that he was nothing more than an airman on the run, he also knew that he was totally at their mercy. They could just as well shoot him out of hand with the justification to themselves that he was a spy or part of the Resistance network.

A few days later, Stanley was moved to the upper floor of the prison and into a new cell which he shared with two middle-aged Frenchmen. They had to share a single iron bed and a straw mattress between them. Since they were staunch communists, and blamed Churchill and the evils of capitalism for their current predicament, it was not a happy union.

Stanley soon became accustomed to the prison routines. Along the vast corridors, extending the entire length of the cell blocks, was a sunken narrow-gauge railway line along which was wheeled, at early morning and midday, a huge cauldron operated by two burly prisoners with a German guard. The cauldron contained either the insipid early morning coffee or the much-awaited midday soup:

> *"Within the cells there was a strict rota at the door, for the receipt of the appropriate number of bowls and portions of bread, for he was the person who would have that split-second choice of which bowl had the most soup or which portion of bread had the more bulk. In my case it was never a problem, for the two Frenchmen always fell out over this privilege and I was always the recipient of the last bowl and the smallest portion of bread – as repulsive as it was, it was most acceptable."*

Friday in Block 3 in which Stanley was confined was weekly exercise day when prisoners from each floor level, in parties of approximately 25 at a time, were taken down the open metal staircases to the lower floor and out into a small exercise yard – the same yard where they held almost daily executions. While Stanley was only given a few minutes of comparative freedom to breathe in the clean air, it was a remarkable boost to his morale, notwithstanding his knee still causing him considerable pain.

It was on the second Friday that he first heard English voices among the muted mutterings of his fellow inmates. He now knew he wasn't alone. He also knew that perhaps he might not be shot after all, for why else would they be alive? The following week, his guards organised a reshuffling of cells, and Stanley was pushed unceremoniously into cell 429 in the company of three other prisoners who looked at him with mistrust. Then they began speaking and Stanley experienced the first sense of joy since he had been captured: two of the voices were English and the third Australian. He soon learned that they were all three RAF or Royal Australian Air Force: two sergeant navigators and a flight sergeant air gunner.

> *"After this a whole new world opened out – there was conversation at last, especially when the occupants of cells were rotated, as seemed to be the weekly habit, though for some reason I did not understand I remained in the same corner cell for the remainder of my sojourn in Fresnes. Being at the top of the prison block and at the end of the trolley delivery run the soup, although it had lost much of its heat, was near the bottom of the vat and of a thicker consistency, with bulkier potatoes or beans, and the portion was*

distinctly more generous than we had been used to on the lower floors. Life was slowly taking a turn for the better."

Life was indeed becoming more tolerable, and a fair way of rotating use of the single bed and straw mattress was found. Despite their privations, none of the men talked 'shop', lest walls had ears, and there was a palpable silence should they find themselves in the company of any USAAF airmen with a German-sounding name. From the small window in their cell they could detect the smell of fresh bread being baked every morning from a small boulangerie to the rear of the prison. One of the airmen fashioned a set of playing cards and they passed the time playing bridge and other games which allowed their minds to briefly escape from the suffering they were enduring.

It was now more than two months since Stanley had set out to bomb Trappes, and so much had happened. The raid itself had been a success. A contemporary newspaper report claimed that Trappes "had been given another pasting" and that "seven enemy fighters had been accounted for".[64] News of the Allied advance and breakout from Normandy also reached them in the most unexpected ways. For toilet paper they were given torn-up sheets of newspaper, from which a surprising amount of information could be gleaned before they were put to their intended use. Stanley's principal worry was still personal hygiene. He remained dressed in a shirt caked in dried vomit and would occasionally pass blood in his urine. With no way to properly wash, shave or brush one's teeth, he felt, looked and smelled awful.

Rumours began spreading around the prison that salvation was near. The behaviour of the German guards began to change. Some became more friendly and benign, perhaps trying to ingratiate themselves ahead of what was to come. Others became more unpredictable and dangerous, insistent that the men would not be leaving the prison alive. In the end it didn't matter.

None of the prisoners knew that their real journey into hell was only just beginning.

CHAPTER FOUR
BUCHENWALD

On the morning of 9 August, Marjorie Booker opened an envelope with a London postmark to receive some good news at last.

While it was not specifically about her husband, it did relate to one of his crew. Eileen Stokes wrote that Snooky had been confirmed as being a prisoner of war in Germany. She had received a card from him saying he was safe, and she was not to worry. If Snooky was safe, there was a very good chance that Stanley might be safe also, and that at any moment she might too receive a card that would finally bring her nightmare to an end. Eileen didn't say (but perhaps she didn't then know) that her husband had been badly injured when he landed, and the loyal Frenchman and his wife who had found him were obliged to hand him over to the Germans – and received a beating for their pains.

Ten days later, another letter did arrive, this time from 15 North Terrace, Yeovil. The handwriting on the envelope was unfamiliar, but the news it contained made her heart leap. Cliff Hallett, the mid-upper gunner, was not only safe, but back in England, and had every reason to believe Stan was still alive. While he feared their pilot, Sandy, may have been killed, he'd been told that one of their number was in a hospital and four others were hidden close by.[65] With Clifford, that made seven.

Clifford had been the first to jump. With the aircraft badly damaged, Sandy had given the order to bale out. Clifford had dropped down into the fuselage, clipped his parachute pack to his harness and opened the rear exit door. Peering out into the darkness, he could clearly see an enemy fighter flying on a parallel course to their own aircraft, about 150 ft below. He watched it overtake and accelerate away, its job done, by which time he'd been joined by the rear gunner (Terry) and the flight engineer (Jack), the latter shouting at him to jump. Clifford left the blazing bomber feet first, pulling the ripcord almost at once, and soon after seeing the stricken aircraft hit the ground and explode with a bright flash.[66] He landed safely, and after hiding his chute, harness and 'Mae West' life jacket in a gorse bush, he crawled across a wheatfield and hid in a small wood until morning when he heard voices and the barking of dogs. Daring to take a peep, he was horrified to read a sign on a fence that declared '*Eintritt Verboten*'; he had dozed off beside the boundary of a Luftwaffe military base, Saint-André-de-l'Eure.

Slipping away quietly and unnoticed, Clifford wandered the French countryside with little in the way of a plan until accosting a friendly farmer who offered to help with coffee, bread and a bed. He was introduced to a giant of a man, 'Michel', a member of the local Resistance, and his identity was checked. Once Michel was satisfied, they burned Cliff's RAF uniform and gave him new clothes to wear. Then he was driven in the boot of an old Fiat to La Madeleine-de-Nonancourt where he was hidden for three weeks by a farmer of Armenian descent, Elie Thorossov,[67] before being moved to another safe house and thence driven from a café with three other airmen to the edge of the Fréteval Forest. In the wood was a secret camp occupied by airmen of many nationalities, clothed and fed through the good auspices of MI9, the British escape-and-evasion organisation. Complaining of abdominal pains, Clifford was treated by a local doctor and diagnosed with internal injuries caused from his parachute fall. He was also told by the camp leader, Wing Commander Lucien Boussa, that should their hiding place be discovered, Clifford would have to be left behind! Happily, it never happened; the camp was liberated in the middle of August by a spearhead group of Belgian and British special forces troops of the Special Air Service (SAS) and Clifford and 131 other airmen bussed to safety.

He wrote to Marjorie again a few days later, by which time he had learned that Snooky was in one piece. Until then he had feared that the escape hatch might have jammed, and perhaps none of the crew at the front of the aircraft had made it out at all. But since Snooky could not leave the aircraft until Stanley had vacated his escape route, now there was every reason to think Stanley had made it out too.

But where was he? And why had she heard nothing from the authorities? It was perhaps as well that she didn't know that her husband's nightmare was only just beginning.

The logistics of dealing with many thousands of prisoners held in overcrowded gaols in Paris and other cities that would soon be in Allied control had been exercising the minds of the German authorities for some time. British agents, local Resistance fighters, and others who worked for or ran escape lines could not be allowed to fall into enemy hands, and many were destined to disappear without trace under Germany's '*Nacht und Nebel*' (Night and Fog) decree. Their files, along with the 168 Allied airmen at Fresnes, had been stamped with '*Rückkehr unerwünscht*' to denote that their return was not required. Mass executions at the prison in Caen (on 6 June) had set a precedent.

On 8 August, Raoul Nordling, the Swedish consul, visited the German ambassador to France, Otto Abetz, to plead for the release of the prisoners in Fresnes. He argued that by placing them in the care of the Red Cross or a neutral country, they would be out of the Germans' way and would therefore not impede the retreat of German troops. He submitted a summary of his proposals two days later. At much the same time, Pierre Laval – the Vichy prime minister – arrived in Paris, in a last-ditch effort to prevent de Gaulle's supporters or the communists from seizing power.

With the threat to the prisoners increasing by the hour, plans were being discussed for ways to attack the prison without provoking a widespread massacre. It did not look hopeful. Nordling's proposals were elevated higher up the chain of command to Carl Oberg, a senior SS general of police. Nordling also sought to garner support from various other players, including the archbishop of Paris, who may have had an influence, as well as requesting meetings with Dietrich von Choltitz, the city's military governor, and later the man credited with being the city's saviour.

On 11 August, those whom the Germans considered the most dangerous among the Resistance and many of the captured agents of Britain's Special Operations Executive (the SOE – famously tasked with "setting Europe ablaze") were evacuated. Two days later, another trainload departed Paris for Germany. A last desperate message was conveyed to London by Alexandre Parodi, a key figure in the Resistance movement, warning the British authorities of a possible slaughter.[68] Elsewhere, Oberg rejected Nordling's plan, and the fate of the Allied airmen appeared to be sealed.[69]

The night of 14/15 August 1944 was a noisy one in Fresnes prison. Cell doors were constantly being opened and slammed shut. Men were shouting. The occasional pistol shot echoed off the concrete walls. No coffee or soup was forthcoming, though earlier in the day they had been fed well. Order appeared to be breaking down. Then the SS reappeared to take charge.

One by one the cells were emptied, and prisoners huddled together until separated into distinct groups. What seemed at first to be a random selection of men was in fact more orderly and controlled until a group of almost two hundred airmen were together, some delighted at discovering the fate of friends they had not seen since being shot down and didn't know were still alive. Among them, Stanley spotted Jack, whom he had not seen since they had been separated at the safe house. Clearly their journeys had followed a similar route.

A dozen or so different nationalities were represented among the Allied prisoners, and a Dutchman – an RAF pilot fluent in German – stepped forward to help convey the Germans' instructions as a form of liaison. He immediately fell under suspicion.[70] The prisoners were told to arrange themselves into groups of 25 to 30, with each group allocated two armed guards. They were to be taken in a convoy of old buses to a railway siding and warned that any attempt at escape en route would result in immediate execution.

Flight Lieutenant 'Tommy' Blackham, one of the British prisoners who'd been on the run since May, remembered the moment: "A German Hauptmann ordered two of his men to cock their machine guns and told them to fire if we made any noise."[71] Peter Phelps also recalls the hatred in the guards' eyes, describing them as "almost inhuman".[72]

Any initial excitement that their ordeal might soon be over was almost immediately quashed as the buses pulled into the vast freight yards adjoining Gare de l'Est, where an ominous line of cattle trucks stood waiting. The dawn of realisation was fast in coming – that this was to be their transport to a destination as yet unknown. They were also dismayed to see that most of the trucks were already packed with prisoners, with an armed guard posted on every door.[73]

As they waited, another procession of vehicles arrived and offloaded their sorry cargo. A group of around two hundred women of various ages were kicked and beaten from the buses onto a platform and into the three cattle trucks at the rear of the line, 70 or so to each truck. Only then did the Germans turn their attention to the Allied airmen, and Stanley recalled:

> *"When all of the buses had arrived the Allied prisoners were lined up, counted and likewise marched across the yard and crammed into the remaining three trucks – one of which already contained 30 French prisoners. Conditions*

were appalling – we had between 80 to 85 in each truck. I was in the second truck in the line. Throughout that long and hot August day the train remained motionless, and despite the sliding doors being allowed to remain open the distressed inmates rapidly became exhausted through the lack of air and water."[74]

In such extremes, military discipline often comes to the fore, and so it proved:

"Morale was still quite high – the situation, although far from good, was not hopeless. We found strength and hope from the knowledge that we were now in the midst of close friends, a proven body of disciplined young men, with a will to live and succeed. The future was far from clear but at least was a contrast from the boredom and uncertainty of the prison cells."

The trucks were too crowded to permit anyone to relax or more than half to sit on the floor at any one time. A single oil drum served as the toilet. Some black bread and water were distributed, but without any knives to portion the bread it proved an unhappy operation.[75]

The light was steadily failing before the guards once again became more agitated and the shouting started again in earnest. The great doors on each of the trucks were slid shut and bolted, heightening the sense of claustrophobia within, the men enclosed in what felt like an inky-black coffin. There was some relief as the train gathered speed, forcing air through the two small barbed-wire openings at either end of the truck, and the men settled as best they could for the long journey ahead.

In one of the trucks, some of the men began scraping at the rotten timbers in the floor with whatever metal accoutrements they had managed to smuggle from the prison. It was no simple task. The thick, rough planks had been there for years, engrained with muck and filth from a thousand other ironically less-bestial journeys, and the heads of the nails were buried and worn, and difficult to extract. And yet, somehow, the men managed it. Having forced an exit, several of the prisoners escaped, among them an American flying with the Royal Canadian Air Force, Joel Stevenson, who eventually made it home.[76] For Stanley, this achievement nevertheless brought danger:

"The following morning when the missing floorboards were discovered, at one of the early halts in a siding, all hell was let loose with the SS making the most

terrible threats of executing hostages and whole truckloads of prisoners if such an attempt was made again. After emergency repairs to the flooring had been undertaken, the clothing and shoes were taken away from the occupants of both trucks where the breakouts occurred, and they were left naked to suffer the added discomfort of the rough splintering timbers of the moving trucks."

Yet morale remained high. Despite the appalling conditions, the RAF boys and their US counterparts had much to discuss, though there was some understandable fear that their train might be attacked by friendly aircraft. Any transport now seen moving around France, day or night, could fall victim to a rocket-firing Typhoon or Mosquito intruder whose sole purpose was to seek out and destroy the enemy.

On the third day they had their first experience of SS bestiality close up. A teenage French boy in a neighbouring truck put his arm out of the truck 'window' while the train was moving and was shot at by a guard seated above, wounding him in the hand. A signal was given, and the train stopped, after which the boy was dragged from his truck and shot in the back, in "just another episode of German Kultur", as one RAF airman would later sardonically recall.[77] An RAF sergeant, Andrew Rowe, and Leo Grenon, a Canadian air gunner, were given shovels with which to dig the boy a shallow grave. As Grenon says: "No names or numbers were taken and he was only one spadeful deep in an unmarked grave."[78] They were then warned that, if there was any further trouble, 45 British and American prisoners would be taken out and shot. It was a brutal hint of what was to come.[79] As brutal, perhaps, was the lack of care afforded to one of the Canadians in Rowe's carriage, Flying Officer James 'Pep' Prudham, who suffered an epileptic fit. Rowe asked the guard for medical attention, or at least some water, but both were refused.[80]

Their departure from Gare de l'Est had not gone unnoticed; a bridge on the River Marne had been destroyed to halt the train's progress. The Germans got around the problem by marching the prisoners in small groups along the banks of the river to the next road bridge and rejoining the train at Châlons. Some of the airmen were humiliated by having to carry their SS guards' kit, and being beaten for their trouble. One, a Kiwi squadron leader by the name of Phil Lamason, was clubbed to the ground and kicked by an SS NCO for failing to comply quickly enough with the German's command.[81]

The end of the fourth day finished all hopes that the airmen were to be separated and taken to Dulag Luft at Frankfurt and processed, as was customary, prior to being sent to a POW camp. Frankfurt came and went, and the train continued on its journey, although some still maintained they could be skipping interrogation and being taken straight to the camps, of which at least one was known to be further east.

It was on the fifth day, the morning of 20 August, that the train drew slowly to a halt in the busy railway station of Weimar. Here it made a lengthy stop whilst the three trucks allocated to the party of French female prisoners were detached and shunted away to an unknown destination. Later it was learned that they had been sent to the notorious Ravensbrück concentration camp, north of Berlin.

> *"We were sorry to lose their company for somehow we had established a silent bond of affection, and personal guilt, for they had been our immediate neighbours throughout that nightmare of a journey, and many of us could not help feeling that probably many of those brave patriots were only in this dreadful predicament because they had sacrificed so much by giving shelter and aid to Allied airmen on the run. Many comforting words, in halting French or in broken English, had been furtively exchanged over the past few days, when, during the infrequent halts en route, and two at a time under the eagle eyes of the leering SS guards, we prisoners were allowed out and permitted a few hurried minutes in order to undertake our personal toilet in between the trucks, always a difficult undertaking in view of the limited time available and with over 80 other prisoners shut up within the truck demanding their turn and an opportunity to stretch their legs."*

The numerous Germans waiting on the busy station platform, both in uniform and civilian clothes, appeared to be completely unconcerned at the distress of the hundreds of prisoners packed into the long line of cattle trucks, with their full loads of human misery. Only later would Stanley come to realise the notoriety of Weimar as a stopping-off point for trains coming from every corner of occupied Europe, and their onward journeys to indescribable hells. They paid no attention as they had seen it all before and were numb to it.

The train was not long in the station after the women were unloaded; nor was their journey to their new home a long one. It was a camp that was originally going to be called Ettersberg, after the hill in Thuringia upon whose north slope it had been established. The Germans, however, had had a change of heart, and since it was situated by a beautiful forest of beech trees they opted instead for its German name, Buchenwald.

As the train broke out into the sunshine at the crest of the wooded Ettersberg ridge, it drew slowly to a halt in a large clearing containing several railway sidings. Along the perimeter was a large industrial complex comprising numerous long hangar-like buildings, secured by a high and electrified double fence:

> *"An astonishing sight was to meet our eyes, for like a colony of busy ants, dozens of skeleton-like figures with shaven heads and eyes sunk deep in their sockets, uniformly dressed in blue-and-white-striped two-piece suits, were scurrying about their various tasks."*

This complex was the famous Gustloff-Werk munitions factory where various components essential to the Nazi's V-2 rocket programme were made. These components were later assembled in the vast underground rocket factory in the Nordhausen-Dora concentration camp, situated deep in the Harz Mountains a few miles to the north.

> *"The bewilderment and speculation at our situation soon came to an abrupt end by the arrival of shouting SS soldiers armed with heavy sticks, whips, and many with vicious Alsatian dogs. The sliding doors of the trucks were thrown open and the occupants herded out onto the platform and hustled away to an assembly area at the end of the track. The dogs freely attacked any unfortunate prisoner who did not respond quickly enough to German orders whilst others were subjected to cruel blows from clubs and rifle butts. Eventually some form of order was restored, and under continuing harassment from the guards and their snarling dogs our wretched column of some 1,650 prisoners shuffled down the shabby lane known as the Caracho Weg – 'The Road of Blood' – which extended for nearly a mile before terminating outside the double-storied gateway to the encampment."*

Surmounting the gateway was a clock tower and platform upon which several heavy machine guns were mounted covering the new contingent of prisoners. Either side of the gateway was a block of shuttered bunkers and cells. In the centre were written the words *Jedem das Seine* ("Each to his Own") – a nod to the superiority of the Germans and their right to destroy whom they wished.

"Entering through the gateway the new arrivals were confronted with an indescribable sight – as far as one could see were row upon row of shabby hutments, mainly windowless, laid out in orderly lines in front of which was a vast open 'parade ground', onto which streaming masses of emaciated individuals, poorly clothed in various striped and odd garments, were assembling in orderly rows likewise under harassment from bullying SS guards."

Hanging over the camp was a pall of acrid smoke, its foul stench pervading every part of the camp, coming from the crematorium whose furnaces appeared to be running 24 hours a day.

"Our arrival into the camp had been a shock to us all and we were still in a daze, as once again we were lined up. If too slow to react, rifle butts, kicks and loud shouts assisted us to a quicker understanding. Clearly this was not a POW camp and a new understanding of our guards and prison was the immediate problem."

Their understanding would not have been helped had Stanley known how he had been classified. Far from being a POW, protected by the Geneva Convention, he was deemed a 'police prisoner' on the authority of the commander of the security police in Paris (*Befehlshaber der Sicherheitsdienst Paris*) with a special instruction that he was not to be transferred to another camp (DIKAL – *Darf in kein anderes Lager*). It seemed Buchenwald was a one-way ticket. As Peter Phelps recalls: "Buchenwald was a death camp. It smelled like death, felt like death and looked like death."[82]

The airmen were marched beyond the crematorium to the *Effektenkammer* – the prisoners' effects store – to the continued shouting of their guards. Half of the party was American, and the other half primarily British and Canadian, with a handful of Australians, New Zealanders and a Jamaican – 168 in total.

The men were herded into a shower block and told to strip. While their filthy clothes were searched, they washed with a primitive soap and attempted to remove the layers of grime that had accumulated at Fresnes and in the subsequent railway journey. The shower was surprisingly refreshing, but their pleasure was short-lived. Still naked, they were ordered into a neighbouring annex where they were shaved from head to toe with what seemed to Stanley to be electric sheep shears. Their naked bodies were then liberally painted with a cresol solution that stung for several hours afterwards. An interpreter, who they later learned was Christopher Burney, a captured agent of F (French) Section, SOE, quietly told them not to resist in any way, nor to make eye contact with any of the SS guards. The first lesson in staying alive was to be anonymous.

Like newly shorn sheep they were pushed into the main administration area, located on the lower ground floor of the vast *Effektenkammer*, where a team of SS clerks and prisoners from the political department undertook to meticulously record all personal details onto various cards and documents. It was here that Stanley was issued with his camp registration number, consisting of five figures, crudely stamped on a strip of cotton cloth to be later sewn onto his camp uniform.

> *"All items of clothing and what few personal possessions remained were taken from us and carefully recorded.[83] We gathered our camp clothing, taken from a pile on the floor, not a set of striped pyjamas as issued to the French prisoners but rather a shabby jacket, shirt, an odd pair of trousers (without a belt or other means of support) and a rough pair of underpants. No footwear of any sort was issued and once again we were herded out into the open clutching our ill-fitting attire."*

The party was then led away from the *Effektenkammer* to an area resembling a derelict shanty town, separated from the main camp by an electrified fence.

> *"It was an unbelievably squalid and evil-smelling nightmare of a scene. We saw a jumbled mass of narrow huts and a couple of very large, tattered tents. Everywhere were signs of filth and decay. It was inconceivable that anyone could exist in such wretched conditions. Every available open space appeared to be occupied by little groups of sorry-looking, unshaven individuals – the great majority of whom were wearing odd and shabby clothing."*

They were now inside the dreaded 'Little Camp', the quarantine area, where all new arrivals to Buchenwald were initially incarcerated, usually out in the open, and until such time as the SS medical officer undertook a cursory examination to assess the degree of fitness for manual work. There then followed an allocation to a working Kommando either within the camp, in one of the two large munitions works, or for transfer to one of the many outside working parties. Many more were destined to be deployed to one of the 136 secondary working camps under the control of the Buchenwald administration.

The SS escort departed, leaving the men, somewhat bewildered, to sort themselves out. It was getting dark, and they had no food, no water and no shelter. What they did have in abundance was fear. Stanley looked at those around him. Faces that had grown familiar were now unrecognisable, and bald heads took on different shapes. Only their voices remained the same. Jack was there, of course, and another he recognised: Terry Gould.

Terry had landed not far from the others by the airfield at Saint-André-de-l'Eure and lost a boot in his descent. After two hours of walking in the dark, he decided to rest and take stock, hiding in a haystack. As the dawn broke, he spotted a young man walking close by and called out to him. The man, Maurice Porcher, was a loyal Frenchmen and took him to his farm where he was introduced to Maurice's wife, Fernande.

The Germans were now all about and it was only a matter of time before they searched the farm. Terry was just donning a farmer's jacket as a disguise when a patrol entered the farmyard, giving him just enough time to jump out of the back window. Landing in a pigsty, he grabbed a pitchfork and made out as if he was working in the pen. The German soldiers thought nothing of it, nor did they question him, and were soon on their way.

On the first night he slept out in the woods until they were confident he was safe. The next night, he slept in a neighbouring cottage which the family also owned. It was dangerous for Maurice and Fernande to shelter the airman any longer than was necessary. Being so close to a German airfield, the soldiers would often appear unannounced to buy eggs or milk, and would be suspicious if they were turned away.[84]

The mayor of Lignerolle, Monsieur Guicheux, paid a visit, after which Terry was given new clothes, a pair of shoes and a bike, and then followed the mayor to his home a few kilometres away.[85] Here he stayed for several weeks, at one point under the very noses of a party of Luftwaffe officers billeted there; he took the opportunity to pour sand into the petrol tank of their car! He was eventually driven, with three Americans, to Paris, and accommodated with around two dozen Allied airmen in a private house awaiting onward transit to Spain. The next evening they clambered onto the back of a crowded truck for what they believed was the last leg of their journey. After only a few minutes, however, the truck stopped, and they were ordered out and into a building where they were told they were all saboteurs and would be shot. Within hours, Terry was in Fresnes.[86] Now – like Stanley, Jack and 165 other aircrew – they awaited their fate.

Quickly, military discipline again took over. The British and Commonwealth flyers formed one group – with Phil Lamason, the squadron leader who had earlier been clubbed to the ground, as the senior British officer (SBO) – and the Americans another, arguing among themselves who should take charge. They sought accommodation, unaware that they would be sharing it with another 6,000 prisoners in their current environment, and a further 38,000 beyond the wire in the main camp. With little room to spare, all were obliged to sleep on the rocky ground out in the open, grateful that it was still August, and that the weather was still comparatively warm.

Then a tiny miracle happened. From one of the huts, a small party of living skeletons emerged dragging a barrel of soup and a small container of cold potatoes, still in their jackets. It was the first proper nourishment the men had received for some time, though without bowls or utensils they had to cup what little soup they could in their hands, or drink like animals at a watering hole. Stanley was somewhat overcome:

> *"This was the first act of kindness since our capture, seemingly a lifetime previously, and was to prove to be the first of many quite often anonymous gifts or services from complete strangers, many of whom could not communicate in any form of common language. Already, in that short time, news had spread that there was a party of Allied airmen in the camp."*

Within comparatively short order, the Allied airmen came to the attention of the commandant, Hermann Pister. He would periodically wander into the Little Camp and hurl abuse at the men, screaming that they were "Terrorflieger" and murderers and would face dire consequences for their bombing of Germany.[87]

Born in Lübeck, Pister, who had been in the German navy in the First World War and joined the Nazi party in 1932, had taken over from Karl Koch, whose wife Ilse became a byword for cruelty in the camps. Pister, though, was no less cruel, and under his rule life for the prisoners at Buchenwald went from bad to worse.[88] As Stanley remembers: "Pister was rough, uneducated, but equally as ruthless as his predecessor."[89] Notwithstanding his crude, sadistic manner, Pister came to grudgingly admire the Allied airmen for their organisation and discipline and would soon come to benefit from these qualities in the days ahead.

Meantime, further acts of kindness touched the men in captivity. Some blankets were donated by fellow prisoners – dirty, threadbare but nonetheless welcome – with one blanket being shared between groups of five. Despite improving conditions, the men rarely spoke. There was little conversation, each man alone with his thoughts. And they weren't especially uplifting. Stanley wondered if anyone knew they were there, and who might come to their rescue. There was only one guaranteed way out of Buchenwald, they used to joke, and that was up the chimney.

With the dawn of the first morning, a harrowing scene began to be played out with which they would become familiar. In the main camp, hundreds of emaciated prisoners emerged from the huts, many wearing conspicuous Stars of David on their jackets, and began forming into regular lines, with ten in each. Within moments the guards appeared, each carrying a club with which to beat the prisoners for any misdemeanour, or simply for the fun of it. The now-familiar screaming began as the SS barked out their orders and the prisoners quickly obeyed.

Two of the guards headed for the party of Allied prisoners and similarly began kicking and beating the reluctant airmen into a parade. Some were less inclined than others, until the Dutch pilot interpreter impressed upon them the urgency of doing as they were told. This was not a POW camp; there would be no second chances.

An *Unterscharführer* (approximate equivalent to a corporal in the British army) by the name of Alfred Hoffman took charge, winding himself up to a dangerous and unpredictable state of fury and hatred.[90] The airmen quickly learned never to look him in the eye and to avoid standing at the front, where they were almost certainly going to be struck, for he was never without a 20-inch club in his hands and would use it with alacrity. After what seemed an age, the ordeal ended with a blow of a whistle. In the main camp, the block supervisors took over, hated almost as much as the guards themselves. After the prisoners were fed their meagre rations, they formed into parties and were marched off to work to the sounds of a small orchestra, dressed in incongruous circus attire. In the Little Camp, the airmen had not yet been allocated any duties, nor was there a routine. They were marched to a brick building known as the canteen, used by the SS for special assemblies and lectures, and from where they could buy beer and cigarettes using Lagergeld – a special camp currency.

"Inside the canteen we were instructed to remove our clothing and each in turn, standing completely naked, was photographed holding a small tablet

onto which was chalked his camp registration number. With this exercise complete we underwent the now-accepted harassment by the escort, were marched back into the Little Camp, again being left to our own devices – hungry, uncertain and with so much going on which was totally foreign to our normal way of living."

A block supervisor took a small group of prisoners away with him to initiate them into camp routines for drawing soup and coffee rations from the main camp cookhouse. They were allowed to be accompanied by their own 'bodyguards', lest they be ambushed by other prisoners on the way back from the cookhouse to their camp, which was quite a distance. The German *Lagerschutz* (camp police) turned a blind eye.

The first sortie to the cookhouse resulted in a veritable feast of hot soup, potatoes and bread, though it proved to be a false dawn for they were never to eat so well again.

While eating, the men began to talk and share what little information they had gleaned thus far. They now knew about the main camp, and the prisoners with their coloured stars to denote their status as Jews, homosexuals, gypsies, Jehovah's Witnesses, criminals or political agitators. They learned also that in Block 17 of the main camp was another party of 'police prisoners' who wore neither striped uniforms nor stars. They had arrived a few days earlier and, while Stanley did not know it at the time, they were all agents of the SOE. The Germans simply referred to them all as "commandos" or just "parachutists".

As spies – and therefore actual terrorists in the minds of their captors, caught in the act of committing terrorist crimes – the fate of the SOE prisoners had already been decided, and it was just a matter of time before they would be executed. Among their number was a squadron leader who introduced himself under an assumed name, Kenneth Dodkin. Phil Lamason, who by an unlikely twist of fate had known the real Kenneth Dodkin, was immediately suspicious.[91] "Half of his own blokes didn't want a bar of him," Lamason recounts, "and even for my own guys he became a matter of concern."[92] The officer seemed excited by the prospect of having another two hundred or so men in his 'army'. The fact they were trained aircrew was even better. He was hatching a plan for them to break out of the camp en masse and make for the nearest airfield. From there they could steal a quantity of aircraft and fly to safety. Only later would the true identity of the mysterious officer and his madcap idea be revealed.[93]

What Stanley and the others learned about the camp did nothing to lift their spirits. While it may not have had a gas chamber, Buchenwald was one of Germany's worst concentration camps – used to gather undesirables for disposal, as well as to provide a source of expendable labour to aid German industry. Built in 1937 to house 7,000 prisoners, it now held 38,000, and its numbers continued to swell as the Russians began to overrun the extermination camps further east. As well as prisoners literally being worked to death, there were also terrible experiments being undertaken in Blocks 46 and 51 that led to many hundreds of horrific deaths as a result of prisoners being injected with deadly viruses. There were no Red Cross parcels or monitoring by any international protecting power, and only the knowledge that they were not alone kept them going:

> *"Provided we could stay alive we would be able to give support and strength to each other, especially fortified with the knowledge that we now had some of our own kinsfolk already well established within the camp to give guidance and assistance as situations arose."*

One of the most essential tools for staying alive was a 'gammel':

> *"It has to be stressed – the absolute necessity for acquiring and retaining a food bowl. There was no way of receiving your ration of soup or coffee if you didn't have a container, and nobody would lend you one. It was a question of one's very survival to own a soup bowl. It went everywhere with you. No gammel – no food. It was a hard fact of life."*

For the next two weeks they remained out in the open as no accommodation had yet been allocated.

> *"The SS took little notice of us except for their taunts, at the morning and evening roll calls. Once a day a barrel of thin and insipid soup was provided, whilst in the evening there was an issue of some form of hot mint tea, with a portion of black bread and a slice of gristly salami-type sausage."*

Peter Phelps remembers that the roll calls (Appells) were a challenge in themselves:

"On a good day it would last one and a half hours. Mostly it lasted longer. The longest I experienced was four and a half hours in the rain. You just stood there and if you wanted to do anything you just did it where you stood and cleaned up afterwards. No matter what the conditions you just stood there and if anyone collapsed, he just lay there. Quite often some were dead when they were moved. It would appear that the dead would have to be counted as being alive and crossed off the following day."[94]

Despite their predicament, the men discussed the idea of escape, though Stanley had little expectation of success:

"To escape in our present condition, living out in the open, was out of the question – there could be no attempts at constructing elaborate tunnels, such as those undertaken by POWs in the seclusion and security of their own barrack blocks. With our prison attire, lack of hair, shoes, money and personal documentation, we appreciated that we could not get very far under the present circumstances."

Unbeknown to Stanley, the mysterious squadron leader was still actively pursuing his plan for a mass breakout. Not many were willing to give it a try, least of all the Russian contingent who thought the squadron leader "just a bloody idiot".[95] The airmen were similarly unimpressed and had one advantage over the ordinary prisoners in the camp: they had first-hand knowledge that the war was coming to an end. While it was true that the communists had managed to get their hands on a veritable arsenal of weapons, it was still a highly risky business, and dozens – maybe hundreds – would be killed if they decided to put the squadron leader's plan into action. If they could sit it out, remain as inconspicuous as possible, and not draw attention to themselves there was a chance – albeit a slim one – that they might still make it out alive.

For some, however, death came from a most unexpected and ironic source.

CHAPTER FIVE
AIR RAID

STANLEY SPENT ANOTHER COLD AND miserable night under the stars, and the usual roll call was followed by the arrival of two Polish medical orderlies wearing white gowns and carrying surgical trays. On each of the trays was an assortment of evil-looking syringes, with needles much longer than Stanley had ever seen before.

As a serviceman, he was used to injections. Operational aircrew received annual anti-tubercular therapy (ATT) and typhoid, paratyphoid A and paratyphoid B (TAB) injections, and Stanley had received his most recent dose in April. But this was different. Anxious to learn what was in the syringes and conscious that the two men had emerged from the sinister medical block, they were told nothing other than it was related to typhus:

> *"We were forced to line up and the two medical orderlies, each armed with one of the large syringes, proceeded to give every airman an injection on either side of the breastbone – not a fleshy area at any time. It was incredibly painful. The same needle was used for the entire party."*

Stanley's concerns were well founded. The Germans were already using phenol in human experiments at various camps, and in Buchenwald itself doctors had developed a method of individual execution by injecting Russian prisoners with phenol and cyanide. Those same doctors were also experimenting with other poisons and their impact on the human body and afterwards killing those who survived in order that they could then conduct post-mortems. Stanley's fears were heightened when, within a little while of receiving his dose, he began feeling slightly disorientated, as though having an out-of-body experience.

Stanley did not have long to dwell on his discomfort, however, for all around him men were pointing to the sky, and in the distance he could just make out the contrails of a large formation of aircraft approaching from the west. They could only be Allied bombers, probably B-17s heading for a target further east in support of the Russian advance. Steadily, an air-raid siren began to sound its mournful tune, accompanied by shouting and running as the guards and prisoners alike headed indoors for what little protection that afforded. An eerie silence descended on the camp and only the distant drone of the aircraft could be heard, getting louder as they approached at 22,000 ft with their bomb doors open. The target wasn't further east; the target was the factories around Buchenwald.

Professional eyes confirmed this was indeed a formation of around 60 Flying Fortresses, the lead aircraft appearing to drop a white flare as it reached the edge of the camp. To the RAF it held no meaning, but for the American airmen it meant that disaster was imminent, a fact confirmed as the first of a series of whooshing sounds could be heard followed by explosions terrifyingly close to the airmen still standing in the open air and – with nowhere to run – scaring them out of their wits.[96]

The air was suddenly full of smoke, and desperate cries of help could be heard in the distance. Panic started to spread on the other side of the inner wire where hundreds of inmates ran across the parade ground away from the crematorium, behind which was situated another munitions works manned by prisoners – the *Deutschen Ausrüstungswerke* – from which smoke and flames were beginning to rise as the American 500-lb bombs struck home.

> "As we recovered from the shock of this, our first ever air raid witnessed in close proximity, our attention reverted back to the sky where to our anguish we watched the approach, from the same direction, of another large formation of B-17 bombers. This time, to our horror, we observed the white marker dropping considerably further to the north than that from the first formation. We shook ourselves out of a state of extreme shock to find smoke and debris clouded the sky – shortly to be filled with many thousands of leaflets that fluttered down like a snowstorm. We felt very naked and exposed, in our vulnerable position out in the compound, as we anticipated the sickening

> *swoosh and thud. Simultaneously hundreds of high-explosive bombs burst on the edge of the camp, much closer than during the previous attack."*

One of their own number, Canadian Flying Officer Frank Salt, was struck by flying shrapnel and badly hurt. He was taken to the infirmary which was already overflowing with the dead and dying. The main camp was in a state of utter confusion and the munitions works (one of two factories neighbouring Buchenwald) and a number of prisoners' huts were burning fiercely. The barracks, however, appeared at first to be untouched and, with the aircraft now departing, stunned and bewildered guards began to emerge with pistols drawn and headed straight for the airmen:

> *"To a man, we each thought: 'This is it – this really is going to be the chop'. It is truly amazing, under such situations of extreme stress, just how calm and composed one becomes. As we commiserated together afterwards, most of us wondered just how they would execute us and our main concern – just how our loved one would ever get to know. We seemed to float over the events of the past few minutes, and the shouts and hostility of the guards – it all seemed so unreal somehow. Unreality was soon lost when we came across the utter chaos that prevailed – the whole eastern side of the camp was an absolute shambles. Flames were not only coming from the two damaged factories, but at least one of the barrack huts and from within the SS administration and domestic areas."*

Various small groups began streaming back across the *Appellplatz* carrying the wounded by any means possible, but none of their actions or the Germans' response appeared co-ordinated. The SS did, however, quickly set up a machine gun on the main entrance to deter any thoughts the prisoners might have of rushing the gates in all the confusion.

One of the SS NCOs who appeared more lucid than the rest gave instructions to the airmen to salvage whatever documents they could from the various administrative buildings and rescue any persons trapped in the damaged factory:

> *"Left much to our own devices we attempted what we could, in the areas where we had been directed to. Many more documents were consumed by the flames than were saved, but our main concern was recovering the bodies that were*

lying around unattended, many in considerable pain and in need of urgent medical attention. Casualty assembly points were quickly established in the nearby canteen building with the dead being crudely dumped in heaps outside of the crematorium. The less severely wounded were carried to the Sonderbau (the camp brothel) located next to the infamous medical experiment block, where we thought the medical facilities could be used to better effect."

Some hours later they drifted back into the Little Camp, exhausted and not a little sickened at some of the horrendous sights they had seen. But they did not return empty-handed – everyone seemed to have taken advantage of the situation, and all had acquired shoes or wooden clogs. Blankets had been 'borrowed', bowls and eating utensils abounded and various miscellaneous items secreted about their persons, including at least one automatic pistol which was given to the squadron leader to add to his secret arsenal.

Some three hundred tons of bombs had fallen in the vicinity, taking out the electricity and water supplies which hampered the rescue efforts and led to a desperate water shortage in the weeks that followed. An air-raid shelter housing various SS families received a direct hit. An official report compiled a few days after the attack (on 27 August) by the senior SS medical officer for the Weimar region, Hauptsturmführer Gerhard Schiedlausky,[97] listed the casualties as follows:

"SS members: 80 dead comprising 30 Buchenwald camp guards and 50 from the SS transport unit; 65 missing comprising 17 SS personnel and 48 'others'; and 238 wounded and in the General Hospital comprising 75 SS and 163 'others'."

To the number were added 24 SS dependents or family members killed, and 43 members of the Fichtenhain VIP special complex dead, missing or wounded. In terms of prisoners, 315 were listed as dead, 525 seriously wounded (many of whom would later go on to die) and 900 with slight injuries. "There is a possibility," Schiedlausky noted, "that included in the prisoner total there is a number of unidentified civilians and SS other rank dependents."

In an official HMSO report[98] published soon after the camp was liberated, the death toll included 400 German servicemen, 200 prisoners, and 150 female dependents including the wife and daughter of the camp commandant, Hermann Pister.

Mission 132 comprised 129 B-17 Flying Fortresses of the 613th Bomb Squadron, 401st Bombardment Group flying from RAF Deenethorpe. Their target was the *Gustloff-Werk II*, the aircrew simply being told that it was "engaged in the production of V-2 rocket weapons". Buchenwald was mentioned by name, but not its function.[99] A summary report (dated 3 September) benefiting from post-raid photo-reconnaissance undertaken by an American 14 (Photographic Reconnaissance) Squadron Spitfire PRXI from Mount Farm[100] suggested that five concentrations of general purpose and RDX (devastating cyclonite/hexogen) bombs and two concentrations of incendiary bombs covered the entire target area. Hits could be seen on ten large workshops: three were completely destroyed while three others were at least partly destroyed and still burning late in the attack. Indeed, fires were widespread and damage to the area was deemed to be "extremely severe".

As well as the workshops, the boiler house received a direct hit, and hits were also recorded in the garage and stores area. The rail sidings received at least ten direct hits, and considerable damage was done to the rail infrastructure and rolling stock. Two small office buildings – believed to be the HQ of the local Gestapo – were also destroyed by heavy explosives.

Understandably, Stanley and his compatriots expected immediate retribution, especially given the casualties among the SS guards' families and Pister's own family; now would be a good time for the airmen to disappear. Some, like Peter Phelps, began shaking hands with their friends, convinced that they had only moments to live.[101]

The response from the Germans was unexpected:

> *"The extreme accuracy of the bombing was held in high regard by many of the prisoners and made us quite the centre of admiration. News had spread of the valuable assistance that we had rendered the injured, many of whom had been French prisoners employed in the two munitions factories.*
>
> *"Later we were to hear through the offices of the senior communist prisoner responsible to the SS administration for the internal running and administration of the camp that the calm and efficient manner in which the Allied prisoners had taken over the casualty recovery and clearance had not gone unnoticed, and it was grudgingly conceded that it was fortunate that we had been available to undertake such an operation almost without supervision. This we did not know until much later when we had settled into*

a barrack hutment where the block supervisor, one of the better long-term German prisoners, was reasonably sympathetic to our sorry plight. He made our daily existence as tolerable as was practicable, under the circumstances, and sheltered us from the usual excesses of the SS authorities to which we had previously been vulnerable.

"On the day following the raid, whilst still left to fend for ourselves out in the open, we were cheered to receive a welcome delivery of blankets, bowls and spoons. We liked to think of these as a token reward for our services to the community the previous day – most certainly many prisoners owed their lives to the orderly manner in which the emergency recovery was effected for which we could claim much of the credit."

After two weeks living out in the open on the 'rockpile', the airmen were allocated space in Block 58 adjoining the medical block where the experiments continued and from where Stanley counted anything up to 30 bodies being removed every day. It was disturbing to witness death at such close quarters, and the threat of immediate liquidation hung over his head like the proverbial sword of Damocles.

Inside Block 58, conditions were scarcely better than out in the open. The hut was raised off the ground, and every morning the wooden floor was washed and covered with quicklime. It gave off a pungent smell of chlorine gas but was a small nod to maintaining some level of hygiene.[102] Along the length of the hut were four rows of wooden shelving, partitioned off into lengths of approximately five feet, which provided spaces in which to sleep, four men in each. No palliasses or mattresses were provided, and they had only a handful of dirty blankets under which to keep warm. The smartest among them took the higher berths, for sanitation was almost non-existent, and constant bouts of dysentery resulted in the men above involuntarily defecating on their fellow prisoners below.

"The stench in the hut was unbelievable, especially when, during rainy weather and after a prolonged sojourn standing to attention at evening roll call, the prisoners returned with drenched clothing. Drying garments was impossible, and the problem was aggravated when anyone fouled his clothes – which proved difficult to clean without toilet paper or any washing or laundry facilities. The problem became more acute at night."

The only prisoner afforded any degree of luxury was the block supervisor, who had his own room complete with stove and metal bed with a mattress and sheets. The supervisors were primarily German, and often long-term prisoners of proven organisational ability. They were assisted by two *Stubendiensten* for maintaining discipline. These were ordinarily thugs, encouraged to use their rubber truncheons at will, or blatant homosexuals under the protection of the block chief. Stanley's block supervisor was a man named Max Back who, they later discovered, had been a prisoner since 1938. With only one leg and several fingers missing from one hand, he struck an oddly comic figure – though there was nothing funny about him. He was, however, marginally more benign than many of his peers, and certainly better disposed to the Allied airmen than many others:

> *"At first he was very aloof, and made it known that we were unwelcome enemies who had brought them much hardship with the raid breaking up the camp routine. But gradually he mellowed, and we found ourselves being given favourable treatment, a fuller portion of soup, lighter domestic chores, and protection from the ever-lurking SS when there was trouble about. He was obviously pleased at the way that we used to organise the Appell roll call, by quickly getting into our ten lines, and helping to get the other disorganised foreign prisoners into shape – it made roll calls so much quicker, and gave the SS less time in our vicinity, to the advantage of us all, many of whom had dysentery problems making standing in line for any length of time a very trying problem.*
>
> *"We kept our portion of the hut cleaner, but we quickly learned to never accept his offer of 'extra soup' in his inner cubicle – on those occasions we always ensured that we went in at least pairs, never alone. We could never get used to the cruelty, the brutal punishments in public, the bodies – it was all foreign to us, even as servicemen. Perhaps had we been trained solders things might have been easier, but as professional aircrew we had lived a more sheltered life, free from bloodshed and squalor. We had to control our emotions and reactions with difficulty, bullying was foreign to our nature, and it was hard to stand by helplessly whilst the most brutal atrocities were perpetrated.*
>
> *"Yet in the midst of such cruelty and hostility, we met so many cases of genuine acts of kindness and friendship from complete strangers, many using hand signals to make their feelings known. A little bundle of some*

precious commodity, a few sheets of precious paper, perhaps a pair of crude sandals for our bare feet – little acts of warmth, and sometimes a few words in broken English, expressing their feelings. In all the expressions of hope and support, there was love and affection in amongst the terror and fear."

The men had very little energy. Typically they would form into small groups to allow some to sleep while the others kept watch. The risk came mainly from the other prisoners, intent on stealing what few possessions or food they might have managed to scrounge. Pain was a constant companion, especially from hunger. Stanley tried to pass some of the day when not sleeping by playing chess on a makeshift chessboard with one of the Russian prisoners:

"*It was the highlight of the day, after the long evening Appell and the guard had got the roll call correct, to return to our barrack where our little Russian friend would call, and we would gather round and play a simple game. It bought such joy and happiness. We could neither of us speak a word of each other's mother tongue, but he had great patience and understanding.*"

He also talked, when he could, to some of the handful of prisoners installed in the camp from the Channel Islands.[103] He had little to do with his crewmates, Terry and Jack. Not out of any ill will or disregard for their well-being, but more because a group system that Phil Lamason had devised to keep each another safe and avoid unnecessary beatings tended to keep them apart. They were attached to a different group.

The fear of being beaten every day was nothing compared to the fear of being ordered to the bunker block – which Stanley learned meant immediate execution, not unusually a public hanging. On one occasion, a Russian prisoner was chained to a set of gallows all day and then hauled up on a rope to be strangled to death.[104] On another, the Germans broadcast a running commentary of the execution of a group of Polish prisoners who had attempted to escape. It included a dramatic drum roll to heighten the tension and the fear and act as a deterrent for anyone else who might be so inclined.[105]

Throughout the day, the Germans also broadcast a continual string of names, and each of the airmen listened intently lest their name be called. On 9 September, 16 names of British agents were called out and Christopher Burney had the sad duty of telling Stanley and the others that they had been executed and cremated on

12 September.[106] Their end had been especially grim: each had been hung by hooks on the wall of the crematorium and died through slow strangulation, piano wire biting into their necks.[107] On 5 October, a further 15 British and French names were read out. One man from the group had succeeded in changing identity and was recorded as having died in the camp's hospital, but the other 14 had nowhere to hide. The party earned respect for the way in which they formed up outside their block and marched, heads high, to their deaths before a firing squad. Only ten SOE officers now remained, and Stanley knew that if the Germans were executing the SOE, there was a very good chance the airmen would be next. Indeed, little did they know that their executions had already been ordered.[108]

To protect those agents who had thus far avoided execution, individuals were moved into other blocks on a simple theory of 'out of sight, out of mind'. Lamason was approached and asked if some could become part of his group of airmen, but he refused. He knew the consequences if one of the agents was later to be found hiding among his small cohort of men.

Just as the Germans were accelerating their executions of the British SOE contingent, the mysterious squadron leader disappeared. An officer who had already assumed a false identity once now swapped identities again, and this time with a corpse. 'Kenneth Dodkin' ceased to exist, allowing his impersonator – whose true identity was Squadron Leader (later Wing Commander) Tommy Yeo-Thomas – to become Maurice Choquet. The famous 'White Rabbit', as Yeo-Thomas was known, was able to slip under the SS radar and was eventually transferred to a different camp, and away from any immediate danger. Yeo-Thomas was a senior agent of RF Section of SOE, the element that reported to de Gaulle's Free French authorities. Later awarded the George Cross, he was nevertheless described by Phil Lamason as something of a loner and an egotist who many in the camp – including his own people – wanted nothing to do with; his departure passed with little remark.[109]

Through Christopher Burney and Phil Lamason, the Allied airmen were in contact with the influential communist underground resistance committee within the camp. From them they learned that an order had been conveyed from Berlin to the commandant that the men were to be executed, a fact that Lamason decided to keep to himself for the time being. They had become an embarrassment to the Germans, but their deaths needed to be concealed. It would take careful planning if the outside world was to believe that they had all died from natural causes. Burney asked that a message be smuggled out via one of the communists engaged in the construction of a nearby German airfield. In the meantime, a complete nominal roll of every airman was prepared, together with a brief background account of their capture and imprisonment in Fresnes prison.

The plan appeared to work. A message was indeed communicated to the German Luftwaffe who discovered, seemingly for the first time, that Allied airmen were being held at Buchenwald.[110] The news allegedly not only ultimately reached the ears of Hermann Göring, the Luftwaffe chief, but also the British government in London:

> *"A few days later, and completely unexpectedly, the entire Allied party was assembled and marched over to the canteen building where they were addressed by two fluent English-speaking German air force officers from Dulag Luft. They gave an undertaking, provided we could satisfy them of our bona fides, that there would be a speedy transfer to a recognised POW Camp under Luftwaffe control and where the airmen would receive correct treatment under the protection of the International Red Cross.*
>
> *"Each airman was given the standard, but false, Red Cross form in use at Dulag Luft which – apart from the regulation questions: number, rank and name, religion and next-of-kin address – contained the usual, but improper, questions of military interest about which all aircrew were warned at pre-flight intelligence briefings.*
>
> *"The Red Cross forms were duly completed, only partially in many cases, and the Luftwaffe officers who expressed their genuine concern at the appalling conditions that we were being subjected to indicated that the transfer would be effected as soon as the necessary administration was completed in Berlin."*

The forms were only 'partially' completed as some of the airmen were still disinclined to advance any more information beyond 'name, rank and number'. Eric Davis, a wireless operator with 83 Squadron shot down on the night of 7/8 July 1944 remembers: "The information requested was far in excess of the Geneva Convention . . . I ignored it."[111] James Stewart did the same: "Some of us just refused."[112] Phil Lamason took the view, however, that – as so many months had now gone by since they had been shot down – any intelligence the Germans could glean would be historic, and of little use. Conscious that the men faced imminent execution, he saw no benefit in unnecessary delay.

Among those involved in the saga, and given credit for pressing home the airmen's case, was one of the Luftwaffe's leading fighter leaders, Hannes Trautloft. While a loyal officer of the old school, he was by no means a Nazi, and had fallen out openly with Göring. Trautloft had been seen visiting the camp on the pretext of inspecting the bomb damage from the recent raid and assessing its impact on Luftwaffe supplies, and was appalled by what he saw. An American airman, in perfect German, called to him from behind the wire and told him of the airmen's whereabouts and predicament. Whether this was the catalyst for the subsequent intervention is difficult to confirm, but the coincidence of the message being smuggled out by the working party and Trautloft's subsequent visit is perhaps sufficient proof that it was.[113]

A few days passed and their hopes began to wane:

> *"The routine in the Little Camp went on unchanged, except that the weather was now turning very cold. The Russian barber shaved our heads once again, and we had the usual delousing inspections, and the regular daily visit from the little Russian peasant soldier. He had adopted his Allied 'capitalist' airmen and, over the many weeks, had spent hours making little chessboards and whittled down the little chess pieces with his razor-sharp pocketknife. Nobody could speak a word of the other's native tongue, yet he, like so many other complete strangers in the camp, was an absolute boon to one's morale. We were the first Englishmen they had ever seen – we liked to think that, in turn, we were good ambassadors for our nation."*

On the afternoon of 18 October, a list of names was sent to the block of those required to report to the main gate the following morning. It included Stanley, Jack and Terry and everyone else with the exception of 11 who were suffering from pneumonia and pleurisy and deemed too ill to travel.[114] It also didn't include the name of Flying Officer Philip Hemmens, a very popular young 49 Squadron navigator who had died of rheumatic fever at the end of September, having also endured a series of beatings that resulted in a broken arm.[115] Hemmens was remembered in a simple memorial ceremony in the Little Camp, led by Squadron Leader Lamason, and piecing the Order of Burial together as best they could from memory.[116]

Stanley vividly recalls the last moments of their time in the camp:

"Much to everyone's surprise, and relief, during the morning of 19 October 1944 our block chief (the *Blockältester*) passed on an instruction that the entire Allied contingent was to report to the *Effektenkammer* for immediate release from the camp. The prisoners were given a hot shower and their original French-issue clothing, now cleaned, together with the shoes and the remainder of their personal possessions confiscated upon arrival (and that had not disappeared). Our bags were sterilised with a hydrogen peroxide spray.

"After this we were formed up and marched across the *Appellplatz* for the last time, and after being subjected to a thorough personal count and identity check, against the camp master record cards, were handed over to a party of Luftwaffe NCOs and airmen. These were mostly elderly and relaxed individuals who seemed to have no respect for the surly SS, who were maintaining their haranguing attitude towards us airmen to the very last."

The long-awaited moment had actually arrived; the day had started out no different to any other – now suddenly everything had changed. It was bitterly cold and raining heavily, and the biting easterly wind threatened snow. The Luftwaffe officer in charge insisted the men stood under shelter while they waited to be marched off – the first real hint that perhaps their ordeal was truly over. They were alive. They had survived. And whatever challenges lay ahead, nothing would ever match the nightmare of Buchenwald.

CHAPTER SIX

STALAG LUFT III

As Stanley, Jack, Terry and the party of airmen were being marched back down the Caracho Weg, in England a letter was being dictated and typed at the Air Ministry that would be received by Marjorie a few days later informing her that there was still no news of her husband.

The letter held out little hope that Stanley was alive: "In view of the absence of news for so long a period," it read, "it is felt that you should be informed of this Department's grave anxiety for his safety, but action to presume that he has lost his life will not be taken until evidence of his death is received, or until such time has elapsed that it is considered there can be no longer any likelihood of his survival."

Marjorie, however, remained more positive. She had now learned from other members of Stanley's crew that there was a good chance Stanley had made it out of the aircraft. Cliff Hallett had confirmed as much, and the Air Ministry later repeated Hallett's assertion that he was "probably safe". But if he was safe, then where was he? Or if he was dead, then why hadn't he been found?

More than six hundred miles away, Stanley could scarcely believe that he was now in safe custody, free from the daily barrage of blows from rifle butts and heavy truncheons, from snarling dogs and hateful handlers. Accompanied by a small escort of benign Luftwaffe guards, they were marched to the railhead, their spirits lifted by the scene of devastation at the once-bustling V-2 rocket factory. A train awaited with what looked like familiar cattle trucks, bringing thoughts of another grim journey ahead. On closer inspection, however, the trucks had in fact been converted into troop carriers. Wooden benches had been fitted and the floors covered in clean straw. In the corner was an iron grate upon which a hot beverage was simmering.

Some 25 prisoners, plus two guards, were allocated to each wagon – the doors of which remained open throughout the journey eastwards. Some preferred to stretch out on the luxury of the clean straw whilst others positioned benches around the open doors and conversed with the elderly guards, who were as interested in hearing of their horrific tales as the prisoners were in their accounts of the paradise for which they were destined:

> *"Each of us was given a loaf of bread, some margarine, a large portion of salami sausage and warm ersatz coffee was readily available. The absolute contrast to our experiences of the past months was unbelievable. The guards were chatty and told of the facilities within the main Luftwaffe POW Camp (Stalag Luft III) at Sagan near Breslau in Poland. There we would receive weekly Red Cross food parcels, letters from home, all the sports facilities we could wish, libraries of books, theatres and music concerts. It all seemed a dream and too good to be possibly true."*

The journey quickly progressed with regular issues of bread and soup, halting at several locations that provided proper facilities to wash and get clean, and which had obviously been built to service troop convoys. Only during the hours of darkness were the wagon doors secured, with one guard remaining on duty. Phil Lamason, who was severely weakened from diphtheria and dysentery, had ordered the men not to try to do anything stupid – even though escape, at this time, was furthermost from Stanley's mind, as they were all too mentally and physically exhausted and rejoicing in their new-found security. Silently, he gave thanks for his deliverance from the evil he had witnessed and thought only of home, and of getting word to his wife that he was safe.

It was on the third day that the train arrived at its final destination, the Luftwaffe-run Stalag Luft III POW camp at Sagan in Lower Silesia (now Żagań in Poland). The men waited anxiously for the first sight of their new home, and the company of fellow prisoners.

They did not have long to wait. Word had quickly got around that a new consignment of prisoners was due to arrive, and as Stanley and his fellow inmates marched, ill-dressed and unshaven, towards the prison gates, they were greeted by the sound of cheering:

"As we marched up from the railway station, passing through the pine woods, we could hear sounds of laughter, and an obvious football game in progress. The camp came in sight – there was no electrified fence, and within the open compounds, little groups of officers in clean RAF uniforms with caps and boots wandered at ease, relaxed and obviously without fear or stress."

Ivan Moody, an American prisoner at Sagan, remembers the new arrivals were in a pitiful state: "They had no shoes except for pieces of blanket wrapped around their feet and scraps of clothing. They were on the verge of pneumonia and were actually starved. They were in a dazed condition and looked like they didn't care whether they lived or not."[117]

Peter Phelps recalls: "We arrived looking like tramps. I had lost a third of my body weight."[118]

The condition of the men was a clear embarrassment to the senior German officer who greeted them for the first time, correctly and somewhat apologetically, as servicemen. In short order they were taken for a shower and issued with clean uniforms and underwear. They were also each given a Red Cross parcel containing a towel, razor blades and a pack of scented toilet soap. They also had soap with which to shave and – most precious of all – a toothbrush and toothpaste, the first they had seen for several months. They couldn't fix Stanley's teeth, but it was a start. They were photographed and their particulars taken down, including the names and contact details for their next of kin. Stanley was given his prisoner number: 8045.

Robert Key, a prisoner in the camp who had been shot down while minelaying earlier in the war, recorded their arrival: "One autumn evening in 1944, 20 new prisoners arrived in the compound unexpectedly. Their closely cropped hair and the drawn, pale look of hunger in their faces gave them that terrifying animal uniformity which falls over all human beings in permanent physical distress. The stories told by these prisoners of the camp from which they had come stirred the most lethargic and bore-minded five-year man. We heard of daily torture, public hangings, guards who walked about with whips, gas chambers, castrated children and prisoners who lay dead for hours in the communal beds. It was almost impossible to believe. As I listened to the stories of these prisoners it was difficult not to be overwhelmed with feelings of hate and revenge. The camp and many others like it had been in existence for years. I felt ashamed for having loathed my own life for so long. None of us had ever heard the name of the camp before. It was called Buchenwald."[119]

Key's recollections are at odds with Stanley's own. Stanley was angry that soon after being processed the officers and the NCOs were separated, the latter destined to remain at Sagan as orderlies to those of commissioned rank. Given all that they had endured, Stanley found this new situation "shameful". His memory was still bitter, 80 years after the event:

> "This unhappy course of action was to cause much enmity to the RAF/Commonwealth party, both officers and NCOs, all of whom were quickly becoming embittered at the hostility and obvious resentment from most of the well-organised POW community – many of whom had been safely cocooned in the camp for several years and spared the horrors and high casualty rate of the later bombing operations of 1944. The party of new arrivals had been accepted into their community with poor grace. Everyone was eager to talk about his adventures over the past few months and ask questions. They all had a story to tell, but few wished to hear – much less believe – the extraordinary brutality and privations 'claimed' to have been experienced."

Not everyone felt the same. Ken Chapman, a fellow Buchenwald inmate, and one of Phil Lamason's crew, remembers things very differently:

> "I told them all my experiences. My shaven head amused them. The tales most of us told were as true as possible and evidently they sounded pitiful and gruesome. The lads were extremely kind and gave me useful articles of clothing and, above all, a free hand to the communal stock of cigarettes and tobacco, of which they had 20,000 of the former. This was indeed a grand state of affairs."[120]

Whatever their experiences, the men were quickly absorbed within their new community, each being allocated to a room with ten or so other prisoners. After the privations of the past few months, Stanley could scarcely contain his wonder at his new-found bounty:

> "There was an abundance of books, a gramophone with classical and popular records, chess sets, playing cards, Monopoly and a variety of other games – family photographs hung over most bunk beds. All in all, it was not unlike many less comfortable Royal Air Force overseas messes."

There was also the thrill of opening a Red Cross food parcel for the first time, and jealously guarding its contents:

> *"Little did we know that we were apparently committing the unforgiveable offence, and breaking the established custom, by not sharing the contents of the parcel other than the large tin of Klim powdered milk and tin of Nescafé. How could the others have known that this was our first taste of real chocolate, cheese, butter, biscuits, dried fruit and the like, since taking off for our final mission?"*

Perhaps the biggest thrill of all was being given a pencil and a Red Cross letter form and the chance to write his first letter home. But where to start? What could he say about where he had been and what he had experienced? And did his wife know that at least two of his fellow crew members were dead, and that he owed his life to their bravery? He wrote:

> *"My Dearest Darling,*
>
> *At last dear here I am able to write and let you know I'm safe and well, having just reached this camp. What a terribly anxious time you must have had pet, I have been thinking of you the whole time, missing you oh so terribly. Still Darling I'll be back with you very soon. How I am longing to see your loving smile once more, bless you. Don't worry about me love. I'm feeling very fit and well, just longing to be with you again, how heavenly it will be dear, like starting life all over again, even lovelier than before. I've had many adventures since I was shot down unfortunately, but I am now safe and very comfortable here. I had a miraculous escape getting out of the aircraft love. God was kind, we were hit and blew up, but I managed to bale out safely and landed unhurt. Sandy and Taffy were killed unfortunately but two of the others are here. Snooky broke his leg and was taken prisoner also, but not here. How are you keeping dear? Looking lovelier than ever now you've had this news. How I am longing for a letter love, to hear all the news. Were you working near home? The money should be nice now – £200 I've worked out. Let me know please dear. God bless you my dearest, all my dearest love Stan. X"*

On the same day, he wrote a second letter, which in the event was the first to arrive. In it, he addressed more practical concerns:

> *"My Dearest Darling,*
>
> *Here I am again, my second letter. The Red Cross has rigged us out but there are a few things I could do with now that winter is coming, if you can manage love, I understand how difficult things are. The Red Cross allows you coupons and four parcels. Send them off all at once, before things end as we expect. Roll necked sweater; socks; undies (short); gloves, scarf. Shoes 9½, hankies; blades (3 hole); shaving soap, hairbrush, toothpaste, towel, pyjamas, Brevet (Obs), tooth brush, photo and any space left – you can put in chocolate if they allow you. It looks very formidable, but I know you will try love. Please send me some cigarettes then I can exchange them for chocolate. Great thrill this morning, I had my first Red Cross parcel, and they're fine. Shall be thinking of you at Christmas dear but will be with you very soon."*

The weeks that followed Stan's arrival in Stalag Luft III proved disappointing after the initial rush of euphoria had evaporated. He was still bitter about the fate of the NCOs with whom they had shared such distressing times, and the lack of any personal mail or parcels from home drove a wedge between the old guard and the new. The latter felt like outsiders and, in Stan's opinion, they were treated as such. Apart from a few toiletries they had no personal possessions of any kind. They did, however, have the compensation of an excellent library (with books to suit every taste) and camp variety and orchestral performances that were of an almost professional standard. Fellow prisoners played football until the pitches froze – at which point it became a skating rink for those (especially the Canadians) with an abundance of skill or an absence of fear. There were English doctors and dentists to care for their physical well-being and Stanley's teeth, and a padre to look after their souls.

Soon Stanley settled into the routine of camp life and noted in particular the impressive way in which the camp intelligence and security was organised. He looked forward to the daily 'Jimmy' – a BBC news bulletin – which suggested the war could not last much longer but that it was the Russians who were most likely to reach the camp first. While only six months had passed since the famous 'Great

Escape' prison break that had ultimately led to the murder of 'the fifty', escape was never far from some of the prisoners' minds:

> "The Senior RAF officer responsible for security and intelligence was remarkably well informed on all matters associated with civilian train timetables and travel restrictions, special travel documents and passes in current use, and the like. All documents that were essential for an escapee to make his way, via public transport, to the Baltic or the Swiss frontier could be forged by the unique camp 'Dean and Dawson' counterfeit section supported with identity-card and document photographs prepared from cameras smuggled into the camp.[121] The clandestine radio receivers ensured that every prisoner was able to hear the BBC news bulletin each evening – the officer recording the information, in shorthand, would visit each barrack hut and, after confirming there were no Germans in the vicinity (or under the floor), read the bulletin to the inmates assembled in the central corridor."

What still rankled in Stanley's mind, however, was the way that nobody in the camp appeared to have any real knowledge of the ruthlessness of the SS, or the existence and locations of the concentration camps. To some, the Gestapo was almost something of a joke, comic-book villains associated with fruitless searches of the prisoners' huts:

> "These operations were usually treated quite light-heartedly by the inmates who ensured that suitable items were discovered to satisfy the needs of these disagreeable visitors from Berlin. The association of the Gestapo with the earlier excesses experienced in Fresnes prison and at the interrogation centre in Paris was not allowed to pass unnoticed by those of us who knew better. But such excesses would not be accepted by the long-term inmates of the camp. It was all contrary to the Geneva Convention of which Germany was a signatory. The weekly arrival of Red Cross food parcels, the daily delivery of mail and family parcels, the regular visits by the representatives of the Swiss and Swedish protecting powers contradicted such national bestiality. What we had to tell from our own experiences simply did not fit into this pattern of Germanic efficiency and correctness – as was practised by the Luftwaffe. We became quite disaffected – something that even the SS and their Gestapo masters had been unable to achieve."

Another Christmas came and passed, and the war rumbled on. Stanley wrote to Marjorie on Christmas Day, wondering where she was and whether she was happy: "We will make up for it next year," he opined. "We will have the Christmas of our dreams then."[122] For the time being, he was relegated to looking his best on Christmas morning by smearing his butter ration into his hair in lieu of Brylcreem!

With some of his strength now returned, Stanley filled his time by volunteering for extra kitchen detail, peeling potatoes while listening to the camp orchestra practising in an adjoining room. The Red Cross provided the instruments. He also attended various lectures – anything to pass the time – while others applied themselves to more serious academic study, gaining professional qualifications under Swiss supervision.

The winter in Sagan was a particularly cold and uncomfortable one, temperatures falling to minus 20 degrees at night, and the New Year of 1945 brought heavy falls of snow that made pounding the circuit more exhausting. News from 'Jimmy' suggested the Russians had reached the Oder river, and a major offensive was underway. The first German refugees fleeing westwards could now be seen in increasing numbers, betrayed by faces that seemed haunted and hunted. Rumours began to circulate. Plans were laid. By 25 January, the Russians were only 40 miles from the camp. Huts became hives of activity as men urgently prepared for the evacuation that must surely come. Rucksacks were fashioned by improvising Red Cross-issued canvas kit bags, and throughout the camp Kriegies (prisoners) began ruthlessly disposing of many precious personal belongings that they had so carefully acquired and hoarded during their many months of captivity. To Stanley, it was like Christmas in happier times:

> *"From friends and strangers alike, we were bombarded with an avalanche of hitherto jealously coveted items. Extra blankets; shirts; ties; pyjamas; underwear; long johns; and even the gift from one of the Canadian pilots of a pair of magnificent combinations with a practical trapdoor flap at the rear. For the first time since our arrival at Sagan we were able to dress respectably which proved an immense boost to morale."*

The non-smokers, in anticipation of the eventual evacuation of the camp, had carefully hoarded their weekly Red Cross issue of cigarettes and their special 'barter goodies bags', fashioned from pillowcases, were packed with cartons of Camels,

Players and other well-known brands together with wrapped toilet soap, Hershey chocolate bars and small tins of Nescafé obtained from the United States parcels. It was a wise precaution, since all would become essential 'currency' for what lay ahead.

Every usable piece of timber, including numerous bed boards and barrack room doors, was used in the improvised construction of simple sledges onto which it was planned to lash the heavy backpacks. A large stockpile of Red Cross parcels which had been assembled in anticipation of the camp having to fend for itself at the end of the war was now plundered, and the camp soon became littered with hurriedly opened food boxes from which the most attractive and easily transportable items had been removed.[123]

Evacuation commenced during the night of 27/28 January 1945 with the occupants of the various compounds moving out in sequence and marching off in a general westerly direction, away from the advancing Russians. The east compound, which housed the RAF and Commonwealth element of the original Buchenwald contingent, was the last vacated at 0600 hrs.[124]

The night had been clear, and the temperature was now 12 below zero. Each column marched under separate command, having little contact with those in front or behind. At the start the column held together, but over time it became more stretched out as the men struggled along in smaller groups – winding their way in a long procession over the congested and snowbound roads, westwards, through eastern Germany. The chief enemy quickly proved to be the extreme weather, even for the Canadians for whom snow was no stranger.

Whenever a column halted, the cold soon became difficult to bear. Boots and clothing which had become coated with snow quickly froze solid. Frostbite became a problem as did the loss of the initial supply of bread which had frozen and was therefore inedible. Before the end of the first day, it became clear that no proper arrangement for the issue of rations had been made, and the German officer in charge had to scrounge whatever he could from the various villages en route. As there were no medical facilities, those prisoners that fell by the wayside suffering from exhaustion or severe frostbite had to be left in the care of the local German people, hopeful of eventual transfer to a military hospital.

Before their departure from Sagan, orders had been received from General Eisenhower's headquarters that prisoners must stay together, and for the individuals' safety there must be no attempts to escape. Discipline in the columns depended entirely upon the prisoners themselves, and any serious attempts to guard them were abandoned almost immediately after the march began.

The German guards were mostly elderly and often in poor health. They were clearly demoralised and anxious for their future and the fate of their own families. As the march progressed and the conditions grew worse, it was not unusual to witness prisoners putting the guards' heavy packs, and at times their weapons, onto the larger sledges and hauling them along with their own kit. Rumours were rife that companies of the dreaded SS were not far behind:

> *"This was bad news, especially for the ex-Buchenwalders who had first-hand experience of their ruthless treatment of prisoners – the friendly, harmless old Luftwaffe guards were infinitely preferred to the younger, fanatical SS."*

The villages along the way were already crammed with sorry-looking families of refugees, and the streets were jammed by carts of all descriptions, laden with household possessions. Overnight billets became increasingly difficult to find, especially for the columns to the rear. After many hours spent standing around in the cold, schools, churches and large barns were commandeered – providing basic shelter for the remainder of the nights and quite often the opportunity to scrounge welcome hot water from the villagers to make tea. The friendliness of the villagers came as something of a surprise to the war-weary men:

> *"Farmers quickly learned to co-operate and made their produce available including tins of delicious home-cured pork. More than once the favours of the farmer's wife were offered, when the temptations of the real Virginia cigarettes became irresistible. Perhaps for the first time in their lives, prisoners gave thanks for the hours spent persevering at school with their German-language studies – certainly they were the ones who went to sleep with a full stomach and a little extra to start the following day."*

After several days of struggling against the appalling weather conditions, disaster befell the retreating columns. A sudden thaw set in overnight, quickly turning the road surface to slush along which the improvised sledges could no longer be dragged. Packs now had to be carried, and excess personal baggage abandoned.

An immediate search was made for handcarts or any form of wheeled vehicle. Prams, trollies and carts were quickly 'liberated' and many a heartbroken young child was to be seen by the roadside, usually clutching a carton of cigarettes or a chocolate bar in lieu of payment and to salve a no-doubt guilty conscience. The columns eventually converged upon the small industrial town of Bad Muskau where the thousands of prisoners were able to enjoy several days of relaxation in the shelter of a vast glass factory and warehouse, where the warmth and opportunities for bartering with the mixed French workers proved to be a blessing.

Some form of organisation at a higher German level must have taken place during this respite, for smaller columns were gradually reassembled and marched away, this time under more favourable conditions. Their destination proved to be a small railhead where an attempt at making a realistic roll call was made, the first since departing Sagan, before despatching the prisoners in small parties to three different POW camps in Germany:

> *"The Americans were the first to leave, destined for Moosburg near Munich. As it happened, they were the first to be liberated. The RAF columns were delayed while further rolling stock was assembled and eventually despatched to Spremberg where they were reunited with our Commonwealth colleagues and despatched to either Tarmstedt near Bremen or to Luckenwalde some 40 miles south-west of Berlin."*

Whereas the prison camp at Sagan had been built for the express purpose of holding captured Allied airmen, Luckenwalde had been a First World War infantry depot. It comprised dozens of uniformly styled single-storey barrack blocks, non-partitioned and completely devoid of any heating, internal toilets, warm water supplies, showers and other domestic amenities.

The camp appeared to be little more than a dumping ground for prisoners of all nationalities, for added to the 1,500 or so British and Commonwealth prisoners were almost ten times that number of servicemen from France, Poland, Russia, Yugoslavia and Norway (including the entire Norwegian general staff). The contingent also included a newly arrived and very demoralised United States Army artillery unit. They were kept secluded outside the camp perimeter in a very squalid tented enclosure. The men had arrived in Germany during early December 1944 and were immediately overrun by the advancing German armies in the battle named after the bulge they had created.

Conditions within the camp were deplorable; there was a complete absence of any Red Cross parcels for the RAF men, who were by now on a near-starvation diet. Morale was noticeably low, even though the end of the war and eventual freedom were in sight. Nightly raids by British bombers on the German capital 35 miles away to the north meant the camp was often plunged into sinister darkness. "Oh how depressed and miserable we felt," one prisoner remarked.[125]

Andrew Wiseman, a Halifax observer who had also been shot down in 1944, described Luckenwalde as little short of a disgrace: "We had grown used to being deprived and did not expect the Ritz, but Luckenwalde was more squalid than we could have possibly imagined. The huts were virtually uninhabitable, there was little sanitation, and no cooking facilities for what few provisions we had managed to save. Not surprisingly, many men already weakened by the forced march fell victim to dysentery, and there were neither sufficient drugs nor food to improve matters."[126]

Stanley, and the handful of ex-Buchenwalders who remained, perhaps coped better than many, for however bad Luckenwalde might be it was paradise compared to the hell of a concentration camp. It was, Stanley says, "just another experience".

Stanley's principal concern was that he had still not had any word from his wife. He therefore had no idea if she knew whether he was dead or alive. At Sagan, he had written more than a dozen *Kriegsgefangenenpost* cards to Marjorie that had all gone unanswered. Marjorie had, in fact, received his second letter and responded, but her reply had gone astray. Her letter to Wing Commander Radford at 10 Squadron, however, informing him that Stanley was "safe, well and a prisoner of war in Germany", received an immediate response, as did her letter to the Air Ministry. The latter wrote back to say that since confirmation had been received through the International Committee of the Red Cross that Stanley was alive, steps were being taken "to officially classify your husband as a prisoner of war". A few weeks later they wrote again, this time informing Marjorie that Stanley's pay would be issued, monthly in arrears, "subject to a provisional deduction at the rate of £5.8.0" which was being made from the pay of prisoners of war, of the rank of flying officer, "in respect of sums understood to be in issue to them by the German Government". This was followed a few weeks later with a letter to say that a further £3.0.3 was being deducted for an unpaid mess bill. It was the start of a long saga that has yet to be resolved, 80 years after the event.

After the brief hiatus of the move, Stanley resumed his letter-writing from Luckenwalde in the hope of receiving a reply. "Never," he wrote, "have I seen so much snow."

Conditions slowly improved, helped enormously by the sterling efforts of the SBO, 'Dick' Collard, who instilled discipline back into the men and into the camp. Some of the servicemen in receipt of Red Cross parcels began sharing their provisions with the British, all except the French who failed to lift any finger to help.[127]

On 15 April, after several days of rumours, the men were paraded with their kit and marched to the local railhead. A locomotive was to transfer them to another POW camp at Moosburg, but the locomotive failed to arrive, and the following morning – after an anxious overnight stay in an ubiquitous cattle truck – Stanley was marched back to Luckenwalde. It was a relief, for none of them fancied a train journey in daylight when the risk of attack by Allied fighters was so great. Indeed, part of the delay had been down to an insistence by the SBO that the Germans painted RAF roundels on the wagons as a condition of going anywhere.

A few days later, the Germans left. It was 21 April. Collard, working closely with the Norwegian general Ruge, issued orders that no man was to leave the camp without official leave to do so. All food stores were to be issued on a pro rata basis, regardless of consignee. Allied personnel were divided into three units and a senior RAF officer appointed to command each unit. Thus, they prepared to protect themselves against the threat of any last-minute Nazi death squads.

Then one morning, a Russian armoured car appeared at the gate and the interpreter was called for. The officer was lost and seeking his unit. With cheers and much backslapping, a map was found, vodka shared, and he was on his way. Twenty-four hours later, a large force of Russians arrived, and the camp was officially 'liberated'.

Any hopes that the British would immediately be set free to return home, however, were quickly dashed as they found themselves pawns in a political game. The prisoners would be allowed to leave only after the Russians had accounted for the thousands of Soviet deserters then in British hands, and claimed other prisoners of interest for the peace to follow. It was a long and protracted affair before a solution was finally found, and the repatriation of RAF prisoners under Russian 'protection' could finally begin. Relief, in Stanley's telling, had an air of Whitehall farce:

> *"When the Soviets received authority for our release they lost no time in assembling a ramshackle collection of lorries, filled them with the excited prisoners, and set off like a bunch of competing rally drivers going hell for leather down the undamaged parts of the old Autobahn, overtaking in the most haphazard and frightening manner but clearly enjoying the privilege*

of taking their 'Comrade Angliskis' on their way home to their loved ones. There were genuine tearful farewells when the river Elbe was reached, and swapping of souvenirs, not that we had much apart from cigarettes and trinkets."

At Halle airfield near Leipzig, Stanley penned a long and detailed letter home, unencumbered by space or word count. He still had no idea whether or not Marjorie knew he was alive:

"It has been a long and weary year, especially as I haven't received any letters from you at all. You have no idea just what a feeling this is to be free love, after being shot down and shut up for a year. We reached the American lines last night. Actually, we had been liberated by the Russians, but it was not a picnic with the local fighting going on, and a misunderstanding about going home which has resulted in all this delay, but now we are in our own lines, and everything is arranged. I will be with you by the end of the week – oh it seems so wonderful."

For the first time, Stanley recounted the hell of his incarceration in Buchenwald, eight weeks of "hell, disease and hunger". He described the "paradise" of Sagan, and the misery of the Long March and the men having to survive on a sixth of a loaf of bread, a pint of soup and six potatoes a day. He wrote of the help of the Russians in driving them to the airfield, where he now waited patiently for an aircraft to fly him home. After two days of "real coffee, real doughnuts, and real indigestion" came the spectacle of more than a dozen C-47 transport aircraft coming in low over the airfield before landing and taxiing to dispersal. The flight home, even for experienced aircrew, was more than a little hairy:

"The hour that followed, flying in tight formation, in and out of low cloud and hedge-hopping over the ground, proved a nightmare. Faces were getting greener and clearly the air of apprehension only compounded the unrest. Following the enthusiastic Russian driving experience a few days previously, going home now in the hands of the obviously highly professional but casual US pilots wasn't quite the joyful experience we had been dreaming of. The relief when Brussels came up out of the murky clouds was profound indeed. The Canadian Army's welcome at the nearby

transit camp was equally enthusiastic. The substantial and well-meant meal took its toll but the clean bed and sheer sense of light-hearted freedom that prevailed was a tonic in itself."

The following morning, groups of 25 or so POWs were emplaned on Bomber Command Lancasters for the final leg of their journey. Operation Exodus, the repatriation of more than 340,000 POWs from Germany, was in full swing. Some wept at the sight of Beachy Head and the White Cliffs, feeling the same sense of patriotic fervour experienced by the great First World War aviator Victor Yeates, and recounted in his 1934 semi-autobiographical novel *Winged Victory*: "This was England. Wandering lanes, hedged and ditched; casual opulent beauty; trees heavy with fulfilment. This was his native land."

The Lancasters landed at RAF Dunsfold in Surrey, each greeted by a pair of airmen wearing respirators to douse every passenger with a liberal spray of DDT. Then Stanley was ushered into a reception tent, where a mug of tea and a thick corned-beef-and-onion sandwich was thrust into his hands. From Dunsfold he was transported to Guildford, and a train to RAF Cosford, where he was again greeted by eager WAAFs, keen to process each of the men as quickly as possible so that they could be reunited with their loved ones to enjoy eight weeks' leave.

The eagerness of the RAF reception centre staff, while welcome, was to create a number of unintended consequences.

CHAPTER SEVEN

HOME

From Cosford, Stanley sent a telegram to advise Marjorie that he would be home the next day. He was examined by the medical officer and given a fistful of food and clothing coupons, and then deposited at Wolverhampton railway station to fight his way onto a packed train:

> *"I spent a miserable four hours standing in the corridor all the way to Sheffield, the pongos (British Army soldiers) wouldn't move over in the first-class compartment, but it mattered not. At Sheffield they had a splendid voluntary scheme whereby a roster of local businesspeople held themselves in readiness to be called out and take any returning prisoners home. In no time at all I was in a splendid Daimler being driven by one of Mr Firth's daughters and at 1.30 a.m. on 29 May 1945, just four days short of a year, I was knocking at the door to the fantastic homecoming that had been the one thought every free moment of the long, long year that had passed."*

After breakfast on that first morning home, and dressed in his 'best blue', Stanley and Marjorie headed for York, from where they took a taxi to RAF Melbourne. Stanley had lost a considerable amount of weight and was conscious of how his uniform hung loosely on his bony frame. He was also, officially, absent without leave.

'Shiny Ten' was no longer equipped with Stanley's beloved Halifax. It had changed duties, and was now part of Transport Command, with row upon row of rather less warlike Dakotas sitting on the tarmac before a silent control tower. They were met and entertained by the station adjutant who, Stanley recalls, "put on a good show but could not possibly have remembered who I was". The new squadron commander[128] was also alerted, and over lunch in the mess listened patiently to Stanley's account of where he had been and the suffering he had experienced.

The CO explained the squadron's new role and that they would soon be departing for the Far East where the war against the Japanese was heading towards its conclusion. He asked Stanley whether he'd be interested in rejoining as navigation leader, an offer that met with a kick under the table from Marjorie that left Stanley in no doubt he was not to accept.

In the late summer of 1945, after the dropping of the two atomic bombs had precipitated the Japanese surrender, Stanley was sent to RAF Church Fenton in north Yorkshire. He was one of thousands of former prisoners of war who now needed to be 'sorted' by way of returning to civilian life or continuing their RAF careers. As a former apprentice clerk on a 21-year engagement, Stanley had never considered a life outside of the military, and as such his stay at Church Fenton was short. He was posted to HQ 41 Group at Andover in the role of ORG IIA – responsible for "the calculation of the manning levels and periodic on-site Establishment Reviews with the Air Ministry and Ministry of Aircraft Production specialist administrators".

With the war at an end, many hundreds of surplus aircraft of all categories had to be stored, sold, prepared for 'long-term storage' or simply and wantonly scrapped. There were at that time more than 30 major aircraft storage/maintenance airfields dotted across the country, many with their own minor sub-storage sites staffed by civilians, RAF servicemen, or a mixture of the two, making the essential manning requirements for more than 30,000 aircraft unusually difficult to calculate. A constantly changing political landscape, and deciding who could buy aircraft from whom, added to the challenge, as did the future role of the Women's Auxiliary Air Force personnel in the storage and handling process.

> *"To visit such units as 29 MU at RAF High Ercall was a sorry experience, where there were hundreds of splendid Halifax bombers in rows just waiting to be broken up, apart from a small allocation set aside for the French government. At RAF Polebrook, a recently vacated US Eighth Army Air Force bomber airfield, and still with vivid reminders of its US occupation,*

> there was the sorry spectacle of many dozens of once-proud Stirling bombers also waiting to be disposed of. Some had only their delivery mileage hours in their F.700 service logbooks.
>
> "Up in Scotland there were many fine Sunderland flying boats lying derelict at Wig Bay like stranded whales littering the shoreline. Over in Northern Ireland there were masses of splendid Catalina flying boats, Lend Lease aircraft the US didn't want, waiting their turn for the knacker's yard. Nobody wanted to buy any aircraft except perhaps the Israelis who were anxious for desperately needed spares for aircraft they had 'acquired' from other sources. Alas, as I found to my cost, it was not appreciated for a young junior officer to expound the national shame that nobody in high authority would have the foresight to preserve a few specimens of each type, of which hundreds abounded, and preserve them in museums for posterity and other generations to enjoy. It was not a happy day when many years later I was asked to sacrifice half a day's pay to help fund an RAF expeditionary team to recover the wreck of an early mark of Halifax discovered at the bottom of a Norwegian fjord!"[129]

Stanley's new job, however, had its perks, not least the opportunity to visit isolated areas of the British countryside where eggs, poultry and other such luxuries were in plentiful supply. His ORG I was Wing Commander Roger Porteous, a famous wartime Mosquito pilot and former commanding officer of 487 (RNZAF) Squadron, who had taken part in the low-level attack on the Gestapo headquarters at Aarhus in Denmark to destroy vital records. Porteous was unhappy and bored 'flying a desk', but always made sure he had an aircraft close to hand that he could fly:

> "With so many thousands of aircraft on our charge it was no problem at all to have one or two 'private hacks' available for 'familiarisation and staff visiting' purposes. With the local Andover airfield being so small and without hard runways, Porteous had an arrangement by which his own Mosquito was always available at nearby Middle Wallop, whilst at Chilbolton airfield a few miles on the eastern side of Andover he kept a specially modified Mitchell with empty bomb bays lined with hooks to enable a large number of turkeys and such like to be filled for special mess occasions, collected by arrangement over in Northern Ireland where there weren't too many prying eyes to tell tales to the press."

The posting provided Stanley with a soft reintroduction to service life and proved beneficial in rebuilding some of his lost confidence. He was, however, far from fully fit, either physically or mentally, and conscious that his personality had changed. He feared and hated large crowds and became increasingly withdrawn and antisocial in the mess. His sleep was frequently disturbed, with heavy night sweats, and it was not uncommon for him to lash out in the dark at imaginary characters whom he was convinced were trying to kill him. He was in the early stages of what would now be diagnosed as post-traumatic stress disorder but was at the time ignored.

A year after his return from Germany, the RAF allowed him to use his annual leave to return to France to try and discover the fate of his pilot and wireless operator, still officially 'missing'. It was also a chance to visit and thank the elderly widows who had sheltered him after being shot down and who had remarkably survived, despite his own betrayal. With the help of his wife Marjorie and two ancient borrowed bicycles they searched the highways and byways around Saint-André-de-l'Eure, stopping at every churchyard or shrine for any sign of the lost crew. Then, on one of the very last days of their holiday, they came across a former German military cemetery, in the corner of which was a carefully tended plot with six wooden crosses, each with the words *Englander ohne Nummer* (literally, 'an Englishman without a number') but with a date and location of where their aircraft had crashed. Stanley was convinced that Sandy and Taffy had at last been found, one a proud Scot, and the other an equally proud Welshman!

Stanley wrote to the Air Ministry Casualty Branch to report his discovery. While they accepted that one of the graves was that of his pilot, and that his name had been recorded by a graves registration unit, they could not confirm the resting place of Taffy Williams until such time as a final report had been received from the RAF's Missing Research and Enquiry Service, tasked with locating missing airmen. "Your contention that the grave bearing the same date and place of crash is that of Warrant Officer Williams is generally accepted," the latter ran. "When definite identification of Warrant Officer Williams' grave has been made, you will be advised."[130]

Definite identification was forthcoming when their bodies were exhumed, and the remaining graves identified as holding four Canadian aircrew whose bomber had also crashed in the area. All six were given official Commonwealth War Graves Commission headstones, and Stanley was contented that he had at last honoured the memory of the men whose bravery had allowed him to live.

* * *

By early 1947, the RAF was experiencing a shortage of operationally experienced navigators, and the call went out for all those in staff or other ground appointments to volunteer to undergo refresher training before returning to an operational squadron. Having flown regularly with Wing Commander Porteous, Stanley felt ready to resume his navigational duties. He'd also been offered an extended service commission in the substantive rank of flight lieutenant, and was posted to RAF Bircham Newton for a navigation refresher and beam approach beacon system (BABS) landing course. The start date of the course coincided with the eagerly awaited birth of his first daughter, Patricia, which had to be accomplished, with much dashing around the country, before he could officially launch himself back into the real flying world. After ten hours of BABS practice flights in Oxfords and Ansons, he was assessed as 'proficient'. Having also attained sufficient proficiency in his ground exams, he was classed as having reached a standard comparable with transport commander category 'D'.

Transport Command was to be his safe refuge and master for the following four years with his new and expanding family in tow. His initial posting to 77 Squadron at RAF Manston should have been idyllic. As a 'Man of Kent' he was returning to his roots, and had his parents close by. Not everything, however, went according to plan:

> *"After arriving at Manston late on the Friday evening I lost no time in seeking rented accommodation, followed by a long train journey to Yorkshire to collect my family and return to our newly acquired lodgings. On the following Monday morning, instead of the anticipated welcome upon reporting to the new squadron commander, I was greeted by the adjutant who told me it was not worth unpacking as I was being posted back to Bircham Newton. Apparently, the following course was undersubscribed, and each squadron had to send a junior navigator to make up the total. As I was the newest arrival (albeit not the least experienced), I was dispatched back from whence I'd come to the prospect of repeating the previous three months' instruction. It was thus with much bad feeling that I demanded an interview with the air officer commanding to resolve what I saw as an obvious injustice as well as a waste of service time. A few days later I returned to the squadron to find I was not very popular because someone else had had to be sent away at very short notice. I also discovered I had been chosen to be the navigator*

of a Dakota detachment based at RAF Honington in East Anglia, which was being used for the twice-daily delivery of reconditioned engines from the maintenance depot at Honington to the Transport Command bases at Lyneham, Abingdon and Dishforth. There was thus the frustration of living in the officers' mess at Honington while my family was now located on the opposite side of the Thames Estuary watching the remainder of 77 Squadron flying around on their daily training duties."

While Stanley's future was being sorted out, and prior to being ostracised to Honington, he had a little time for what he called some "light trading". His logbook entries for the first few days of September 1947 hide the extent of his under-the-counter dealings:

"The Dakotas from Manston would go up to Northolt to pick up the Queen's Messenger and fly him with all his secret files and documents to Warsaw. That meant stopping overnight in Berlin which was always popular. At the back of a Dakota by the toilet there was a section of the floor that could be lifted up and where we could fit about ten boxes. So we used to pack these boxes with cocoa and other goods, and when we got to Berlin, we'd park the Dakota in a hangar near the woods and wait till dark. We'd be met by a coach driver who'd take our boxes away and then we'd fly on to Warsaw. On our way back from Warsaw, we would land at Berlin, park in the same hangar, and be met by the driver who would now have boxes full of tea sets or china or whatever else you fancied to take home."[131]

Stanley's somewhat mischievous routine was shared with one of the flight commanders, Michael Wainwright, a former Battle of Britain pilot.[132] Their antics, however, did not always go according to plan: on one occasion, another aircraft due to fly back from Berlin to Manston had trouble with its engines, and so Stanley's aircraft was given over to the crew. Since this crew were following a similarly nefarious routine, there was a frantic transference of boxes from under floorboards, and from under the noses of the authorities!

When 77 Squadron, which at the time was commanded by Wing Commander 'Pete' Peters DFC,[133] was depleted to form 62 Squadron, under the command of Squadron Leader Douglas Hoare,[134] both squadrons began operating in a 'three-prong system' along with 53 and 18 Squadrons from RAF Waterbeach.

Stanley found himself initially at Honington and then part of a new detachment of Dakotas based at RAF Bückeburg in Germany flying 'trial support sorties' into Berlin as a prelude to a remarkable humanitarian aid effort that was to follow. He was also, in the spring of 1948, appointed the 62 Squadron intelligence officer with Flight Lieutenant Richard 'Dicky' Thornborough as his deputy.

Reposted again to 206 Squadron at RAF Lyneham in the late autumn/early winter of 1948, Stanley was now flying in the Avro York, a four-engined transport aircraft whose design had derived from the more famous Lancaster with which it shared many common parts. It was, he said, "a very gentle, much-loved beast that caused very few problems". His posting followed a short conversion course at 241 CU at Dishforth, where he had arrived to find there were no aircraft on which to train until a single York and two instructors returned from Wunstorf near Hanover three weeks later![135]

With 77 and 62 Squadrons he had flown with many different pilots – including multiple trips as a spare navigator with Reg Housby, Albert Duffield and Keith Davey, the latter having earned the DFC.[136] He also flew with Squadron Leader Patrick Shaughnessy, who'd been an early 'bomber boy' from 1940.[137] At the conversion unit, however, Stanley once again became part of a regular crew with a regular skipper, Bill Drinkell. Like Stanley, Drinkell had been an apprentice, but at Halton. It meant he spent the first part of the war as ground crew before volunteering and being selected for pilot training. He initially qualified as a flying-boat skipper, before the heavy losses experienced by the bomber boys led to a sideways step into Bomber Command and a posting to 50 Squadron. He received a DFC for his first tour, the citation making note of his "untiring enthusiasm, courage and skill". He demonstrated similar skill later in Japan, on one occasion coming to the aid of six RAAF Mustangs lost in bad weather and helping them down.[138]

> *"We were a good team. Bill didn't drink or smoke, and when time allowed, we would head into Hanover to buy presents for our respective families."*

With 206 Squadron, under the command of Squadron Leader Ernest Moody, the crew was deployed to Germany. Europe was once again in crisis with the very real threat of war against the Soviets. In 1945, at the Potsdam Conference, Berlin had been divided into four zones, co-ordinated through the Allied Control Council comprising members from the US, UK, France and the Soviet Union. When in early 1948 the three western Allies began secretly planning the creation of a new German state, and a European Recovery Program engineered by US Secretary of State George Marshall, their plans were discovered and the Russians withdrew from the council. In June 1948, without informing the Russians, US and British policymakers introduced the Deutschmark "to wrest economic control of the city from the Soviets, enable the introduction of the Marshall Plan, and curb the city's black market".[139] The Soviets responded by issuing their own currency, the Ostmark, and blocked all major rail, road and canal links to West Berlin, thus starving it of electricity, as well as a steady supply of essential foodstuffs.

As history records: "Based upon written agreements with the Soviet Union in 1945, the only connections to Berlin left to the western Allies were air corridors from West Germany used to supply Berlin by air. The administration calculated that if the Soviets opposed the airlift with force, it would be an act of aggression against an unarmed humanitarian mission and the violation of an explicit agreement. Thus, the onus of igniting a conflict between the former allies would be on the aggressor."[140] The United States launched Operation Vittles on 26 June; the UK followed suit two days later with Operation Plainfare.

The West, including the Americans, was short of everything needed to mount such an unprecedented exercise. It lacked aircraft, crews, airfields, navigational aids, traffic controllers in the air and on the ground, equipment for rapid loading and unloading and much else besides.[141] Somehow, however, Anglo-American resilience paid off. The Berlin airlift was on.

The Soviet blockade of the capital lasted from June 1948 to the end of September the following year. As each aircraft landed, it was met by teams of German civilians who unloaded each precious cargo within minutes. Between them, British, Commonwealth and American crews made almost 300,000 flights into Berlin and delivered more than 2.3 million tons of supplies. At the height of the emergency, one aircraft was said to be landing in Berlin every three minutes – the shortest time in which three aircraft could be fitted onto the runway: one approaching; one turning off; and one departing. It was, in the words of one veteran, a modified version of musical chairs:[142]

> *"We operated on an exhausting 21-day flying schedule, making two return flights daily round the clock in all weathers taking supplies into the former capital. We had to fly with great precision to remain on track, with plus-or-minus-25-second timing within each wave of a dozen or so transport aircraft*

all making for the same place – Gatow for the RAF and civilian tankers and the Berlin main civil airport of Tempelhof for the US transports. We often carried coal, because it was easy to load/unload into a York, thanks to the low-ground-clearance fuselage. It was ironic that we were now helping the besieged former capital which was the very same 'Big City' that only a few years earlier many of the crews had bombed."

As well as coal, Stanley's crew carried flour, dried potatoes, meat and fish. A Red Army barracks was located near to Gatow, and as such many RAF crews – especially when taking off in the early morning – stayed as low as they could for as long as they dared to disturb the Russians' sleep. The pace was relentless:

"On the 24th day of each month of the deployment the crew would normally fly an empty York (packed with three or four other crews) back to Lyneham or Abingdon for a well-earned rest while the aircraft was inspected and cleaned. We would have just a few days' stand down during which time we had to spend several precious hours 'bashing the circuit' at Lyneham, simply to fulfil our mandatory monthly continuity training. We would all pray for good weather and a serviceable aircraft so we could dash off to Swindon railway station to disperse and make our various ways home to our loved ones for a very few precious hours of family bliss. This schedule was to go on throughout the following summer."

Stanley's logbook attests to the extreme pressure the crews were under. He flew his first airlift sortie on 1 November 1948 from Wunstorf to Berlin and back, a round trip of around two hours. By the end of November, he had made no fewer than 20 trips, half of them at night. A similar pace was maintained throughout December (he flew two trips on Christmas Day) and into the New Year, the reliability of the aircraft a great testimony to the hard work of the ground crews in keeping them in the air. For his 95th trip he had a different captain, Mike Ensor, one of the squadron's flight commanders and a highly decorated wartime wing commander.[143] Ensor described that period as "the best flying practice I ever had". He also joked: "In the beginning, God created heaven and earth. Then he created the Berlin airlift to cure keen pilots of their sinful desire to fly aeroplanes. The assorted smells of previous and present loads wafting through to the cockpit were something no veteran of the airlift will ever forget."

On 24 March 1949 Stanley recorded his 100th trip, this time in the company of Flight Lieutenant Morden. He flew his 200th sortie on 13 July and finally closed his account on 11 August with his score standing at a remarkable 227. His total flying time night and day from start to finish of the airlift amounted to a staggering 480 hours. In all that time they only once lost an engine, and on one of their last trips they overshot the runway while landing at Wunstorf. While Russian jet fighters were occasionally seen, they remained at arm's length:

> *"We flew our final Berlin sortie on 11 August 1949 and a few months later our fine 206 Squadron was disbanded, and many of the crews either chose to leave at the first opportunity or found themselves back in Bomber Command, now flying Avro Lincolns or the newly arrived B-50 Washingtons.*[144] *Most of us were never given our promised annual leave which should have been accrued during the emergency."*

With his departure from 206 Squadron, Stanley was offered the post of navigation leader at 99 Squadron, also at Lyneham. It was a chance for him to fly in the new Handley Page Hastings aircraft, which had only recently entered service and which supplemented and eventually replaced the York.[145] Having previously attended the staff navigation instructors' course at RAF Cranage, Stanley was promoted to become the flying wing navigation training officer.[146]

The three Lyneham-based squadrons were increasingly undertaking longer-range sorties, and 99 Squadron was no exception. Stanley flew most of his sorties with Flight Lieutenant Crosbie or Flight Lieutenant Gardiner from Lyneham to Malta and beyond to Habbaniya (in Iraq), Mauripur (Pakistan), Negombo (Ceylon, now Sri Lanka) and Changi (Singapore) in the Far East, and over territory that was often hostile. Survival training became a key focus, as did a renewed emphasis on search-and-rescue operations and intelligence gathering, and as such Stanley was sent on a five-week RAF general intelligence course in London. It was an environment in which Stanley thrived, and his enthusiasm translated into impressive results in his final exams. He thus came to the attention of a rather mysterious squadron leader who congratulated him on his achievement and on his end-of-course lecture on his survival as an enemy 'Terrorflieger' in a wartime Nazi concentration camp:

> *"He asked me how well I could speak German. Being apparently reassured by the short conversation we had, he went on to say that my annual RAF*

1369 confidential report continually referred to my 'apparent retiring nature' and 'avoidance of mess social functions' and would I therefore be interested in a posting to Germany where there would unlikely be many such events, and which clearly for reasons of my own I was happy to avoid."

No details of the nature of the posting were given, but the officer was happy to respect Stanley's acceptance, provided Stanley could be certain that his young family would also be posted with him. With the assurances duly given, Stanley was attached as a supernumerary to RAF Uxbridge from where he commuted into central London every day as a member (and the only military representative) of a small course run by the Foreign Office at Carlton Gardens:

"We sallied each day on strange (to me) excursions to make 'unobserved' rendezvous in such busy centres as Soho and Leicester Square (in those days both active red-light areas where to dally was to be rapidly propositioned), or seeking dead letter boxes in a numbered street toilet in Mayfair (the one I wanted always seemed to be occupied!) and dabbling in 'secret inks' for purposes I was never made privy to. I was to learn everything cloak and daggerish, except what I was actually going to be doing when I got to Germany."

With his course completed, Stanley returned to Lyneham where his absence was difficult to explain. He had been specifically warned not to discuss the events of the previous few weeks with anyone. It was therefore something of a relief when he was summoned to the station commander's office, ordered to clear his married quarters, send his wife and young family home, and report on a particular day and at a specified time to the rail transport officer at Liverpool Street Station:

"I reported to the railway station where to my surprise I was expected and entrained via Harwich and the Hook for HQ Second TAF, then located in central Germany at a famous peacetime spa town of Bad Eilsen, about 50 miles south-west of Hanover."

For the first week Stanley was in the hands of the friendly intelligence staff and studied journals and background folders on the Soviet air force in eastern Germany. This was 1951, and the Russians were rapidly rearming and increasing their numbers of Mikoyan-Gurevich (MiG) fighters and Ilyushin bombers close to the western borders. In 1946, Soviet engine technology was far behind the West's. In the five years since, however, they had made rapid strides, having been allowed access – somewhat incredulously – to technical information and licensed to build the Rolls-Royce Nene, then being used to power the Hawker Sea Hawk and Supermarine Attacker. Adapted for the local environment, a Nene derivative was tooled for mass production as the Klimov RD-45 to be incorporated into the MiG-15 – the aircraft that so shocked the Americans when it first appeared in combat over Korea. The same engine was also the basis of the twin-engined Ilyushin Il-28 then coming into service and which could fly more than 500 miles per hour. It rapidly became the Soviets' standard tactical bomber.[147]

As the new boy, Stanley quickly discovered what he needed to know, and what he didn't, but still fretted that his actual job had not yet been explained to him:

> *"As a stranger I was genuinely reassured when the occasional well-meant social enquiry frequently invoked the question: was I 'one of Ackerman's mob'? When out of sheer ignorance and embarrassment I replied 'yes' there was inevitably a nod and a wink, and everyone seemed to accept the situation. It was only several years later that I actually found out who the mysterious Wing Commander Ackerman was."*

Eric Ackerman was a master of electronic communication, and head of the RAF's air scientific research unit which led to the establishment of the first RAF ground-based intercept station in Germany to 'listen in' to Soviet air force signals. Ackerman and Stanley never met, and Stanley was never in truth one of his 'mob'. The phrase, however, became something of a 'catch-all' for anyone to explain away the mysterious goings-on at the time.

Stanley was put on an express train to Hamburg, but only after he had been issued with a 'special security card' that stated that he was to be given every assistance from both civilian and military authorities in the execution of his work. He also had the necessary paperwork to allow him to wear civilian clothes while on duty and carry a firearm of non-War Department pattern. His Walther PPK – the weapon favoured by Ian Fleming's hero James Bond – was issued to him personally at No. 2 RAF Police Wing by the provost marshal, Wing Commander Champion.[148] It gave him both comfort and fear in equal measure for what he might be letting himself in for.

At Hamburg he was briefed to wait by the station entrance where he was met by a polite but rather shabbily dressed man in a large black hat who introduced himself as 'Jacques'. Jacques, it transpired, was his driver, for Stanley was being afforded an official car. They drove through the ruins of what had once been a beautiful city and along the infamous Reeperbahn to arrive at an obscure British military barracks. It appeared to house a handful of rather bored civilians and members of the Control Commission for Germany (CCG) secretarial staff who greeted his arrival with an air of complete indifference. One of the civilians, however, was not quite what he seemed, for like Stanley he was an RAF officer out of uniform:

> *"He was the man I had been sent out to relieve and for the following two days I was taken in tow as he told more about the role and I was introduced to my local contacts. I was now an actual liaison officer with the British military government. It was only later and almost by accident that I discovered that my 'real' employer was one of those departments that officially never existed."*

Having quickly settled in, Stanley's young wife and daughter travelled out to join him. They were allocated a splendid house on the wooded banks of the Elbe, just a few miles outside of the city. It was not easy appearing to be civilians rather than a service family, and their difficulty was compounded by the proximity of a small cluster of married quarters occupied by RAF families from a nearby maintenance unit. All used the same NAAFI grocery store to purchase various UK 'essentials' and it didn't help when a family arrived who they had known at Lyneham.

Stanley's role was to gather information on what was going on in Germany's eastern zone, controlled by the Soviets. In the first few days after his arrival, he was driven to various safe houses where he occasionally met local German agents who had contacts in West Berlin and who made regular BEA flights to the 'Big City' to collect reports on their briefed targets. At that stage he was to have no direct contact with the East Germans.

Hamburg had been extensively damaged by the Allied bombing. Food was in short supply, the milk was not safe to drink, and men could be seen fishing for eels in the open drain covers.[149] It was still, however, a major port and centre of commerce, which meant there was a regular flow of commercial traffic using the Autobahn between the city and Berlin. The major Autobahns also tended to pass close to various military installations, exercise areas and several operational airfields, so regular travellers were always a good source of information on barrack activities, convoy movements and new military equipment:

> "It was a period when a small number of refugees were still trickling through from East to West and from whom useful background information could be gleaned of interest to the British and their American counterparts. I had specific areas allocated to me, and the more I knew the more I could put strangers at ease when talking with them. It was not so much an interrogation, but rather a conversation made more productive by casually throwing in a name or an incident from the past.
>
> "We patiently built contacts living near or perhaps returning from my area of interest and then seeing them as often as possible to find out what they knew, which was often more than they realised. It was like finding pieces of a jigsaw and fitting them all in place. Sometimes it was down to luck, and sometimes perseverance. You had to be prepared to accept disappointment and never take anything at face value. There was always the danger that an individual might fabricate or embellish an account in an effort to inflate their reward.
>
> "We were dealing with people who had no particular reason to love the British, or any of the occupying forces for that matter, and so you had to always question their motives and ask yourselves why they were co-operating. This was especially the case if they had something to lose by it, for example if they were a commercial traveller whose very livelihood depended on being able to travel without suspicion between East and West. Many of the men I spoke to would have had wartime military experience and doubtless earned a lucrative income by co-operating with the various Allied intelligence agencies."

Freedom of movement was essential for Stanley too, and he needed a regular driver. Jacques was all very well for official business, but much of Stanley's work pushed the boundaries of officialdom. He needed someone who was discreet and would ask no awkward questions when their 'search for missing aircrew' appeared to take them into strange locations and at interesting times of the day or night. He also needed someone who was streetwise. Here he struck gold. Since others on his station were ostensibly civilian, Stanley – as a serving RAF officer – was allocated a rather splendid Opel Kapitän and a former Luftwaffe officer as his driver and unofficial 'minder':

> "My driver had been a regular pre-war Luftwaffe Hauptmann and night-fighter pilot, coincidentally flying Junkers 88s from Saint-André-de-l'Eure in France – the very airfield from which our assailants had taken off on the night we were shot down. He had also flown from various other airfields that were now of interest to me and were undergoing major redevelopment in the eastern zone. The long hours of sharing a car on our daily sorties were indeed a real pleasure, for not only was he a genuinely decent family person, but we also had so much mutual interest – him being a fighter pilot and me in Bomber Command. I like to think that in our own small way we did our bit to rebuild a strong bond of trust and national understanding."

Stanley also sought the assistance of another former Luftwaffe engineer who regularly crossed the border from East to West and back again:

> "He had been responsible for examining recently crashed Allied aircraft to obtain technical and other intelligence from the wreckage and sometimes from the remains of their crews. He could always be persuaded – at a price – to make a special sortie to a location where his specialist knowledge could be put to good use. We were not encouraged to make extensive use of such rogues, however, as they were difficult to control and their loyalty was suspect."

Stanley's time in Hamburg was short-lived and his skills in demand. While much of the information he had been gathering up until that point was broad background, now there was a need for more detailed intelligence, and the type of information that Stanley says was 'out of scope' for his local organisation. It had become clear to him that he was in fact serving two masters: the official, War Office-sponsored German CCG, and another more shadowy department back in London. An occasional appearance in Germany from the mysterious Squadron Leader 'X' and his boss made it clear to Stanley that he was now one of their seconded field officers, and being groomed for bigger things. The Russian threat was developing at such a pace that he needed to be closer to the action to join 'the professionals' of the British Secret Intelligence Service (SIS – or MI6).

And that meant Berlin.

CHAPTER EIGHT

SPY SWAMP

THE LOCALS CALLED BERLIN THE *Agentensumpf* – the 'spy swamp' – and for good reason. The British SIS/MI6, the US Central Intelligence Agency (CIA), and French *Service de documentation extérieure et de contre-espionnage* (SDECE) rubbed shoulders with their East German counterparts in a deadly game of espionage and counter-espionage. Berlin, in Stanley's recollections, was "John Le Carré at its best – a murky world of intrigue and dirty goings-on" in which he felt completely at home, where honey traps and mysterious calls in the dead of night were part of the everyday routine.

The evidence was there for all to see. Much of the information Stanley and his colleagues were tasked with finding was also being sought by other 'friendly' organisations:

> "Some had a surfeit of dollars which worked wonders in loosening tongues and ailing memories – and all too often the truth as well – but it was all part of the game. All around were the visible signs of other 'agencies', perhaps the most obvious being the vast, mountainous artificial mound of building rubble known as the *Teufelsberg* (i.e 'the devil's mount'), upon which, for all to see, were numerous aerials of varying shapes and sizes pointing in various directions, and an occasional RAF truck nearby.
>
> "Anyone living near the vast Olympic Stadium would also from time to time glimpse a battered military Opel Kapitän saloon, laden with three or four male occupants in various assorted items of uniform, flying boots

> *or heavy rubber galoshes dashing up the main highway from the frontier crossing-point to report into their Berlin operation centre – to debrief and hand over photographs of various military establishments in Eastern Germany."*

Under the leadership of section chief Peter Lunn, a former captain of the British Olympic skiing team, employees at Field Station Berlin worked around the clock, and Stanley had to be available 24/7. Some of the benefits he had enjoyed in Hamburg were no more; second-hand Volkswagens attracted less attention than posh limousines with personal drivers, though the Foreign Office had taken over some of the more desirable properties in the Grunewald and Dahlem districts. Stanley and his family were allocated a house in Dahlem that had once been the home to one of Hitler's personal medical team. Built over several floors, it boasted among other things an enormous kitchen, five bedrooms, a cellar and an attic – which Stanley would sometimes disappear into for hours on end to build and play with his beautiful *Märklin* train set which was the envy of all. It had a dumbwaiter between floors that fascinated the children and came with a live-in maid, a *Putzfrau* (cleaning lady) for the more heavy-duty chores, and a gardener who as well as tending the lawns was also tasked with walking Stanley's Alsatian, Prince.[150] A regular policeman was also constantly on duty outside to guard against curious onlookers or visitors, which included the physician's wife who came to the house on the anniversary of her husband's death. While there was a phone, Stanley's two daughters (his younger daughter Cynthia was born in Hamburg in 1951) were on strict instructions never to answer it, and when on one occasion Pat was inclined to disobey, only to find her father on the other end, he was furious.[151]

Constantly on call, Stanley had little time to enjoy his new-found luxury. As Lunn was reported to have told one of his officers in the spying game: "You think it's going to be all wine, women and song. Well let me tell you old boy, it's all beer, bitches and broadcasting!"[152]

Field Station Berlin operated completely independently of the Potsdam-based British military mission to the Soviet forces in Eastern Germany (BRIXMIS) and the nearby RAF signals monitoring agency. The stated objective of BRIXMIS and SOXMIS, its Soviet equivalent, was to "maintain liaison between the Staff and the two Commanders-in-Chief and their Military Governments in the zones". Officially, the liaison officers were each issued passes allowing them freedom of travel in all but certain restricted areas within each other's zones. Such 'tours' were conducted in uniform, and in vehicles that were clearly identifiable. Unofficially, both sides used the arrangement to gather intelligence.

> *"For 40 tense years of the Cold War in Europe, a team of British intelligence agents, working under diplomatic cover as liaison officers, ranged like pirates through Eastern Germany in uniform and unarmed. Their target was the massive military strength assembled on German soil by the Soviets for a potential invasion of the West. The BRIXMIS members came from the three armed services, the SAS and the Foreign Office. Fluent linguists, they penetrated top-secret training areas and mingled with troops on exercise. They collected unexploded bombs and snatched video footage of the latest Soviet aircraft. From a light trainer aircraft, they snatched pictures of weapons hidden behind high walls. Their efforts met with violent Soviet response."*[153]

While Stanley says BRIXMIS and Field Station Berlin were independent entities, it would be naive in the extreme to suggest that their paths never crossed. Stanley confirms as much:

> *"From time to time, a strictly unofficial message might reach the station from a friendly, reliable source somewhere down the line, that maybe we should put a check on one of our contacts. There may have been evidence that they had been telling lies or perhaps hadn't been where they said they had been. They may even have been 'turned'. Either way, there was a suspicion that the information we had been given or a report on a particular target could not be relied upon. In such cases the very 'unofficial' and strictly forbidden 'old-boy' service network was put to good use. Over a social, off-duty 'chance meeting', a whisper to take a look at a certain locality when next in the vicinity all too often proved highly successful in catching out some less-dedicated regular contact who had probably not bothered to undertake his regular walk around his local airfield to check the colour and four-figure aircraft number that in most cases identified the actual Soviet air-force formation based on the airfield under surveillance. It was good to have reliable and understanding friends, many of whom were former RAF aircrew contacts from the past, and who were prepared to bend the rules at times all for the good of the cause."*

Much like in Hamburg, Stanley's role was divided between having a specific 'target' and more general intelligence-gathering. A large part of his time was therefore spent at the refugee reception centre in Marienfelde, spotting for possible 'talent' that could be of service to him or stealing them from under the noses of his American and French counterparts.[154] This was no simple task, for as well as the 'legitimate' refugees there was always the risk of a 'plant'. The agents of the East German secret police – the infamous Stasi – and their Soviet intelligence masters were well aware of the targets of particular interest to the Allies, and took every opportunity to infiltrate the refugee stream:

> *"Our American colleagues were known to have been deceived on more than one occasion, which resulted in the odd embarrassing security situation and the unwanted publicity that such planted information could generate."*

There was another, more personal challenge with dealing with the Marienfelde refugees for which Stanley was little prepared. On several occasions he would encounter cases of genuine hardship, which meant a quick return home to raid the family wardrobe and children's toys – and make his excuses later. On one occasion, a white poodle appeared overnight, which Stanley felt no particular need to explain. Neither his wife nor his children had any inkling as to Stanley's 'real' job, only that despite being a serving RAF officer he never wore uniform. Both girls were at an international school, and everyone's father was up to something, which made the extraordinary somehow more ordinary. They were all living a double life.[155] His own earlier privations in Fresnes and Buchenwald no doubt gave him a unique perspective on what it was like to be desperate:

> *"It was a personal weakness, perhaps, but the whole Berlin intelligence scene was a complete enigma, and one had to try and retain a sense of humanity having virtually sold one's soul to the devil for getting so wholeheartedly involved in the often sordid deception game. As we sowed, we reaped, and inevitably one had to take the rough with the smooth when things sometimes went wrong. On reflection one couldn't but think back over the initial induction course set in the relaxed world of the Carlton Gardens' lecture suite where they seemed more concerned with the choice of a good brandy or deciding the suitability of an underground toilet for a dead letter box than preparing us to cope with such problems as midnight resettlement*

of a desperate refugee family and to learn – only by experience – which emergency events were really genuine and which had been organised opportunistically to secure priority refugee recognition and resettlement in the West with a bonus payment into the bargain."

Throughout his time in Berlin his paymasters had a master plan for how all personnel and their agents would be extricated from the city in an emergency. To that end, Stanley always had access to a vehicle, 24/7, with sufficient petrol to reach Poland in a single journey. He would on occasion wake his wife and children in the dead of night to rehearse their escape, leaving nothing to chance should disaster strike. An hour every Saturday morning was also given over to shooting practice, after which, if time allowed, Stanley would take Marjorie, Pat and Cynthia to the *Kaufhas des Westens* (KaDeWe) – Berlin's equivalent of Harrods – where they would be greeted by the doorman with a deep bow.[156]

On the theme of domesticity, Stanley also had legitimate concerns regarding the safety of his own family. While there was a great deal of satisfaction when a rendezvous went well, it also created a state of constant unease:

"At times of local political tension apart from the heightened awareness of the fact that one's family was some two-hours' drive from the relative safety of the Allied zones, I also became more conscious of my personal vulnerability as a result of my current occupation. However cavalier an air we might affect, we knew that we were competing with an all-too-ruthless opposition who were fully aware of our presence and our activities."

To that end, Stanley points to the fate of Commander Lionel 'Buster' Crabb as representing "an unmistakably brutal warning". Crabb was a Royal Navy frogman who vanished during a reconnaissance mission for the British secret services around a Soviet cruiser on a visit to Portsmouth dockyard. It was later alleged that the Russians had been expecting him and had slit his air hose and his throat. His body was never recovered.[157] Stanley also refers to the mysterious disappearance and subsequent reappearance of the head of the West German intelligence service, Otto John, amid allegations that he had been drugged and abducted:

"Whatever the facts of the matter at the time, we in 'the trade' perceived this incident to be another warning. With as many as 80 espionage agencies

said to be operating in West Berlin anything could happen. It would, for example, have been all too easy to present a kidnapping as a defection and it would be very difficult to distinguish fact from fiction. The sense of insecurity is heightened by the presence of one's family. Would the enemy go to the lengths of kidnapping one's children? It was not so far-fetched. There would have been political repercussions, of course, but depending upon the operational advantage to be gained the opposition might have considered this to be a price worth paying."

Stanley had experienced the humiliation and shame of a Gestapo interrogation and knew his personal capacity for pain. What he didn't know, however, was how he would cope if either Patricia or Cynthia was being threatened:

> "These thoughts led to a great deal of heart-searching during the long restless nights. Was I being selfish keeping the family together under these circumstances? I was not alone in having such misgivings; several of the other seconded service officers confided that they had had similar doubts. Most of the full-time SIS men, more or less conditioned to permanent overseas assignments, elected to send their children to boarding schools in the UK. Perhaps with hindsight we should have done the same. To have made such a decision would have required some pre-knowledge of what lay in store for us, of course, but there had been no briefing on the implications of being involved in liaison duties. Indeed, few of us ever knew where we were going let alone what we would be required to do."

Stanley's time spent at the refugee centre was never wasted. He was particularly interested in any individuals employed by Bau-Union Brandenburg (BCB), the East German airfield construction company, who might, therefore, have intelligence relating to Stanley's priority 'target' – Gross Doelln.[158]

> "The heavily guarded and obviously secret Soviet airfield at Gross Doelln had been my responsibility since its inception. Construction was being monitored virtually around the clock by a variety of independent sources providing constant updates on the laying of concrete. With typically Teutonic efficiency, each concrete section was allocated its sequential identification number, and we used these to keep track of the locations of drainage tunnels,

electrical ducting, inspection access points, and so on – indeed anything that might one day be useful, perhaps for a sabotage operation. Construction work on the runway – 3,500 metres long and 80 metres wide and made of unusually heavy load-bearing concrete – was undertaken by the BCB. When they had finished, the Bau-Union Sud (BUS) took over to co-ordinate the activities of a variety of contractors who completed the necessary electrical installations and built a semi-underground fuel depot alongside the airfield rail spur."

Stanley's responsibility for determining what was happening at Gross Doelln became almost an obsession. Nothing of its kind had been seen before, and the Allies were becoming understandably nervous about the possible threat that the construction posed. Not having been trained in what he calls "Foreign Office journalese", Stanley's regular reports were dozens of pages long, flying in the face of accepted doctrine that reports from field officers should be concise, easy to read, and contain the "absolute minimum technical content possible".

"This was not an easy dictum to follow. Soviet airfield construction projects were complex, and as such it was necessary for me to go into the considerable technical detail for our ultimate customers – the Joint Intelligence Bureau (Airfields Division) and AM DDI (Tech), both based in Northumberland Avenue in London. Their desk officers were practical, down-to-earth types who relished the depth of content including detailed technical drawings and photographs which my bulky reports contained and helped them be more certain of their authenticity."

As the principal 'active source' for the Gross Doelln material, preparing and updating reports placed considerable demands on Stanley's time. Help came in the form of a highly formidable Foreign Office career secretary, with a heart of gold and a weakness for gin. Stanley's life was transformed:

"We became a most unusual but highly effective team. She would gently say to me: 'Now Stanley, it is not the great volume of content of our reports that is essential to please the great man, but the way in which they are laid out and presented. That is what immediately catches their eyes and that, in the end, is what they want and must get. Be concise and to the point and your

reports will be appreciated. They will demand more and be acknowledged'. They proved to be very wise words."

At Gross Doelln, the departure of the BUS was almost immediately followed by the arrival of the Soviet air force (SAF).

> *"They moved in with a convoy of extra-large five-axled fuel bowsers (never seen before) suggesting the imminent arrival of aircraft so large that the standard bowser would be inadequate. That same afternoon the first of a series of special aviation fuel tanker trucks were shunted down the airfield spur to start stocking the new fuel dump."*

The SAF at that time had two principal long-range bombers – the Tupolev Tu-95 and the Myasishchev M-4 – and their 'imminent arrival' was indicated. The former, given the codename 'Bear' by the Allies, was only just entering service, and its four 15,000-hp turboprop engines gave it a top speed of 575 mph and a range of 9,300 miles.[159] It could carry up to 15,000 kg of ordnance, including cruise missiles armed with thermonuclear warheads. The latter, codenamed 'Bison', was also 'new'. It was a four-engine turbojet bomber with a similar top speed to its contemporary (588 mph) but a shorter range (around 5,000 miles). The range, however, was sufficient to reach the shores of the United States, and it could carry two nuclear bombs.

Gross Doelln had long been a major source of curiosity, indeed concern, to the entire Allied intelligence community. It was a recognised indicator of Russian intent that a third world war may be imminent. The Joint Intelligence Committee recognised that its construction and the bearing capacity of its runways were "far in excess of the requirements of tactical light bombers". What they needed answers to was whether it was going to be a base for heavier aircraft, or whether the Russians, perhaps, had developed some kind of new fighter aircraft with a "prodigious take-off run". Very soon they would have their curiosity satisfied.[160]

Within moments of the new fuel being delivered, a litre sample had been 'liberated' and was in the hands of specialist analysts to be tested. The following night, the peace around the airfield was shattered by the arrival of the first aircraft – not the feared long-range bombers with their stand-off weapons but another type of bomber altogether. 'Bears' and 'Bisons' failed to materialise, and a unit of twin-engine Ilyushin Il-28 'Beagles' flew in. In Stanley's words, having monitored the building of the airfield with such diligence, they had "hit the jackpot" as the first of the Allied intelligence services to be out with the news. The spying machinery sprang into life, and Stanley despatched an emergency 'FLASH' signal to London:

> *"Very important persons were woken, and there was a quick invitation to the station head's office to receive the official 'pat on the back' from the 'man on top' (especially as we had beaten the Yanks to it, which was all that seemed to have mattered seeing as World War Three hadn't broken out)."*

Stanley's euphoria was short-lived, however. In his enthusiasm to be the first with the news, he had failed to clear the FLASH signal with Peter Lunn:

> *"This was the most hideous crime for an amateur who wasn't 'in the club' and was a seconded RAF officer to boot. Thus, after nearly four years of hard work and now at my moment of glory, when I might have expected a glass of champagne and an immediate knighthood, it all ended with the most tremendous dressing-down for my unforgivably wicked deed."*

In reconsidering his feelings at the time, Stanley later recognised that the rocket from his boss was fully warranted. While he had no hesitation in trusting the information he had been given, sinister forces were at play within SIS/MI6 that would soon have devastating consequences for the intelligence community generally, and Stanley personally. For the time being, however, he was content with an 'off-the-record' congratulations from his chief, and a hint from his secretary that his contribution had been reported to the prime minister in person.

The weeks following Stanley's Pyrrhic victory in that spring of 1955 were something of an anticlimax. The Beagles returned shortly after to Poland, to be replaced by a unit of MiG-21 fighters.[161] While interesting, they posed little threat, other than if the West decided to make the first move and attack the East.

Stanley was involved, however, in another significant operation during his first tour of Berlin, and one which eclipsed the Gross Doelln affair: Operation Gold.[162]

Operation Gold involved digging a tunnel under the feet of the Berliners to enable the underground cables carrying Soviet military communications to be tapped. A joint CIA/SIS project, the idea was modelled on a successful British operation to dig a tunnel in Vienna which had been masterminded by Peter Lunn during a previous posting.[163] At 70 ft in length, this was a modest affair, but it had allowed a theory to be proven in practice. The tunnel under Berlin was destined to be something in the order of 1,500 ft, and referred to by the Americans as the biggest wiretap in history:

> *"The mother lode of Operation Gold was the KGB headquarters compound located in the Karlshorst district of the city. The Berlin phone system had been set up before World War Two and remained intact with just a few modifications reflecting post-war realities. The city was "second only to Moscow in the Soviets' communications network" – a fact that made tapping into the lines nearly irresistible from an intelligence standpoint."*[164]

By tapping into Soviet communications traffic in Berlin, the intelligence services recognised they would not only have an accurate picture of what the Soviets were thinking and doing in East Germany, but also further afield in Warsaw and Bucharest.

Approval for the scheme was given on 20 January 1954 by US Director of Central Intelligence Allen Dulles, and Bill Harvey, Peter Lunn's US equivalent, put in overall charge.[165] Construction began the following month. In terms of who did what regarding the physical labour, the US team was responsible for procuring a suitable site from which the tunnel could commence and driving the tunnel to a point beneath the target cables. At this point, the British took responsibility for driving a vertical shaft from the end of the tunnel to the targets and then effecting the cable taps such that they delivered a usable signal to the tunnel head for recording.

The engineers had no doubt that the tunnel could be built, assuming they had the money and resources they required. The biggest question, and one that was said to haunt the minds of the project personnel for many weeks,[166] was what to do with the estimated 3,000 tons of excavated soil that would need to be disposed of.

It was to this challenge that the intelligence services looked to a number of former Allied prisoners of war for their advice and ideas. Stanley was consulted, as was another former inmate of Stalag Luft III, 'Jimmy' James. Jimmy and Stanley had adjoining offices, though initially neither party knew of the other's imprisonment in Stalag Luft III, nor of their respective experiences of a concentration camp.

Shot down on the night of 5 June 1940, Jimmy had been closely involved with digging several tunnels during his five-year incarceration as a POW, most famously the tunnel from which he took part in the Great Escape and became one of the few to be recaptured but not shot. He was, however, sent to a concentration camp (Sachsenhausen) from where he tunnelled out again, only to be caught while sleeping in a wood. He was fortunate not to be returned and executed.

In Stalag Luft III, Jimmy was responsible for disguising and/or dispersing the sand excavated from tunnel 'Harry' and worked out a way of hiding more than 80 tons under the camp theatre and the shaft of a further tunnel, 'Dick'.[167] The intelligence services clearly thought this was knowledge worth harnessing, especially given that the soil was of a similar complexion, which would mean that it was not only difficult to hide, but would also impact the way in which the tunnel was constructed to prevent its roof from collapsing. (Jimmy could also speak Russian, which endeared him to the service even more.)

In the event, the solution was one that had originally been put forward, somewhat facetiously, to dig another hole and put the dirt in that, much as Jimmy had done with Dick.[168] Engineers therefore created their own version of the Stalag Luft theatre, acquiring a warehouse with a huge basement in which the soil could be stored, while on the first floor of the building they could install their recording and signal equipment.

Local engineers were told the warehouse was an experiment. Half of the building would be above ground and half below, with a ramp to run forklift trucks from the basement to the first floor. They were told Berlin had been selected because the labour rates were low so construction would be cheap, and the work would benefit the Berlin economy. The basement was able to be dug in plain sight of the border guards and provided the hole for the soil excavated from the tunnel.

The tunnel ran across the border at a depth of around 20 feet, and the cable to be tapped ran less than 20 inches below the bustling *Schönefelder Chaussee.* The tunnel had to be sufficiently robust to withstand the possibility of heavy Soviet and East German tanks trundling across the ground above. It was a major engineering challenge made more difficult by an unexpected leak when the diggers encountered ground water at 16 ft while digging the vertical shaft, instead of the predicted 32 ft. A clay layer existed that created a perched water table in that spot. Pumps were installed to remove the excess water and the dig continued.

Construction was completed on 28 February 1955 at a total cost, including equipment, of $6.7m – a staggeringly large amount of money for the time. Indeed, everything about the project was impressive: three cables were tapped containing 273 metallic pairs capable of transmitting a total of approximately 1,200 communications channels. The maximum number of channels in use at any one time approximated 500. On average, 28 telegraphic circuits and 121 voice circuits were recorded continuously. In the period during which the programme was fully operational, approximately 50,000 reels of magnetic tape were used – the equivalent of 25 tons of recording material.

In addition to the small processing unit maintained at the Berlin site, there were two facilities in London and Washington, together employing more than 650 personnel. In London 20,000 Soviet two-hour voice reels containing 368,000 conversations were fully transcribed. In addition, 13,500 German two-hour voice reels were received and 5,500 reels containing 75,000 conversations were processed. Some 17,000 of these conversations were transcribed.

The team in Washington was similarly busy. Some 18,000 six-hour Soviet teletype reels and 11,000 six-hour German teletype reels were completely transcribed. The potential of any given six-hour teletype reel was approximately 216 hours of teletype messages, either in plain text or encrypted. The daily output was about 4,000 feet of teletype messages. Printed in book form these messages would have filled a space ten feet wide, 15 feet long and eight feet high! The material gathered resulted in a total of 1,750 reports being generated and 90,000 messages or conversations being translated and transcribed.

Information was disseminated in a closely controlled system called 'REGAL'.[169] REGAL gave US and British intelligence services a source of information of a kind and quality which had not been available since 1948. And some of the information – both political and military – was dynamite. It revealed, for example, the Soviets' intention to form a dedicated East German army, allowing foreign ministers to be warned in advance of a high-level conference in Geneva and respond accordingly. It gave a clear picture of the unpreparedness, confusion, and indecision among Soviets and East German officials whenever an instance occurred in East Berlin involving citizens of one of the Western powers. And it traced the progress of Marshal Zhukov's attempts to curtail the influence of the political officer in the Soviet armed forces – an attempt that later contributed to his downfall.[170]

From a strictly military perspective, REGAL revealed Soviet plans for reorganising and reducing the strength of its military while developing an improved nuclear delivery capability in the Soviet air army in East Germany. It highlighted the air army's plan to introduce new bomber types and twin-jet interceptors, as well as doubling its bomber strength in Poland. And it identified many hundreds of individual military leaders and personnel by name – as well as several hundred personalities associated with the Soviet atomic energy programme.

The rich source of high-quality intelligence was stopped dead in its tracks when the tunnel was 'discovered' by the Soviets on 21 April 1956 after 11 months and 11 days of operation. Heavy rainfall had apparently entered a faulty cable, requiring sections of the cable to be dug up for repair. While the CIA and SIS had assumed the Soviets would keep quiet about their discovery, at the risk of being humiliated on the world stage, the deputy Berlin garrison commandant did the exact opposite and invited the Berlin press corps in to take a look.[171] It thus became, in the words of a report made after the event, "the most highly publicised peacetime espionage enterprise in modern times prior to the U-2 incident".[172]

If the Soviets thought the world would come out in unison to condemn the West for its underhand tactics, they were sorely mistaken. There was universal admiration on the technical excellence of the installation and "the imaginative nature of the undertaking". It indicated that the "US, almost universally regarded as a stumbling neophyte in espionage matters, was capable of a coup against the Soviet Union, which had long been the acknowledged master in such matters."[173]

One US newspaper proclaimed: "Frankly we didn't know that American intelligence agents were that smart. In fact, we were beginning to think that what the CIA needed was a few lessons on the fundamentals of espionage from some defected Russian agent. But now we take it all back. If the Soviet charges are true American intelligence agents have actually collected some important information concerning Soviet military operations and installations in East Germany."[174] The broadcaster NBC announced: "Presumably we should be embarrassed but nobody in Berlin is. In fact, there is a hint of American and West German pride in knowing that we pulled off an espionage trick on the Reds for a change."

The Americans, West Germans and British were indeed proud of their achievements, and Stanley was proud of his small part in its success:

> *"Such operations were rigidly confined to the specialist individuals concerned on a strictly need-to-know basis, which was just as well in the light of the terrible damage that the station's mole was doing to the organisation."*

The 'mole' to which Stanley refers would only be unearthed sometime later, and for now, after more than six years in shadows, the Air Ministry wanted him back. Stanley's work was coming to an end. As well as Gross Doelln, other airfield-related 'targets' in Stanley's orbit, including the woodland tactical forward airstrips being constructed at Allstedt and Mahlwinkel, were also now near completion, such that his work in this arena was effectively done.

An acting squadron leader despite never having worn the uniform, Stanley reluctantly reverted to the rank of flight lieutenant, gathered his family and headed for home.

CHAPTER NINE

ALL AT SEA

Stanley had been serving in Germany and away from flying for more than five years. Only rarely in that time had he returned to the UK for briefing, and usually in the company of a particular source or 'special contact' for whom he was the armed escorting officer. They involved short, furtive trips to RAF Northolt in an HQ 2 TAF communications flight Anson (or a twin-engined Pembroke and its much roomier cabin), being nodded through with a flash of his special passport and firearms certificate, and a whispered 'six' to the customs official that seemed to explain everything.

Being back in the bosom of the RAF proper, and back in uniform, was both a comfort and a shock. Much had changed in those five years he had been away, and his contemporaries had advanced in both rank and flying experience. The aircraft too had changed with the acceleration of the jet era, which Stanley describes as "a challenging period of adjustment which brought its own reward". Importantly, they were together as a family once again, with no more lies and deceit, and no unexplained absences in the middle of the night. He had neighbours that spoke English, and life was once again 'normal'.

The first requirement on his return was to get Stanley back up to speed with modern navigational thinking – which meant a navigation refresher course at 1 ANS at RAF Topcliffe.

Topcliffe was not the most welcoming of stations for an old hand. As a proper 'school' in its own right, it reminded Stanley of his apprentice days, being surrounded by several flights of eager young officer cadets – very smart, single minded and serious. The veterans, many of whom had been away on jobs far removed from the flying world, helped bridge an obvious gap between the 'old' RAF and the 'new':

> *"In the past it was survival of the fittest, but textbooks, lectures and meticulous flight discipline were now the order of the day. For the 'old hairies' it was a relief to fly in older and much slower aircraft, just like wartime Wellingtons – steady and gentlemanly – rather than the jets. We would fly in pairs, choosing close friends to regain our confidence, and cheating where necessary, furiously creating 'non-available sextant star and sun shots, with the deep winter weather making the skies obscured' from actual live radar plots."*

He took his first flight on 12 December 1957 (he had last flown on 1 February 1951) as a navigator on a Handley Page Marathon, an unusual four-engine transport aircraft that proved disappointing for both the RAF and the manufacturer. Topcliffe had 16 on its books as well as a small number of the Vickers Valetta, the military version of the Viking civil airliner which had been turned into a flying classroom. There were regular incidents involving collapsing undercarriage, including one on 11 February 1958 while Stanley was coming to the end of his course. The aircraft (XA268 – a Marathon T11) was damaged beyond repair after its nosewheel became detached:

> *"My time at Topcliffe was softened by sharing the debilitating experience of having to virtually start right from scratch all over again with another former senior intelligence specialist who was coming up for retirement. Between us we 'paired off' and gave each other mutual support over those difficult weeks. Fortunately, Coastal Command was seeking a new intake of navigators for their Shackleton long-range force down in Cornwall, and so on completion we headed west."*

Avro Shackletons were developed from the Avro Lincoln bombers (which were themselves a development of the more famous Lancaster) specifically for use as long-range maritime patrol aircraft and in response to the need to keep an eye on the rapidly expanding Soviet navy. As well as having a reconnaissance role, it also became the RAF's front-line anti-submarine warfare (ASW) aircraft, a duty it would perform until steadily being phased out by the arrival of the jet-powered Nimrod in the 1970s. It had a range of almost 2,000 nautical miles and an endurance of more than 14 hours.

In preparation to flying the Shackleton, Stanley was posted to 15 Maritime Operational Training Unit on the Moray Firth. The unit had formed at RAF Kinloss, in the north-east of Scotland, in October 1956 to centralise all Coastal Command's advanced training and was equipped with a dozen of the four-engine 'Shacks'. Here, Stanley was able to get to grips not only with the aircraft, but also its radar and ASW equipment which would fall partly under his remit, taking part in various sonar and submarine-tracking exercises. The aircraft was both loved and hated by its crews in equal measure, one contemporary remarking: "To many, the old grey lady was a dirty, noisy, smelly and supremely uncomfortable home for up to 15 hours at a time."[175]

Kinloss was in complete contrast to Topcliffe. It was, in Stanley's words, reminiscent of an "old-world gentleman's club". Whereas Bomber Command was filling its ranks with a new generation of younger airmen to pilot and operate the similarly new generation of Canberra and 'V' bombers,[176] Coastal Command appeared staffed with the older generation of highly experienced flyers:

> *"The navigation was pure and professional, just like the basic Dead Reckoning days back at Llandwrog where one respected the weather and became expert in interpretation and acceptance. The flights over the sea were lengthy but always rewarding, and brought the excitement of fighting with the navy and the thrill of the chase on anti-submarine patrols."*

He found the experience stimulating and the surroundings akin to a paradise:

> *"There was such a vast open world to explore with all the northern and western islands, each having their own characteristics, and proving a navigator's dream with headlands and lighthouses to aim for as landfalls after some 12 hours or more out over the drink. The Northern Lights in spring were an experience one would never forget. Good old-fashioned bombing practice was a feature of every trip, and in the modern world of submarine detection there wasn't any room for a second chance once the hunt was on. The old observer's brevet worked a charm; the technique hadn't changed a bit. Real contact and crew co-operation at every stage, each*

The young apprentice.

Marjorie, a nurse, and the love of Stanley's life.

Portrait of Stanley with the white hat band to denote aircrew under training.

Left: *Stanley and Marjorie on their wedding day. Their enforced separation was keenly felt.*

Below left: *Stanley as a newly qualified observer. 1944, before being shot down.*

Below right: *Clifford Hallet who took only seconds to decide to become an air gunner.*

Gordon Culverhouse, Stanley's flight commander at 10 Squadron, who wrote the word 'missing' in Stanley's logbook. (Courtesy of Rob Culverhouse.)

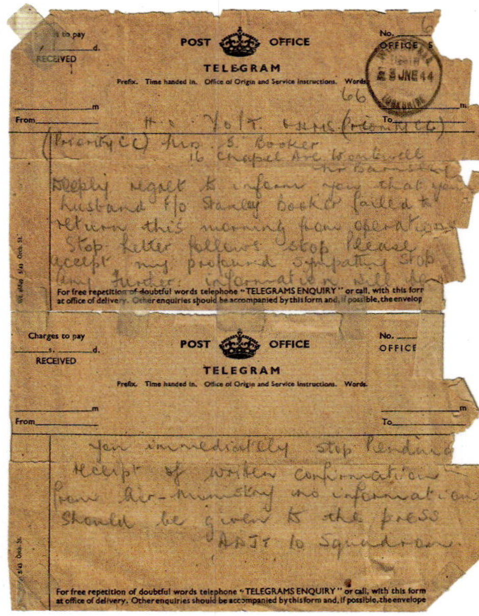

POST OFFICE
TELEGRAM

Charges to pay ___ d.
RECEIVED

No. 6
OFFICE S

Prefix. Time handed in. Office of Origin and Service Instructions. Words 66

29 JNE 44

From ___ To ___

(Priority CC) Mrs. S. Booker
16 Chapel Ave Wombwell
Nr Barnsley

Deeply regret to inform you that your husband F/O Stanley Booker failed to return this morning from operations. Stop. Letter follows stop please accept my profound sympathy stop any further information will be

For free repetition of doubtful words telephone "TELEGRAMS ENQUIRY" or call, with this form at office of delivery. Other enquiries should be accompanied by this form and, if possible, the envelope

POST OFFICE
TELEGRAM

Charges to pay ___ s. ___ d.
RECEIVED

No. ___
OFFICE

Prefix. Time handed in. Office of Origin and Service Instructions. Words.

From ___ To ___

you immediately stop pending receipt of written confirmation from Air Ministry no information should be given to the press

Adjt 10 Squadron.

For free repetition of doubtful words telephone "TELEGRAMS ENQUIRY" or call, with this form at office of delivery. Other enquiries should be accompanied by this form and, if possible, the envelope

The dreaded telegram informing Marjorie that her husband was missing.

A Hercules-powered Handley Page Halifax similar to the one in which Stanley's tour of operations came to an abrupt halt.

Photo of Jack Osselton from his forged identity papers while on the run.

Terry Gould, the 'lucky' man of the crew.

Stanley's logbook. The latter entries are in obviously a different hand.

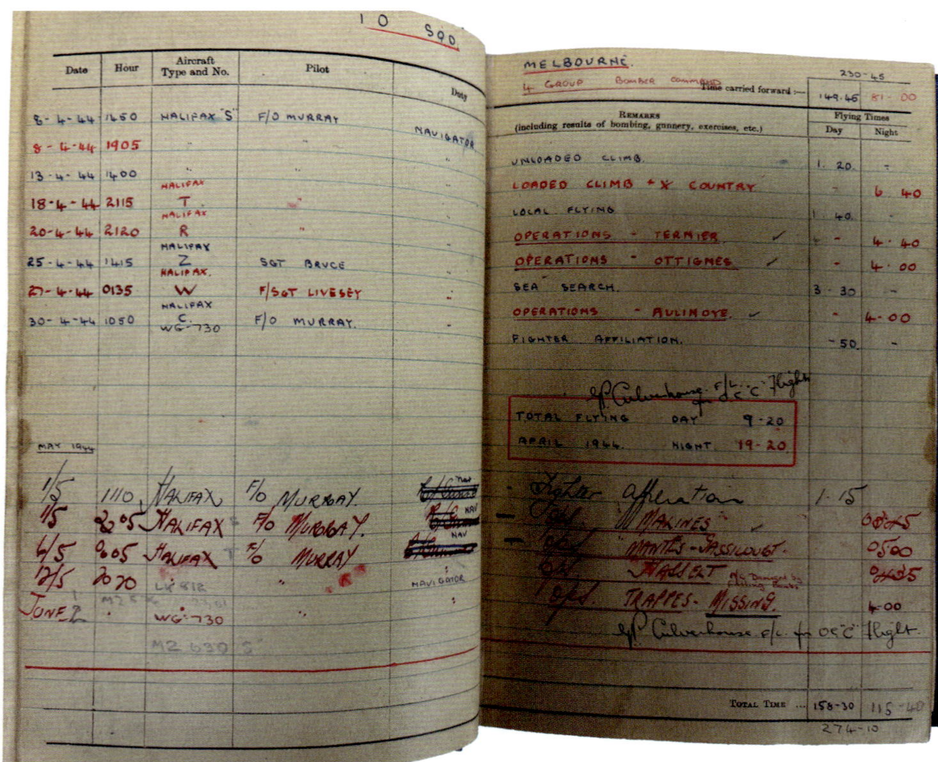

The graves of Sandy and Taffy, killed when Stanley's Halifax was shot down.

Francis Dablin – codenamed 'Mathurin' – helped verify Stanley's identity.

Madame Orial, one of the first to come to Stanley's aid.

The home of Englishwoman Madame le Fèvre — an evader's dream.

False papers identifying Stanley as a gardener 'Pierre Lecomte'.

N° 1267 Série 19.

CARTE D'IDENTITÉ

PREFECTURE DE EURE

Nom LECOMTE

Prénoms Pierre

Né le 25 Avril 1922

A St Vigor le Grand

Département Calvados

Domicile Beaumontel Eure

Signalement

Taille 1m85

Cheveux Noirs

Nez Court

Forme générale du visage ovale

Néant

Empreinte digitale.

Signature du Titulaire : Pierre Lecomte

A EVREUX le 26 MAI 1943

POUR LE PRÉFET :

PREFECTURE DE L'EURE EVREUX

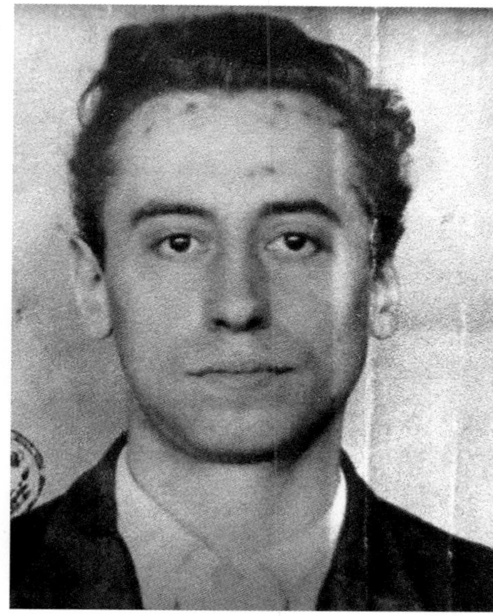

Above left: *Geneviève Desnos, the 18-year-old maid to the venerable Madame Orial.*

Above right: *Jacques Desoubrie, the man who betrayed more than 80 Allied airmen.*

Right: *The French prison at Fresnes from where Stanley was taken for interrogation. (Courtesy the Frank Falla Archive via Paul McCue).*

Below right: *Shocking portrait of Stanley with shaven head and sunken eyes as a prisoner of Buchenwald.*

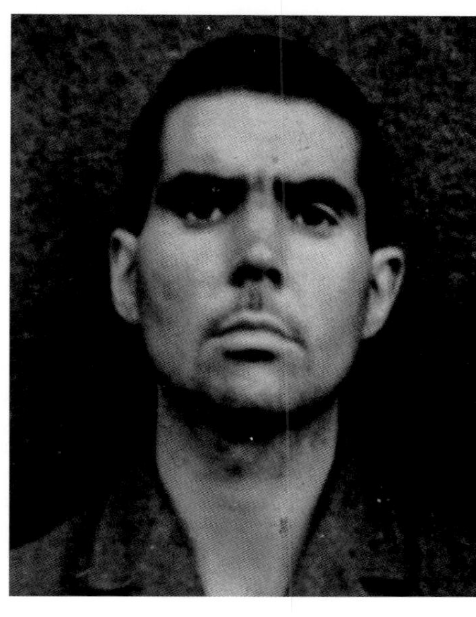

Entrance to the Little Camp where the 168 airmen were originally corralled.

Photograph of Buchenwald taken from the air at the time of the USAAF bombing attack.

The nightmare is finally over for these Buchenwald inmates as the camp is liberated by US forces.

Top: *Marjorie atop a disabled tank on their return to France in 1946 to find the graves of Stanley's lost crew.*

Above: *The Avro York, mainstay of the Berlin Airlift.*

Right: *Stanley (right), Bill Drinkell (2nd right) and crew who flew more than 200 sorties to Berlin during Operation Plainfare.*

Surname / Zuname: BOOKER
Christian Names / Vornamen: Stanley
Sex / Geschlecht: Male
Date of Birth / Geburtsdatum: 25.4.1922
Height / Größe: 6'0"
Colour of Eyes / Augen: Brown
Colour of Hair / Haare: Dark Brown
Other distinguishing marks (if any) / Etwaige sonstige Kennzeichen: None
Signature of Issuing Officer / Unterschrift des ausstellenden Beamten
Date / Datum: 18 Feb 1961

Passport No. / Paß Nr.
Civilian Grade / Ziviler Rang: H.E.O.
Signature of Holder / Unterschrift des Inhabers

Holder's Unit / Inhabers Einheit
Address of Unit / Adresse der Einheit

The Holder of this card is a civilian employee of the War Department or sponsored organisation and is entitled to visit military units in the course of his duties.

Der Inhaber dieses Ausweises ist ein Zivil-Angestellter des War Departments oder angeschlossener Organisation und ist bei Ausübung seines Dienstes berechtigt, militärische Einheiten zu besuchen.

CIVILIAN ESTABLISHMENT AND PAY OFFICE BRITISH FORCES POST OFFICE 40.

A 1961 ID card entitling Stanley — a 'civilian employee' — to visit military units 'in the course of his duty'.

Stanley with his beloved Alsatian 'Prince'.

Stanley giving James Bond a run for his money.

The Olympic Stadium, Berlin. If walls could talk…

Stanley with his younger brother Les who became a Halton Apprentice.

Formal portrait of Stanley while serving with Coastal Command.

An Avro Shackleton, seemingly loved and hated by its crews in equal measure. (via Sean Feast).

Above: *Inside a Shackleton – 'dirty, noisy, smelly and supremely uncomfortable'. (via Sean Feast).*

Left: *Stanley (left) in Gibraltar with visiting VIPs who appear suitably impressed.*

Below: *Gibraltar proved to be one of Stanley's favourite postings.*

Stanley was awarded the MBE in the New Years Honours of 1965 for his work on The Rock.

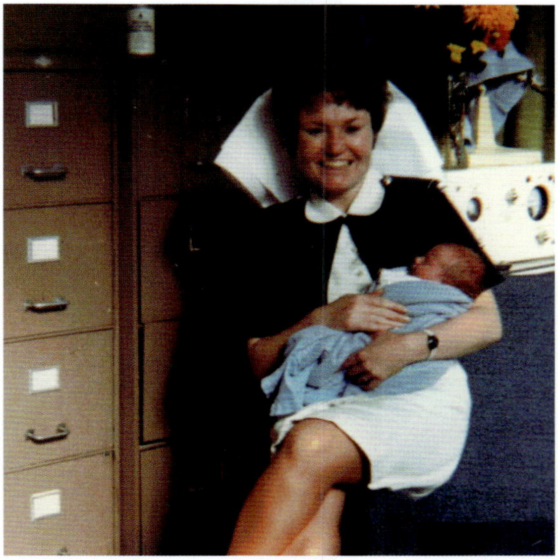

***Right:** Flight Officer Patricia Booker of the Princess Mary's RAF Nursing Service, RAF Halton, 1969.*

***Below:** Teaching an old dog new tricks at the Personnel Selection Training School in 1970.*

Stanley presents a copy of RAF at Buchenwald *to the OC of the AIDU.*

Stanley lays a wreath at Buchenwald as the only RAF representative at the 40th anniversary of the camp's liberation.

The crematorium at Buchenwald, the furnaces of which appeared to be burning 24 hours a day.

Top: *Although Stanley spurned events and reunions, he made an exception for the KLB Club.*

Middle: *Stone tablet remembering the two airmen who died as prisoners of Buchenwald.*

Below left: *The present-day memorial to the agents murdered in Buchenwald who marched to their deaths with their heads held high.*

Below right: *Memorial to the missing men of 10 Squadron on the site of the former RAF Melbourne. (via Sean Feast).*

Above left: Paul McCue invites Stanley to become an honorary member of the Secret World War Two Learning Network.*

***Above right:** Members of the present-day 10 Squadron present Stanley with a framed print of an Airbus Voyager.*

***Left:** Stanley proudly sporting his Légion d'honneur.*

***Below left:** Celebrating Stanley's 101st birthday with friends and family from the UK and France.*

member making his own vital contribution – especially the 'off-watch' crew doing such magnificent work on the galley, serving bacon or egg butties. It was never a chore. There was always so much of interest to do, see and eat!"

For his last trip he was reunited with a familiar pilot whom he had not seen since the Berlin airlift, Mike Ensor. Ensor was coming to the end of his service career, having taken 15 years to climb back to his wartime rank of wing commander. As the OTU's chief instructor, he was having one last 'hurrah'; for despite the need for trained navigators, Coastal Command was a dwindling force whose frontline strength (by March 1959) stood at only 24 aircraft. Stanley joined Mike for a marathon reconnaissance over the Arctic, from which they returned after a flight of 15 hours and 10 minutes, two hours of which had been in total darkness.

Having satisfied the chief navigation instructor that he could be trusted not to get lost, Stanley was given his choice of posting, and decided to exercise his rights under Queen's regulations to apply to return to his previous service squadron:

"There was a wide choice of postings to aim for. Coastal Command was very much an old established firm that treasured its tradition and its crews. The morale was fantastic. Each posting – whether to Malta, Gibraltar, Cornwall, Kinloss or Lossiemouth – would be a boost for the family, having compact stations by the sea, with excellent established school backups and superb recreational facilities. I felt the family deserved a complete break after faithfully living such a sheltered life in Berlin."

Stanley was delighted, therefore, to be posted to RAF St Mawgan, rejoining 206 Squadron, his old unit from Transport Command days. Cornwall, with its beautiful beaches and coastline, was in stark contrast to life behind the Iron Curtain, and Stanley felt truly safe and at peace for the first time in years: "I was back in the 'real' Royal Air Force again and we loved it."[177]

At the OTU Stanley had been trained on Shackleton Mk 1s, but 206 was equipped with the upgraded Mk IIIs which had better soundproofing, crew seats and team positions to increase overall comfort. Stanley flew regularly with one of the flight commanders, Squadron Leader Moss, on search-and-rescue (SAR) and reconnaissance patrols, and to test new radar equipment, including Blue Silk, a new-generation Doppler system. The squadron was commanded at the time by Wing Commander Ronald Billett, with whom he struck up an immediate rapport. It was Billett who on 5 February 1959 rated Stanley as an 'above average' navigator in his annual assessment, confirming that despite his unexplained leave of absence, and lack of flying time, Stanley had not lost his touch.

Stanley spent a happy two years with 206. After the Berlin subterfuge and living a lie for so long, it was a pleasure, he said, to come in to work every day: "It was a wonderful recuperation process; the RAF at its best."

His days were long and busy, and his logbook filled with operational exercises and the shadowing of suspicious vessels in friendly and neutral waters as part of Operation Grape. He took part in several SAR missions, including one on 20 May 1959 looking for an Anson that had ditched off Anglesey, and another on 24 September searching for a jet that had come down near the Isle of Wight. In the case of the former, the aircraft was later discovered having flown into the Tal y Fan mountain in north Wales. All three crew members were killed. The latter involved an RN Sea Hawk on a test flight from RNAS Lee-on-Solent. The control column jammed, obliging the pilot to point the aircraft out to sea and eject. He too was sadly killed.

Stanley retained his 'above average' rating at his next assessment by which time he had a new squadron commander, Wing Commander John Bazalgette DFC, and had worked his way back to the squadron navigation officer role.[178] One day, after they had returned from the RN post-exercise wash-up at the Portland submarine training base, Billett, the wing commander flying, had simply been posted away:

> *"This was not unusual at that time as there was a great deal of activity within the command with the introduction of the new high-tech Nimrod which was absorbing quite a few of the brighter, more experienced 'Kipper Fleet' aircrew."*

Only later would Stanley learn the true reason for Billett's departure.

One day, completely out of the blue, Stanley took a phone call asking him to come to London for an interview. Ominously, he was also told to get any furniture he may have out of storage, for he would shortly be returning to Berlin to pick up where he had left off. In the immediate term he was to report to the College of Air Warfare at RAF Manby to complete a 'rocket familiarisation course' to better understand the capabilities of the Russians' latest surface-to-air missile (SAM) threat.

The plus point of returning to the shadows was that his acting rank of squadron leader was reinstated. But it meant more upheaval for his family and a return to the lies and deceit that he thought had been left behind. A formal letter from the War Office on 17 January 1961 confirmed the offer of "Temporary appointment as Intelligence Officer, Grade 1, with the No.1 Planning and Evaluation Unit in Germany". He was told to confirm acceptance by return, and make his own arrangements to travel out with his family the following month.[179]

Stanley arrived back in Berlin on 15 February having once again been reissued with the necessary documentation and firearms certificate for a new .32 automatic pistol and 25 rounds of 7.5 mm ammunition. He had in fact surrendered his original Walther PPK to the West Riding constabulary in Barnsley, Yorkshire in the period between competing his maritime OTU and his arrival at St Mawgan.[180]

Among his first duties was to report to the public safety officer at the Olympic stadium to be reissued with his various official passes. These included his official identity card that clearly stated he was "a civilian employee . . . entitled to visit military units in the course of his duty".[181] He also received soon after his British Forces Germany driving licence and petrol requisition authority allowing him to draw 190 litres of fuel per month. His address was given as 'The Claims Unit', HQ, Berlin BFPO 45.[182] At the stadium he came face to face with a big cheery group captain, in uniform, about to enter an office marked 'Deputy Officer i/c BRIXMIS'. It was none other than Stanley's former wing commander flying, Billett, who had left St Mawgan so abruptly just a few weeks earlier, without a word.

Despite the initial pleasure at seeing his former 'boss', things started badly. It transpired Stanley's predecessor had been involved in a serious skiing accident just days before Stanley's arrival, and so there was to be no smooth handover or detailed briefing. He was at that time languishing in a US army hospital in Bavaria. It meant that Stanley did not have the keys to the safe, literally and metaphorically, to access the operational contact files and other such important information without which it would be impossible to do his job.

Worse was to follow. One morning Stanley arrived for work to find the place in uproar. Secretaries began dashing around corridors, rounding up their masters, for an important powwow in the head of station's office. This was an unusual event, to say the least, made more unusual by a slight sense of panic in the air. Then the reason for the commotion was explained. A 'mole' had been unearthed:

"This amazed everybody. We were dumbfounded to be advised that back in London a former member of the earlier Berlin staff, who had been highly thought of, had just been arrested and already confessed to his guilt. It ultimately became clear that for many years he had copied everything that had passed over his desk and elsewhere whilst he had been enjoying everyone's hospitality and confidence."

The man in question – George Blake – sat in the next office to Stanley's during his first tour of Berlin. There was every possibility that Stanley's own operations had, in fact, been compromised.

Blake was an unlikely traitor in many ways. Dutch by birth (his family name was Behar), he'd escaped to Britain in 1942, having initially worked against the German occupation as a courier with the Resistance. He was commissioned into the Royal Navy as a sub-lieutenant and was quickly recruited into the intelligence services, joining the Dutch section of SIS/MI6 and working with the SOE tasked with sending agents and supplies behind enemy lines.

With the end of the war in Europe he was posted to Hamburg, interrogating former U-boat captains on behalf of naval intelligence. The service sent him to study languages, including Russian, at Downing College, Cambridge, after which he was posted to the British legation in Seoul, South Korea. While outwardly employed as a vice-consul under Consul General Vyvyan Holt, his real work was as a spy, gathering intelligence on communist North Korea, China and the Soviet Far East.

With the outbreak of war on the Korean peninsula, Seoul was quickly captured and Blake, Holt and other British diplomats taken prisoner. Blake read Karl Marx in captivity and, after witnessing what he believed to be the shameful bombing of North Korea by American B-29 Superfortresses, was determined to become a communist. Having first been awakened to the possibilities of communism at Cambridge, he now took positive action, volunteering his services to the Soviets. He felt, he was to say later, "on the wrong side" and that "it would be better for humanity if the communist system prevailed".

Blake's release from captivity in 1953 was greeted with great enthusiasm and relief by the authorities, who may have felt differently had they known the havoc he would ultimately cause. Blake joined Stanley in Berlin in 1955, in the same station, working as a case officer tasked with recruiting Soviet officers as double agents. Unfortunately, he was no longer working for the British and was instead informing his new masters of the Allies' every move. This included Operation Gold, the secret tunnel project.

Blake's involvement with the tunnel was considerable. He had attended vital meetings and was authorised by his lords and masters to take detailed notes to share official minutes about the tunnel and its progress. What the intelligence services didn't know, however, was that he was also sharing the information with his 'real' masters in Moscow, on at least one occasion meeting his KGB handler atop a London bus. Such was his importance as a Russian 'asset' that it appears the Soviets allowed the tunnel to go 'undiscovered' for some time to avoid any suspicion falling his way. When the programme was exposed, the Allies faced the awful realisation that much of what they had heard may have been bogus.[183]

In the course of nine years, Blake – who Peter Lunn described as his best agent runner – is believed to have betrayed the details of some 40 SIS/MI6 agents to the KGB, disrupting many of the Allies' principal operations in Eastern Europe. Blake himself proposed that number might have been ten times greater. He may also have been the man responsible for exposing a CIA mole in the KGB, Pyotr Popov, who was later executed.

Blake was undone, it is said, by the revelations of a Polish triple agent, Michal Goleniewski, who had received information originating from a mole in SIS/MI6. The mole – Blake – heard the news that the CIA had a top-level informant in Poland and sent word back to the KGB, who passed it on to Polish intelligence. Goleniewski heard the news from the KGB and immediately escaped.

Blake was arrested in London on his return from Lebanon, where he had been enrolled at the Middle East Centre for Arab Studies, a well-known spy school for Westerners. On the third day of his debriefing, he confessed to everything: he had not been tortured by the North Koreans into changing his allegiances; he had converted voluntarily. He also felt no remorse for those he had betrayed, and suggested that he had received assurances that every SIS/MI6 agent he exposed should not be arrested; at least one, however, may have been taken to Moscow and never seen again.

As the full extent of Blake's treachery began to unfold, Stanley and those in the Berlin station were left to deal with the fallout. As a contemporary of Blake, Stanley was immediately eyed with suspicion by those around him. If the station had one mole, then why not two? Within hours, the offices were all but deserted, and the people gone. A handful of secretaries remained to tidy round and collect up what was left by way of personal possessions.

The exposure of Blake led to changes in how the station would operate in future. Several familiar faces had now gone, some never seen or heard of again. Working alongside another former RAF wartime Bomber Command colleague who had also served in 4 Group, the pair spent several months meticulously examining and analysing a copy of every station file on every case to assess the degree of compromise to every agent in the field. Their task in saving agents from the consequences of being known to the East German secret police had to coincide with the need to maintain day-to-day operations and essential intelligence work.

The volume of refugees now spilling over the border reached a new high. Since 1949, more than two and a half million had fled from East to West. On one single day, more than 4,000 refugees registered at the Marienborn reception centre – something of a record.[184] The mass exodus of skilled workers from the East posed a major economic problem[185] such that Moscow decided to take drastic action. During the night of 12/13 August 1961, in a well-planned operation that appeared to take the Allies (or at least the staff at Field Station Berlin) completely by surprise, building began of a Wall that would seal off completely the Soviet sector from the Western sectors of Berlin.[186] By dawn, some 40,000 workers started erecting slabs of prefabricated concrete along the entire three Western sector boundaries, a distance of almost 30 miles. Numerous side streets were closed off with temporary barricades and barbed wire, street surfaces were torn up to make them impassable to vehicles, and the enormous multi-floor tenement blocks that bordered the eastern side of the old boundary roads were cleared of their occupants, the lower windows bricked up, and all exits secured.

The work was accompanied by a show of strength from the East German border guards (the *Grenzpolizei*) at the Brandenburg Gate, supported by water cannon to quell any potential disturbances, and with the ominous outline of Soviet T-55 tanks in the distance.

Stanley and his 4 Group colleague were at the Gate to watch the events unfold and were impressed with the calm showed by the British military police (MPs) who worked quickly and efficiently in sealing off *Strasse des 17 Juni* to control the numbers of West Berliners now congregating in the area. Barbed wire was also placed around the imposing Soviet war memorial 300 metres inside the British side of the Gate, and two MPs were posted to protect the anxious Soviet sentries who were still maintaining their traditional 'guard' of their national tribute to those who had fallen in the 1945 battle for the city.

The orderly conduct of the modest British response at the Gate was in complete contrast with the spectacle a few hundred yards further around the sector boundary where, on the edge of the famous Potsdamer Platz in the US sector, there was every prospect of World War Three breaking out as the Americans deployed columns of noisy M48A Patton heavy tanks supported by M59 armoured personnel carriers (APCs). The handful of Second World War-vintage Comet tanks of Britain's Berlin brigade, and their attendant recovery vehicle, which occasionally clattered across the city to lift the spirits of the local inhabitants, remained steadfastly in the Spandau barracks, no doubt on immediate standby, but certainly not adding to the tension that was clearly building up throughout the course of the day.

With plenty to keep him occupied, it was only much later that Stanley would learn of some of the other covert activities being undertaken during and around that time:

> *"Billett and his number two, Squadron Leader 'Dickie' Dyer, spent many hours over that weekend and afterwards up in their little de Havilland Chipmunk training aircraft taking photographs to assess the extent of the actual build-up of the Soviet military and which we, as local 'information officers', were not alerted to. I was concerned about what might be going on at 'my' airfield, Gross Doelln, but it wasn't going to be me who was going to send off another FLASH signal. I had learned my lesson and had burned my fingers before."*

The immediate crisis that greeted the building of the Wall soon passed, though not without a considerable rattling of sabres between East and West. This included a stand-off between US and Soviet tanks at the famous Checkpoint Charlie where one false move from either side could have ended in calamity in an incident described as "one of the tensest moments of the Cold War in Europe".[187]

A plus point to come from the crisis, however, was that Stanley's role and responsibilities became more formally recognised, and attitudes towards him changed. "We few seconded service 'specialists' became closer members of the professional family," he recalls. He also got to take advantage of reduced staff numbers by revising the Buchenwald *Abcochen* spirit in terms of scrounging whatever they could lay their hands on, and occupying one of the more sumptuously furnished offices which had recently been vacated.[188] "It had thick carpets and furniture that would grace any cabinet minister's office back in the

UK," he said. "If our tours were obviously going to be curtailed, then at least for the few months remaining we were going to live in comfort!"

The end, when it came, was not a disappointment, for a new outlet for Stanley's talents had been found, and in sunnier climes.

While much of the focus of Soviet agitation up to that point had of course been on land (and especially on Berlin), the Soviet Union was also steadily building its presence in the Mediterranean – a presence which posed a new and unpredictable threat. In 1958 they had signed a Soviet-Albanian agreement to build a permanent operating base at Valona to service Soviet diesel submarines, which allowed them to begin regular forays into the central and eastern Mediterranean. By 1960 they had a dozen or so submarines in the area, along with a series of support vessels. That same year they conducted their first major exercise in the Med, involving not only their submarines and surface ships from their Black Sea fleet, but also elements from the Albanian navy:

> *"The Soviets had a new generation of missile-armed warships operating mainly at the eastern end of the Med but also congregating off the coast of Tripolitania. We only had aircraft from Malta to keep an eye on them, namely Coastal Command Shackletons and Canberras from one of our photo-reconnaissance squadrons. The ships were being built in the Black Sea shipyards and then passing through the Dardanelles and out into open waters en route to join their Baltic, northern or Pacific fleets, all of which were a threat. Thus, in early 1962 I was not disappointed when my Berlin deployment was coming to an end to be considered for a role in intelligence in Gibraltar. I knew that having served in Coastal Command I would have an advantage, but it meant reverting back to the rank of flight lieutenant."*

Despite the step down in rank, Stanley was happy with his new role in RAF Int./Ops at the Shackleton base at RAF North Front in Gibraltar, which was very much on the front line of the action. He was a little disappointed at the beginning, however, to find that 'intelligence' on the Rock – as Gibraltar was known – amounted to little more than monitoring the conspicuously unremarkable Soviet electronic intelligence (ELINT) vessel that was always on station, using its sophisticated sensors and communication equipment to 'spy' on NATO and the nearby US Navy nuclear missile submarine base and airfield at Rota in Spain.[189]

"One had to brief one's operational flying crews on the sinister function behind the regular morning daily rotation of the transiting Okean-class trawlers, always dropping their anchors in the same position, opposite the exits to the naval base and right below the flight path to the main runway. The vessels kept themselves apart from the normal whaling and commercial merchant fleet anchorages, and were laden with the most amazing arrays of different aerials way over and above the most enthusiastic of local TV-reception requirements. One had to brief the same aircrew and visiting NATO participants on just why that same innocent-looking trawler had transited the Med at a steady eight knots from its Black Sea base and just happened to find itself right on time and in the middle of the undeclared NATO war games exercise area, or in the nearby Royal Navy trials areas where a new nuclear submarine trial was taking place."[190]

Stanley's arrival in Gibraltar coincided with a change in fortunes for the Soviets in the Mediterranean. The agreement they had signed with Albania was unceremoniously broken, and the abrupt loss of their submarine base was a serious setback. Diesel/electric submarines require extensive support facilities to operate for long periods away from home waters. At the time the Soviet navy did not have sufficient numbers of long-range surface ships or submarines to divert to the Mediterranean; and the Montreux Convention forbade submarines from entering the Mediterranean for combat patrols from the Black Sea. As such they had to make the long journey from the Baltic or northern seas which seriously hampered their operational capabilities.

Soviet naval presence in the Mediterranean became somewhat 'spotty' for a time, not only because of the Soviet Union's break in relations with Albania, but also because Moscow considered the defence of its northern and Baltic maritime borders as more vital.[191] But this period also coincided with the build-up to the Cuban Missile Crisis which required significant volumes of Soviet shipping, both merchant and naval, to pass through the Strait of Gibraltar to reach their destination across the Atlantic. The US deployment of nuclear missiles in Italy and Turkey was being mirrored by Soviet deployment of nuclear missiles in Cuba. Nikita Krushchev, the Soviet premier, had struck a deal with the Cuban revolutionary Fidel Castro to install missiles on the island to deter a future US invasion. Construction of the sites required considerable resources, some of which were being shipped from Russia through the Mediterranean from one of four

Black Sea ports (Sevastopol, Feodosiya, Nikolayev and Poti). It was an exciting time to be in intelligence, and in close proximity to the Shackleton crews engaged in distant reconnaissance patrols east of the Rock:

> *"The aircrew would initially intercept and identify the traffic, taking detailed photographs from all aspects and heights. Their reconnaissance was supported by the regular use of the very enthusiastic local air-sea rescue launch, with the RAF's best photographer on board, to take really close-up photographs of every ship, especially its aerial and radar fit-outs, which could be simultaneously matched with the detailed overhead photographs from the aircraft. Healthy competition was established with the Americans' Lockheed Neptune reconnaissance aircraft from Rota, but regrettably their national publicity policy was more enlightened than ours at the time, and it was their photographs – which were often less detailed than ours – which ended up hitting the headlines at that period of serious international tension."*[192]

Another frustration was having to hand over intelligence to senior staff in the Royal Navy:

> *"The Shackletons and air-sea rescue launch brought the most outstanding close-up intelligence photos of Soviet warships and merchant vessels with their lethal deck cargoes of nuclear missiles. I would often not only debrief the crews but also prepare the background operational reports, only to have to hand them over to the resident director of naval intelligence, who was one rank higher. We got little of the fame and glory, but such is inter-service life."*

The end of the Cuban Missile Crisis in October 1962 did not, however, mark the end of gathering intelligence on the Soviet naval fleet. The 'enthusiasm', as Stanley calls it, continued:

> *"The Shackleton squadron won a much-coveted Command Intelligence trophy as well as other operational efficiency awards, while the SAR crew continued to deliver a regular daily survey of every Soviet vessel at anchor in the bay. This was in a standard 'four-view format', that over the years was to provide a remarkable library of Soviet fishing trawlers and merchant shipping, with remarkably odd aerials, that regularly took anchor each morning. It also*

included photographs of every Soviet vessel passing through our area, many of which were new to Allied intelligence, with prototype equipment that proved to be of considerable interest to the Admiralty."

Gibraltar proved to be one of Stanley's favourite postings, one which he described as "an enthusiastic intelligence officer's dream", apart from the time he had to spend liaising with the international media, a task he described as "anathema to any professional intelligence officer used to maintaining a low profile". As well as his ground duties, he also managed to cadge the occasional ride in a 'Shack' from North Front, primarily taking part in regular SAR exercises to keep his hand in:

"One lived on the edge – if not as an actual paid-up member – of the exclusive sig./elect.int. world in the days when GCHQ was only spoken of in whispers and strictly behind closed doors. Its very existence never appeared in print."[193]

Stanley's RAF intelligence tour at RAF North Front, Gibraltar came to an end in the autumn of 1964 when he was informed that for "career purposes" he needed to get back to flying. Within a few hours of landing back in the UK, however, he received a telegram requiring him to make a reversed-charge call to the MOD. On the call he was advised that he was to take up an immediate special intelligence post in Malaysia – and leave his family behind. It didn't happen, however, and in the New Year of 1965 Stanley was once again back in the flying world, but not before he had taken a trip with his family to Buckingham Palace, having been recognised in the New Year Honours with the award of an MBE:

"Her Majesty graciously said a few very kind words and showed how remarkably well briefed she was. She showed an informed interest in my earlier Berlin involvement. It was a most humbling and memorable experience."

Stanley also received a congratulatory letter from the AOC RAF North Front, Gibraltar, Air Commodore Charles Inness.[194] Inness was delighted that Stanley's 'sterling work' at RAF North Front had been recognised and that he might "return to Intelligence duties in due time thoroughly refreshed".[195]

Stanley was posted to 1 ANS at Stradishall in the spring of 1965:

> *"I was now 43, still a senior flight lieutenant, and after undergoing yet another navigation refresher course – my third – I found myself in Signals Command as a Varsity navigator on their routine flight aids calibration squadron at Watton. Watton was a base known for its history of odd intelligence goings-on in the past but none of which seemed to come my way during my short tour on the squadron."*

His new unit, and the last squadron with which Stanley served in a flying capacity, was 115 Squadron. It had formed originally in the First World War, and in the second had gained the distinction of making the RAF's first bombing raid of the war on a mainland target.[196] Disbanded in 1950, it was re-formed eight years later to become a radar calibration unit.

He took his first flight with the squadron in Varsity WJ887 on 15 May 1965 and flew his last on 5 November the same year. The final entry of his logbook records a one-hour continuation training flight with Flight Lieutenant Welch in Varsity WJ947. His logbook is signed on 9 March 1966 by the OC A Flight, by which time he had flown a total of 2,187 hrs during the day, and 751 hrs and 35 mins at night – bringing a grand total of just short of 3,000 hours of flying time. He had flown in 18 different types of aircraft, from a Lysander II to a Shackleton III. (He also notes a further 100 hrs had been flown between 1945 and 1947 in Lancasters, Mosquitoes and Oxfords while at HQ 41 group, but that the records were not made available to him from the Air Ministry.)

This was not the end of Stanley's RAF career, however. Having attended a staff officers' training course,[197] his final years of service were spent as part of No. 1 Aeronautical Information Documents Unit (1AIDU) at Northolt:

> *"I was privileged to be in charge of the RAF special briefing unit, a compact team of experienced briefing officers which included some somewhat elderly wartime warrant officer navigators and signallers who could turn their hands to anything. They had the most amazing contacts anywhere in the world, wherever we wanted them, and were the salt of the earth in every way. The RAF was most fortunate to have had such remarkable characters in their midst."*[198]

The unit was tasked with day-to-day liaison with crews of the Queen's Flight, then based at RAF Benson, to prepare and publish a notice to airmen (NOTAM) regarding every royal flight and details of the 'purple corridor' – the area to be kept free from commercial and other aircraft to allow the passage of VIP aircraft. Its responsibilities also ran to preparing detailed printed navigation and radio-frequency briefing documents using information from its comprehensive unit library and from the Joint Intelligence Bureau. Royal trips overseas were often complicated affairs, requiring significant input from the team to ensure the safety of those onboard and the availability of essential services (SAR for example) should something go wrong.

> *"It was a demanding but satisfying job to follow the progress of a royal flight, often through the media, and nearly always with our fingers crossed at all times."*

As well as royal passengers, the unit also prepared documents for certain civilian VIPs undertaking various 'hush-hush' duties in far-flung regions of the former empire. On one memorable occasion, the unit also helped support the epic flight of Sheila Scott, the actress-turned-aviatrix, who became the first person to fly over the North Pole in a small aircraft, and the first European woman to fly solo around the world.

During Stanley's time in charge, he also learned of the depth of radar capability being afforded by the US to their European allies, some which he said "we in the RAF had never been fully aware of in any professional capacity whatsoever at that time".

Stanley's time with the unit, and with the RAF, was ending, and a new career in the utilities industry beckoned. He described those last few months as very good therapy:

> *"To be able to give my best and to work with dedicated colleagues who had pride in their work proved a rewarding and satisfying conclusion to my service career."*

But Stanley's relationship with the services was far from done. An even bigger fight was already underway.

CHAPTER TEN

FIGHT FOR JUSTICE

Airey Neave knew something about being held captive by the Germans. He knew something of the meaning of fear. Mobilised on the outbreak of war, he'd been sent to France in 1940 in time for the German invasion of the Low Countries, which forced British troops back to the Channel ports. Neave was wounded and captured at Calais on 23 May 1940 and imprisoned initially at Oflag IX-A/H near Spangenberg, and then Stalag XX-A near Thorn in German-occupied western Poland.

It was from Thorn that he made his first escape, only to be recaptured – finding himself briefly in the hands of the Gestapo. He was then sent to Oflag IVC – Colditz – from where he made further escape attempts, the second of which was successful. Travelling by train and on foot in company with a Dutch officer, Anthony Luteyn, he eventually made it to safety, returning to England almost exactly two years after his capture.

Recruited by MI9, an organisation set up to support underground escape lines in occupied Europe, Neave went by the codename 'Saturday', gathering intelligence on a huge cast of characters involved in helping downed aircrew, including those who were later unmasked as working for the other side. They included an electrician from Tourcoing on the Belgian border, Jean-Jacques Desoubrie, whom Neave described as one of "the most successful of our enemies".[199] It was Desoubrie – also known as 'Jean Masson' and 'Pierre Boulain' – who almost single-handedly brought down the Comet Line, one of the most successful of all the escape lines; it was Desoubrie who was directly responsible for betraying

Stanley, and dozens of others who ended up in Fresnes, to the Gestapo; and it was Desoubrie whom the US military intelligence service described in August 1945 as "a vicious German agent" for whom "every possible effort" should be made to bring to justice.[200]

After the war, Airey Neave became a member of parliament, and it was in this capacity that Stanley and he began to correspond. Four years after the war, a law had been passed in Germany to restore the rights and privileges of those who had been discriminated against in National Socialist legislation. Further, the government in Bonn created the Federal Restitution Law (the *Bundesrückerstattungsgesetz*) in 1957 to compensate and reward "former victims of National Socialist persecution". Whereas many Allied countries whose servicemen and women had suffered under the Nazi regime were quick to engage and settle, the British government began dragging its heels. The level of procrastination was such that the cause was taken up by Neave in the spring of 1964, and his campaign accelerated with the death of Yeo-Thomas, the mysterious squadron leader whom Stanley had known in Buchenwald. Yeo-Thomas, Neave pointed out in a Commons debate, had died in poor health and without ever receiving compensation for the suffering and deprivation he had endured. He went further, stating that the Foreign Office was "very gravely to blame" for its failure to press the West German government for compensation for British survivors of German concentration camps.[201] The foreign secretary promised to look into the case.

Stanley wrote to Airey Neave from Gibraltar on 10 April 1964, outlining his case for compensation.[202] Towards the end he wrote: "As a serving officer, I cannot publicise my experiences . . . Should you be in a position to take any official action with HM Foreign Office then I should be only too willing to give any further facts you desire, and I can substantiate these with official documents taken from the camp records."

Neave responded ten days later, explaining that Stanley's letter had been forwarded to the Foreign Office and promising that he was still pressing them as hard as he could.[203] He also wrote that the FO appeared to be taking a view that it could not establish a complete list of who was entitled to a payout until the total amount of compensation had been agreed with the Bonn government.

Soon after, on 9 June 1964, the British and German governments agreed a compensation pot of £1 million, a wholly arbitrary figure given that they had no idea how many claimants would be eligible, or whether that money was to be shared between five or five hundred. Crucially, in the wording of the agreement, which was published in the national press, the money was to benefit victims of persecution who, as a result, had "suffered loss of liberty or damage to their health". Stanley qualified under both.

Stanley's torture at the hands of the Gestapo had left him with deep physical and mental trauma. Sinus issues that had stemmed from being beaten in the face were a continual problem and at various stages he was unable to fly. He was also denied the opportunity to fly jets: "This alone," he said, "had a bearing on the curtailment of my service career."[204] Chest complaints were common, as were severe pains in the groin. His sleep was disturbed, and frequent, violent nightmares became a regrettable way of life. Headaches were commonplace, and paranoia nagged at his thoughts:

> *"Reclusion and abruptness became an accepted manner and was later to cause family and social problems. In general, I had a growing bitterness and resentment that nobody understood. There was a desire to talk about the horrors I had experienced yet nobody seemed interested."*

In the post-war RAF, which Stanley admits on reflection "was the wrong place for a survivor", he had a growing need to avoid social contact or publicity. He could not settle in crowds or parties. Mess functions became an ordeal, and Christmas parties and summer balls filled him with dread. He was happier when he could escape with the family on holiday to Seville or Grenada but even this could be a strain, and he was inclined to walk off on his own when it all became too much for him. His absence from mandatory dining-in nights was noted and, he felt, directly impacted his prospects for promotion. Before the war he had very much enjoyed socialising and been the life and soul of any party. Buchenwald had robbed him of all that, and his sense of proportion. After starving in the camps, he could not abide to see food being wasted and in such vast quantities. He wrote:

> *"The depression I thought would pass, but right from the first day of returning to England I found myself shunning company and confined spaces. Travelling on buses or trains was agony and unless there was a corridor in the train or a convenient bus stop I could not continue the journey. Whilst this is a state of mind, I know it has had a very serious adverse effect on my service career. I was promoted to the rank of flight lieutenant in 1945 and*

held the same rank after 22 years of service. I was told over and over again this was my own fault. Before I was shot down and fell into evil hands, I was a very gay party-loving individual with a very promising career ahead of me; thus I can only blame my failure on one thing: my internment and mishandling by the SS and Gestapo."[205]

The absence of any medical endorsements that confirmed his wartime experiences in Fresnes and Buchenwald didn't help, and added to the scepticism of those who would later decide his financial settlement. The failure, Stanley felt, to capture his experiences and the experiences of others in the camp had been ignored from the start, from the moment he arrived home to be processed by the RAF reception centre staff at Cosford and his subsequent debriefing by MI9 at the Marylebone Hotel, London on 13 October 1945:[206]

"*The only official interest (from MI9) was in establishing the names of the various French families who had given me assistance after I had been shot down. This was apparently in order to assess the degree of assistance given, so that appropriate 'Tedder certificates' could be awarded to the families concerned.*[207] *To my complete surprise and concern, nobody had the slightest interest in how we were shot down or our crew casualties, nor even how I was betrayed to the Gestapo. They didn't seem to want to know about how I was interrogated or the subsequent incarceration in Buchenwald where we witnessed at first hand the devastating air attack by American bombers dropping more than 300 tons of heavy explosives. Even more of a concern, they had no interest whatsoever of our sharing our captivity with the ill-fated among the party of 37 SOE/SIS agents, including Yeo-Thomas, the legendary 'White Rabbit', and that we had witnessed 31 of their number who had been marched off to their cruel fate in the cellars of the evil crematorium. I could not understand why our own British intelligence was not pursuing these vital events.*"

On 2 April 1965, Stanley was invited by the Ministry of Pensions and National Insurance to attend a medical board in Cambridge (Stanley was living in Yorkshire at the time), where his application for restitution would be progressed. He was invited also to bring "any documentary evidence about the disabilities which were claimed to have resulted from wartime imprisonment".

The medical board, undertaken at the Ministry of Employment's unemployment sickness assessment office, comprised two doctors. In answer to their questions, Stanley showed them the deep scar on his chest, the result of the cigar butt being ground into his sternum, and detailed the disabilities he was claiming due to his wartime deprivations. These included problems with his sinuses, nightmares, testicular discomfort, arthritis in his right knee, anxiety and claustrophobia. He had had three sinus operations at RAF Wroughton and RAF Halton between 1950 and 1953.

The assessment made by the board was at best unsympathetic and, in the light of what Stanley had gone through, verging on cruel. Since he had not had an operation for more than ten years, they did not consider his sinuses to be an issue. His knee did not prevent him from flying, and since he retained his full aircrew medical category, he must be very fit! Since Stanley was unable to provide any supporting documentation with regards to the conditions in the prison or the camp, and since the British government appeared to have no knowledge of any RAF prisoners among the 168 Allied airmen interned in Buchenwald, Stanley was pushing water uphill. And yet they did know, and had they joined the dots and bothered to look in their own archive, the outcome for Stanley and many others would have been significantly different.

Indeed, at the very moment Airey Neave was going public in his criticism of the glacial pace of FO intervention, a file of 'excerpts of information' (*Dokumenten Auszug*) was being handed to the British embassy in Bonn from the International Red Cross tracing service in Bad Arolsen, with full personal details of every former RAF inmate in the camp. Worse, the government had actually received a full report of conditions in the camp and the men incarcerated there as far back as 1944.[208]

All these facts Stanley would only discover later, much to his understandable frustration, but the information should have been used by the Foreign Office to inform the settlement negotiations generally and the specifics of every case, especially in the context of lost liberty or damaged health. As Neave outlined in a further letter to Stanley of 2 November 1965: "The Foreign Office handling of this matter has been most unsatisfactory. They should have been obtaining records from the last 20 years before they made a lump-sum settlement with the Germans."[209]

One of those records in the FO's possession was an official report prepared in Berlin, dated 24 November 1944, by a delegate of the protecting power, Albert

Kadler. Kadler had been sent to compile a special report on the conditions suffered by the RAF prisoners while being transported from Fresnes to Buchenwald, as well as conditions in the camp itself. To do so he interviewed Phil Lamason in Stalag Luft III. The suffering of the prisoners was laid bare. Kadler's report includes details of the beating that Lamason and others suffered; the murder of the Frenchman dragged from the cattle truck; the insanitary conditions of the camp; being made to sleep out in the open for two weeks; the lack of food and water; the constant Appells; the fleas and constant sickness. The death of Philip Hemmens (listed in the report as "Hemmings") is also recorded, as are the names of 11 other Allied airmen who had been left behind, too sick to travel. Five other British subjects, all from the Channel Islands, are also reported.

The fact that this record appears to have been locked away and forgotten is puzzling at best. What is even more puzzling is that the British authorities had knowledge of the Buchenwald airmen even before receiving Kadler's report. The escape of Joel Stevenson, the American flying with the RCAF, had been known since his debrief by MI9 in Paris nine weeks earlier. He had given the intelligence service full details of his betrayal and capture by the Gestapo and his detention in Fresnes in his debriefing on 2 September. Indeed, three weeks prior to that, the authorities would have been aware of the destination of the transport that departed for Weimar (Buchenwald and Ravensbrück concentration camps). Stanley always felt, but could never prove, that there must have been some bigger, ulterior motive for MI9 and the British government at the time not to want to promote the fact that British servicemen had been held in anything other than a bona fide prisoner-of-war camp. The Americans too went even further. A Senate report that followed a meeting to discuss atrocities and other conditions in concentration camps in Germany, requested by General Eisenhower himself, stated:

> *"Before proceeding with detailed statements concerning the several camps visited, we believe a preliminary word as to just what these camps are and just what they are used for would be of value. In the first place, the concentration camps for political prisoners must not be confused with the prisoner-of-war camps. No prisoners of war are confined in any of these political prisoner camps and there is no relationship whatsoever between a concentration camp for political prisoners and a camp for prisoners of war."*[210]

Thus the Americans, in the spring of 1945, were being categoric in their belief that none of their airmen had ever been held captive in Buchenwald. It is little surprise, therefore, in this context, that Stanley's experiences and those of his fellow prisoners were not always believed. It suggests, also, that the US authorities had their own motivation for denial, perhaps linked to the subsequent use of former Nazis to aid the Western cause against a post-war Eastern bloc enemy.

The Americans' position is even more extraordinary in the light of a document dated 22 May 1945 from their own military intelligence service to its British equivalent. In it, Major John F. White Jr writes to MI9 agent Donald Darling – code-named 'Sunday' to Airey Neave's 'Saturday' – regarding a possible merit award to Raymond Picourt. (Picourt had established a network in Dreux in parallel with the Hunter network and which used some of the same helpers.) In it, he says that the group that Monsieur Picourt inspired and directed handled more than 50 evaders, but that unfortunately over half this number fell into the clutches of 'Jean Jacques':

> *'We have recently discovered that the British and American evaders who were in Fresnes until August 15 1944 were on that date sent on a train to Buchenwald. This group contained about 168 British and American soldiers most of whom had been through Jean Jacques' hands or else through the hands of other agents directed by the same German service.'*[211]

Stanley's fight for compensation, inextricably linked with his urgent need to be believed, continued, and his efforts bore partial fruit. In October 1965 he received an initial payment of £136. On 22 February the following year, he received a further lump-sum payment of £680 "based on the percentage of your disablement as decided by the Ministry of Pensions and National Insurance medical board". A final payment of £285 was received on 27 October of the same year as "the final payment taking into account all aspects of the claim".[212] The letter concluded: "The distribution scheme is now closed."[213]

In total, Stanley had therefore received £1,101 – the equivalent today of just over £26,000. The Foreign Office had told him back in March 1965, prior to his medical board, that his compensation would be "dependent on the length of time in a concentration camp" and "not solely on the presence of a permanent disability".[214] His settlement letter of 22 February, however, was based purely on his level of disability; no account was taken either of his time in a concentration camp or – perhaps more importantly – the time spent as a prisoner in Fresnes where he underwent brutal beating and interrogation at the hands of the Gestapo. It did not, therefore, in any way take into account the extreme trauma that Stanley and those like him had suffered with the constant fear of execution. Nor could he make anyone understand what it was like to live in a concentration camp knowing that you were DIKAL – 'not to be transferred to any other camp' – which could only mean one thing: certain death.

Stanley was not prepared to let the matter rest. On 29 September 1972, he underwent a further medical examination which noted a "progressive gradual deterioration of the chondromalacia in the right knee" which resulted in a patellectomy operation at the RAF hospital at Halton, removing his kneecap. The surgeon wrote afterwards that more than 90 per cent of the internal surface of the patella had been eroded, the cause of the significant pain and discomfort Stanley had experienced since baling out 28 years earlier, and the long months afterwards in which he had received no treatment for his injuries.

The following year, upon his retirement from the RAF, Stanley applied to the Department of Health and Social Security (DHSS) for the award of a war disability pension, given the troubles he now suffered as a result of having his kneecap removed. The DHSS accepted that the condition – osteoarthritis of the right knee with patellectomy, and left-shoulder myalgia – "can be accepted as attributable to Service". The degree of disablement was assessed as being between 6 and 14 per cent for an indeterminate duration, putting Stanley's claim below the 20 per cent threshold for a war disability pension. He was, instead, awarded a tax-free gratuity of £561 at which point the assessment was declared 'final'.[215]

That might have been the end of it, had it not been for the establishment of a medical fellowship, created in 1979 to provide a comprehensive investigation into the health, care and compensation needs of veterans and victims of war. The study, which took two years to complete, was published in September 1981 and made a number of recommendations to government. These included the need for a mechanism for identifying former prisoners of war, a review of the existing literature on the long-term effects of war-related deprivation on health, and the establishment of a medical advisory committee to include the health problems of former POWs. The study also included recommendations on how to standardise medical assessment procedures and improve the medical care of prisoners of war and the severely war-disabled. It recommended that regular medical checks should be carried out on all former prisoners of war, and that where there was an element of doubt due to insufficient medical evidence, the benefit of such doubt should be given to those claiming compensation.

The report's authors, Dr Donald Patrick and Dr Peter Heaf, urged government to ensure that all POWs and war-disabled should be informed of their entitlements. Eight months later, an article in *Pennant* – a magazine published by the officers' pension society – reported that "there are still many POWs who are not aware of their entitlement to claim pension for the effects of service and POW experiences and many who may not associate other conditions which may arise in later life with their service in the forces".[216]

Stanley seized upon the findings of the doctors' investigation and the article in *Pennant* to review his claim for a pension which had been effectively dismissed ten years earlier. A further medical examination followed on 1 December 1983 to which the DHSS conceded to add "malnutrition and privation" as historic issues affecting Stanley's current health, but since he had already received a full and final payment in 1973 he was not entitled to any further compensation. Stanley appealed, and on 27 July 1984 the DHSS reassessed his degree of disablement at 30 per cent.[217]

The new award, however, did not take into account a further painful operation Stanley had endured in the meantime involving the excision of a spermatocele, a cyst which had developed in the epididymis, and which he claimed could also be attributed to his time in Fresnes. A further appeal was heard on 10 June 1986:

> *"The Royal British Legion had long been championing the cause of former prisoners of war who had problems with war-related medical difficulties and fully supported the continuing dispute with the DHSS and their reluctance to recognise the background to the complex medical problems that had manifested themselves."*

At the hearing, Dr Pearson, a specialist, provided a detailed medical report that effectively said that they need look no further into the cause of Stanley's spermatocele than the beating he had received from the Gestapo. "The long-term interval," he said, "was not material."[218] Despite this evidence, Stanley had to recount, in detail, the torture he had endured and the issues he had suffered since – and had to do so in front of two female Queen's counsellors:

> *"My QC, who was a last-minute substitute for the QC who had been properly briefed, presented her case solely on the Gestapo interrogations I*

had experienced but that we had not had time to discuss beforehand. It was thus necessary to recall, in exact detail, the privation and emotional shock of being stripped naked, handcuffed, and subjected to repeated blows to the testicles and kidney region, the face and nose, breaking two front teeth, and such like. I was asked how I reacted – as if being violently sick and fainting after the second blow to my genitals was not a satisfactory answer – and had to give details on how I felt on being returned to the prison. Having to relive the very details of events that had long been the root of many years of nightmares and disturbed sleep caused me obvious distress."

Stanley's suffering did not appear to be enough to impress the authorities to change their minds. Since no mention had been made of spermatocele, or any issues related to the testes, in previous medical examinations, they chose to ignore the specialist's report that it was almost certainly the result of Stanley's torture. Crucially, they also stated that there was no reference to any physical mistreatment or torture in Stanley's MI9 debriefing, and therefore no record of any 'torture in captivity'. Thus, 40 years after Stanley's homecoming from the war, the lack of interest shown by MI9 in his experiences in Fresnes and Buchenwald had come back to haunt him. As far as the DHSS and the government was concerned, if there was no record of any torture, then it didn't happen.

The appeal was disallowed, leaving Stanley to take the only course of action still open to him. And a chance to exorcise a particularly haunting ghost.

CHAPTER ELEVEN

RETURN TO BUCHENWALD

THE CHALLENGE OF HAVING TO relive his experiences as a prisoner, and of not being believed due primarily to a lack of supporting documentation, was the catalyst Stanley needed to journey back into his past, and the source of his suffering.

Stanley knew from his Berlin intelligence days that after Buchenwald was liberated on 11 April 1945 by armoured divisions of the Third US Army, it was handed over to Soviet military administration three months later, being in the agreed 'Russian zone'. By that point, all the 21,000 surviving inmates had dispersed, and the camp had been transferred to the Soviets in one piece. The Russians then set about turning the former concentration camp into its own 'NKVD special camp', along with ten other similar facilities (among them Sachsenhausen), to hold captive thousands of former National Socialists and members of the Hitler Youth who posed an ongoing challenge to their authority or who needed to be punished.[219] A number had been former members of the police, Gestapo or SS. They also rounded up other 'undesirables' including those denounced as collaborators or spies, many of whom subsequently 'disappeared'.[220]

Soviet activities at Sachsenhausen camp had been monitored, to some extent, during the Berlin airlift, when selected RAF crews were instructed to make daily innocuous deviations from track whilst approaching Berlin along the northern air corridor and to 'accidentally' overfly Oranienburg airfield which adjoined the camp. With Buchenwald, however, no such 'accidental' detour could be made; it was simply too far off course for a deviation to be seen as anything other than deliberate.

It was in the summer of 1982, when returning from a holiday in the south of France with his family and crossing through the Jura mountain range that marks the French–Swiss border, that Stanley spotted something that immediately drew his attention:

> *"It was one of those hotel information boards which carried an advertisement relating to the Musée de la Résistance et de la Déportation in Besançon, and they had a special Buchenwald museum. We visited at the earliest opportunity."*

The museum was located in the city's famous citadel perched high on a hill – a vast, sprawling fortress that had been the regional headquarters of the Gestapo during the war and in which more than a hundred resistance fighters had been executed. (It had also been an internment camp, in the early stages of the war, for British passport holders.) The curator of the museum, Mme Denise Laroche, who had herself been held at Bergen-Belsen, proved most helpful and understanding of Stanley's mission:

> *"She was only too pleased to welcome another concentration camp survivor and one who had a particular interest in her famous exhibition centre. Whilst she had many excellent photographs of the dreaded 'Little Camp' and the devastation caused by the USAAF bombing raid, she was unable to provide any documentary evidence relating to the detention of Allied airmen in the camp. She was, however, in touch with Barbara Yeo-Thomas, who in turn was well aware of the existence of Allied airmen within the quarantine camp, adjacent to the main camp where her husband had occupied Block 17. She was also able to provide details of the Red Cross International tracing service where, she explained, all the surviving original SS records of the various concentration camps were assembled after the war had ended. This department would be able to issue one of their official 'extracts of documents' which would give full details of all the personal information required associated with any period of detention within the camps."*

In the serendipitous finding of Mme Laroche, Stanley had struck gold. She had recently made the acquaintance of Klaus Trostorff, the then-director of the *Nationalen Mahn- und Gedenkstätten Buchenwald*, preserved by the East German government as a national memorial and museum.[221] Letters were sent to Herr Trostorff, and the directors of the International Red Cross tracing service, enclosing background of Stanley's experiences at the hands of the Nazis, with requests for copies of any archive material that might confirm and perhaps enlarge on his time at Fresnes and Buchenwald. A few months later, Stanley received a package from the IRC containing 'extracts of documents' giving full details of Stanley's transfer to Buchenwald on the orders of the SS Reich security service in Paris. It included the date of his transfer, camp registration number, and confirmation of his special category as a 'police prisoner' with the additional directive on the *SS-Schreibstubenkarte* stating 'DIKAL' – *Darf in kein anderes Lager*. (These were the same documents that had been sent to the British embassy in Bonn 20 years earlier, and conveniently 'forgotten'.)

Soon after, a second package arrived at his Bracknell home from the Buchenwald museum. It was a letter from Herr Trostorff, who confirmed that not only had he been a prisoner in the camp at the same time as Stanley, but that he was very much aware of the illegal detention of the two parties of Allied parachutists (i.e. the men from the SOE/SIS) and the airmen. He advised that the camp archives held records that gave details of the medical examination given by the SS medical officer on 28 August 1944 following the arrival of the entire intake of 1,650 prisoners from Paris eight days earlier, who were categorised for their suitability for work. Of particular importance to Stanley was the fact that a list existed that named every one of the Allied airmen held captive. Beside their registration numbers (in the series 78–266 and 78–443) had been written the word 'Terrorflieger'.

The archive from the Buchenwald museum proved to be the gift that kept giving. Herr Trostorff was also able to provide a copy of the official *Abschrift* dated 17 August which gave the complete nominal roll of the 37 SOE and SIS officers who had arrived at Buchenwald that day from Compiègne, in France, with their personal details, dates of birth and other such particulars. Against 31 of the 37 names was a coloured cross and the date on which they were murdered.

The kindness shown by Denise Laroche and Klaus Trostorff in helping Stanley to scratch an increasingly frustrating itch led to a decision that in his heart he knew he had to make:

"Despite its evil reputation and past unhappy personal associations, for a good many years I'd had the urgent desire to make a return visit to the

> *former concentration camp. I had the certain feeling that only there lay the key to conquering the sickness that lay within and was desperately trying to escape."*

Having determined to return, Stanley was immediately concerned about what he might find when he got there. In venturing East, he was also acutely aware that the DDR authorities might not take kindly to a visit from a former intelligence officer who had until recently done all in his power to undermine their military. It was therefore with some trepidation that in the autumn of 1984 he set off for the border with his wife and a few treasured possessions from his time as a prisoner. These included documents that had been 'recovered' by Stanley's post-war Resistance contacts and were by way of proof of his bona fides to be allowed to travel.

Stanley and Marjorie drove across the heavily guarded East German frontier crossing, where their papers were examined and their reasons for travel explained. Stanley's knowledge of the local language proved a blessing.

The vehicle was subjected to a rigorous search while one of the border guards, an officer, showed particular interest in a note written for Stanley from the Buchenwald museum director and bearing an impressive official stamp. It was the stamp, perhaps more than anything else, that seemed to make the most impression. A more senior officer emerged, a lieutenant colonel, smartly dressed, with two female officers carrying, somewhat incongruously, a Sony video camera. Stanley's Japanese car was something of a rarity in the area, and they were determined to capture its features!

After more than half an hour of searching and general fussing they were allowed to pass, without even having to pay the mandatory ten-Deutschmark 'visitor transfer fee'. The senior officer – in English – wished them a pleasant onward journey. They turned onto the Autobahn, still showing signs of wartime damage and having a pockmarked surface that contributed to an uncomfortable drive. They passed only a handful of other vehicles, noisy Trabants and the occasional lorry, in all cases belching black smoke because of the low-octane fuel which was all that was available for civilian use.

Within an hour they arrived at the rather splendid Hotel Elephant in Weimar, an official visitors' transit hotel which had been welcoming guests since the 1500s. Goethe, Liszt, Bach and Tolstoy had slept under its roof, as had Adolf Hitler, who had his own personal suite designed for him after the hotel was completely rebuilt and reopened in 1938.

In the Elephant, Stanley and his wife were welcomed with genuine warmth. British nationals were a rare commodity in Weimar at the time; a British national who had been a prisoner in the infamous camp hidden in the beech forest just a few miles to the north was rarer still. It was the next morning, after a restless night, that the two drove out to find the camp. The *Nationalen Mahn- und Gedenkstätten* was initially well signposted but then all signs disappeared as they left the city. Roadworks also made it difficult to know exactly where they were going and the route they should take. By doubling back to the main railway station and starting again, Stanley was able to locate the road they needed through the forest to reach their destination. The oppressing darkness of the woods eventually gave way to brilliant sunshine as they summited the hill and parked by the side of what was once the former railhead, the scene of so much cruelty and bloodshed in the past. A large mural had been mounted on a stone platform, depicting the SS reception committee at work. A short walk led to a clearing and the gateway with the haunting words *Jedem das Seine* still prominent overhead.

Stanley was struck by the eerie quiet of it all. There was no birdsong, despite the proximity to the forest, and rabbits and deer remained in the shadows of the surrounding trees, disinclined to break cover. There was not a wildflower nor blade of grass to be seen. It was, as Stanley recalled, as if nature had turned her back on such an evil place:

> "The utter silence met when passing through the gateway was almost frightening. One could already sense uneasy spirits and with little imagination hear screams echoing through history. The squat wooden watchtowers evenly spaced around the perimeter of the camp stood intact, linked by rusting electrified barbed-wire fencing still bearing their rows of white insulators and the fading enamel *Blitz und Totenkopf* shields – warnings of the death that awaited any prisoner who attempted to climb upon them. Before us lay row upon row of grey foundations in absolutely symmetrical lines extending beyond the vast empty *Appellplatz* – all that remained of the former endless collection of shabby wooden barrack huts. To one side, and completely intact even to the carefully preserved lines of ovens in its basement, stood the crematorium with its squat chimney – thankfully no longer belching out its thick, foul smoke which had permeated everywhere with its stench of death. Down in the cellars alongside, linked to the dreaded bunker cell block, were the gallows. The hooks onto which hapless victims were hanged with thin

piano wire were still there on the wall, as were the trollies, though no longer piled high with limp, naked corpses."

Stanley continued his sombre walk through the camp, to the three-storeyed *Effektenkammer* which stood on the lower northern end of the camp adjoining the kitchen block, and then on to the induction and shower block which now housed the museum. Dotted around the former compound were occasional tablets bearing inscriptions and decorated with fading flowers on the site of where the barrack blocks once stood but had now been demolished. Of the Little Camp nothing remained. The entire area was overgrown and had returned to nature. The old barbed-wire gateway lay rusting on the ground. According to a local expert, the Americans had burned the Little Camp to the ground shortly after its liberation, to lessen the chance of spreading highly infectious diseases including typhoid. To Stanley's distress, a model of the camp which featured in the museum and the storyboards around it had whitewashed all mention of the Little Camp from history. In attempting to raise the matter with the East German directing staff, it was clear that any reference to the camp was an embarrassment and further enquiries discouraged.

"Where other former sites and special-interest buildings had been specially signposted, the section of perimeter wire beyond which the former Little Camp had been located was bare, and contained only a temporary, wired gateway secured by several modern padlocks. There were no noticeboards to relate to its former function."

At last, Stanley came upon the prime object of his visit – the spot marked on the official tour guide where a small memorial had been laid to the murdered British and Canadian paratroopers [sic]. The memorial stood between the crematorium and the *Effektenkammer* and comprised a simple granite tablet on a site marked Block 17, with an inscription carved in Russian, German and English. It read: "In honour of the memory of the members of the British and Canadian forces murdered in Buchenwald concentration camp. The lives of four British patriots were saved by the solidarity of German anti fascists. They were imprisoned in block 17."

"A small vase containing a few faded plastic flowers was all there was to honour the memory of the brave friends and compatriots whom we had

left behind with no known graves. There was no scroll, no roll of honour, nor anything tangible to identify their names. There was no official Commonwealth War Graves Commission headstone to record how they had fallen, in dignity, in their own special field of battle."

While some parts of the camp no longer existed, other blocks remained to remind Stanley of the horrors he had endured. They included the block where some of the executions had taken place. It comprised a special room fitted out as a medical reception centre. To the side on one wall was a height-measuring arm against which the victim was stood. In the wall, and directly behind where the prisoner was placed, was a small hole through which a fatal pistol bullet was fired. A tray was placed at his feet to catch the spilled blood. Close by was a stainless-steel trolley on which the dead man was taken away to the crematorium for immediate disposal, and all evidence of the crime committed against him removed.

From the special execution room, Stanley was taken to the nearby quarry, now overgrown, where he again experienced an uneasy feeling of spirits disturbed. Simple stone cairns seemed to whisper to him words he couldn't quite understand; scraps of paper sat among flickering candles, many halfway exhausted, with names and a five-figure number inscribed to the memory of a loved one or fallen comrade. Stanley recalled his own brief experience of the quarry, where he had been sent for two days on a punishment detail for the minor offence of breaking ranks during an evening Appell. He was forced to break huge rocks with only the most basic of tools, until his muscles ached, and his hands bled. He remembered also suffering from a severe bout of dysentery and taking shelter in a temporary lean-to which offered some respite from the horrors around him. In a way he had been lucky; other prisoners had been hanged for less, and it was only the intervention of a comparatively friendly *Blockältester* that had saved him from almost certain death.

The local staff wore no uniforms to distinguish them from the general public, but a few elderly civilians stood at various points around the camp to answer any questions that any visitors might have, and Stanley heard various languages being spoken. A young, solitary Russian soldier, from the local garrison, was also looking with obvious sadness at the grim relics associated with the thousands of deaths from starvation and deprivation of his fellow kinsmen. There were small parties too of East German schoolchildren supervised by grey and somewhat shabbily dressed teachers who had perhaps envisaged something more colourful and fun from their day out of the classroom. It was, however, mandatory for every schoolchild to visit one of three designated camps, and to be educated on the full horrors of the Nazi regime. Nothing was hidden, avoided or excluded, apart from the involvement of the United States Army in the liberation of Buchenwald, or that any US nationals had been imprisoned there. It was, in Stanley's words, a remarkable visit in which the ghost had been laid:

> *"Words could not express our emotions. Somehow one found oneself completely devoid of any expected hatred or even bitterness. I felt numbed by the experience; to have lived through such nightmare all those years ago and to have been so very, very close to the fate that befell so many thousands of others. To have been spared to return to the normal world outside and now to be brought back to the scene of so many horrors. Somehow I felt cleansed and liberated, able to see things at last in a true perspective."*

A few months after Stanley's return from Buchenwald, the Royal Air Force Museum at Hendon learned of his visit and decided to commission a special commemorative cover to fit within its 'wartime escaping' series. Proceeds from the sale of the covers were destined for the Royal Star & Garter Home for disabled ex-servicemen at Richmond in south-west London. In the meantime, Stanley was invited back to Buchenwald by the East German authorities to attend a special international ceremony of the 40th anniversary of the camp's liberation. The RAF Museum recognised this as an opportunity to have their covers specially stamped and signed by as many veterans as possible. Stanley was therefore tasked with taking the entire consignment of 5,000 envelopes over to Germany where the specially acquired DDR postage stamps could be formally 'cancelled' and the covers authenticated. He decided that he and Marjorie would travel with the consignment to Buchenwald, taking the exact same route that he had himself taken 40 years earlier from Fresnes.[222]

Shortly before he was due to go, Stanley answered an advertisement in the *Daily Telegraph* from ITV for veterans to come forward and record their experiences for a special programme on the liberation of the prison camps at the end of the war. They were especially interested in anyone who had experienced life in a concentration camp. Stanley wrote to the programme producer and very soon after was contacted and asked if he could come to the studios by return:

"Immediately upon arrival we were warmly received, a sealed envelope for travel expenses was pushed into my hand, and I was advised that they had a studio ready 'to get an hour's worth of experience down in the can'. We were to set off to Eastern Germany in a very few days, and the success of the final operation would be entirely dependent on the goodwill of the various East German authorities who had, up until then, proved very understanding and co-operative. I explained that I was fully sensitive to the manner in which the media edit their material and often present a completely distorted final version, completely at variance to fact, often causing offence and embarrassment. There was no way I was going to risk them possibly offending the East German government at this late stage, though I did offer to give them every assistance when we returned, which would be in good time for their programme on the VE Day anniversary. Needless to say, we never heard any more from them and it took quite a while and a few heavy letters to get my original supporting briefing material and camp brochures back."

Transporting the envelopes, which comprised six bulky boxes, involved considerable organisation. Special arrangements had to be made with the (then-) Customs and Excise, because the covers would have been subject to a duty for crossing EEC borders on their return, and the value of the postage stamps would have increased after cancellation. He received help not only from the British vice-consul in Lille, but also from the East German authorities, who proved surprisingly accommodating:

"These German authorities gave their upmost co-operation, providing special postage stamps and personal customs clearance both coming into DDR and on departure. The local Weimar head postmaster and his staff also gave full assistance by having each postage stamp cancelled by hand."

The Royal British Legion poppy factory prepared a four-foot wreath for Stanley to take with him; each poppy was triple wax-treated to withstand the rigours of the exposed memorial site along with a simple 'in memoriam' message. The wreath and the covers were conveyed to Paris and the Gare de l'Est, the actual station from where the original transport had departed in 1944, and thence onward through the familiar towns of Metz, Saarbrücken and Frankfurt until they reached their final destination.

> "The event proved to be yet another remarkable experience. In the midst of the estimated 100,000 visitors from all parts of Europe, milling around in small parties within the camp and nearby memorial facilities, were little groups of frail, elderly former prisoners, some wearing their original striped-pyjama suits and others proudly wearing their original coloured triangles – mostly red – featuring their national letter and five-figure camp registration number. The wreath, with its pale blue ribbon and RAF crest, attracted quite some attention when it was placed on the SOE memorial tablet and I heard so many expressions of sincere respect spoken in broken German, French and a smattering of Russian. Some spoke perfect English and conveyed genuine interest in the memory of the brave Allied parachutists and airmen whom they remembered both in Block 17 and in the Little Camp. One fine old Russian gentleman – his Soviet military staff car and senior NCO driver denoting his status – embraced us both with an indescribable warmth of feeling. It was a very moving and unique experience – something never to be forgotten."

On occasion, and much to Stanley's annoyance, he had to jostle for position with various international television crews as they sought their own 'exclusive' content. More annoying – to the point of embarrassment – was the presence of a US TV crew who seemed genuinely astounded to hear English being spoken and who had clearly been poorly briefed for the event they were covering:

> "They had not the slightest idea that there had ever been any Allied servicemen in the camp, much less over 80 of their own aircrew. They had been standing on the ruins of the former *Gustloff-Werke* where their own air force had wrought so much death and destruction and they had not the slightest idea, despite the conspicuous public notice mounted on the ruined site."

While Stanley could overlook the ignorance of the American reporters, he found it more difficult to conceive of the lack of interest from the British press or any official party:

> "There was no British representation at the event: no television team; no visiting dignitaries; and no wreath from the SOE authorities (now the responsibility of the Foreign and Commonwealth Office). After attending

the opening of the museum, now established over all three floors of the refurbished former Effektenkammer, we were privileged to attend the very moving ecumenical service conducted on the barren Appellplatz outside of the former canteen building. It was given by Rabbi Ringer, together with senior clergy from the Catholic, Russian Orthodox, Methodist and Lutheran churches, accompanied by a modest orchestra of young people from the local community. Within the former canteen there was a simple dedication service for the introduction of the new memorial hall of remembrance to which the building had been converted."

For Stanley and his fellow survivors, it was an emotional event, but intruded upon by the press. He recalled how, on that very spot that he now stood, a party of elderly Jewish prisoners had once gathered to await departure to another camp in the East, an event which for them meant almost certain death in the gas chambers of one of the extermination camps. Despite knowing what fate lay ahead, they remained calm and composed as they assembled at this, their final roll call, and after the parade was dismissed held a simple, moving service concluded by what must have been the most haunting musical tribute ever likely to be experienced. Onto the steps of the canteen came a frail, elderly prisoner, imprisoned for a crime that had nothing to do with his faith for he wore no Star of David. As he stood he took out a violin and played – with absolute concert-hall perfection – Bach's haunting Air on the G String:

"There, in the midst of so much squalor, degradation, stench and fear, that solemn music was pure magic – a treasured memory to hold dear for the remainder of one's lifetime."

The ceremony was held over three days, and on the final day visitors were subjected to a series of political speeches from local dignitaries, decrying the decadence of NATO and the West. Elderly former camp inmates had been replaced by a younger crowd, bussed in especially to create an image of superiority for the cameras. Stanley took the opportunity to look more closely at the wreaths and memorials to various other nations who had stood together to fight Nazism and reflected again on the lack of any symbol of British involvement, save for his own small tribute.

"On the massive Avenue of Nations not one of the 18 plinths was dedicated to Great Britain or the Commonwealth, nor was there one Allied statesman.

There was no representative of the Allied armed forces and not one single floral tribute to honour the memory of the fallen. I stood there alone, a proud former member of RAF Bomber Command, from whose ranks alone more than 55,000 aircrew lost their lives, as the sole Allied link with the past in the midst of this huge crowd of foreign nationals. There had been no mention in any of the anti-Western speeches of the many US soldiers who died fighting the SS right up to the very gates of the camp, giving their own precious lifeblood at the closing stages of the war to free thousands of people they didn't know. My wife and I remembered the precious lives lost by so many nations, and we remembered the many who continued to suffer and lived on in their own private hell."

On his return home, Stanley delivered the precious commemorative covers to the RAF Museum. Their sale and distribution proved an immediate success and reached the furthest corners of the globe. Several found their way to a few of the former RAAF camp inmates as well as RNZAF prisoners, among them the indomitable Phil Lamason. Soon after, a handful of British, Australian, New Zealand and Canadian survivors formed themselves into a formal group and reached out to their US counterparts.

The parties soon expanded and gained new members, which Stanley recalls "awakened a close bond of friendship and mutual understanding". The *Konzentrationslager* Buchenwald (KLB) Club – which was founded while the men were still concentration camp prisoners and before being dispersed within Stalag Luft III – was re-energised, with a membership of 84 of the original 168 airman.[223] Art Kinnis, formerly of the RCAF, had kept a diary while in the camp and, at great personal risk, recorded the names of every Allied POW, their registration numbers, and their 1944 addresses. Coming across the document many years later while clearing out his loft, he set about trying to trace as many of the former party as possible. A regular newsletter was created, and international visits and exchanges organised. While the American Red Cross continued to maintain that no US nationals were ever in a concentration camp, the paperwork Stanley had secured by way of 'extracts of documents' from the ITS was sufficient to prompt the Australian and New Zealand governments to award their veterans AUS$10,000 and NZ$13,000 respectively.

Stanley's work, however, wasn't quite done; he still had one final challenge to resolve.

CHAPTER TWELVE

MEMORIAL TO THE FALLEN

STANLEY'S VISIT TO BUCHENWALD OCCURRED just a few weeks after the 40th anniversary of the bombing of Dresden and the media hand-wringing that followed. On his journey out to Buchenwald, Stanley had met a family on the train who were heading home to Dresden for a memorial service. They had suffered terribly in the bombing and, as such, Stanley was understandably reluctant to reveal his true identity as a Bomber Command veteran. They were, however, intrigued by the covers and RAF wreath which he carried, and he told them of his own pilgrimage to Buchenwald and his reasons for going. They expressed tremendous remorse for what the Nazis had done to him, and remorse too for their blind following of a regime that had resulted in the bombing of their beautiful city.

The coverage in the UK press regarding Dresden swung between full justification for their actions and no remorse, to an absolute decrial of 'Butcher' Harris and his boys as outright murderers. Stanley was incensed by what he read, even more so because it flew in the face of his own recent experience abroad. Determined to correct what he saw was 'twaddle' with regard to the bombing of Dresden,[224] he penned a letter to the *Daily Telegraph*:

Sir.

The last thing I would want to do is to revive the argument over the merits of the bombing of Dresden, which as a former member of Bomber Command has hurt me deeply, but I believe that the implications of my recent visits to East

> Germany might be of some interest. Last weekend I attended the celebrations of the 40th anniversary of the liberation of Buchenwald where, together with 75 other members of the Royal Air Force, I was held captive in 1944. I met hundreds of Germans and former inmates of this notorious concentration camp and was left with two outstanding impressions: one that with few exceptions the German people in nearby Dresden have no doubts that they brought the bombing upon themselves by starting the last war, and the other that the British people in Buchenwald will forever be remembered for their patriotism, spirit and discipline. You must forgive me when I say I was almost moved to tears when laying a poppy wreath on the commemoration tablet to those British servicemen who marched as a unit to the gallows to be hanged.[225]

Within hours of the letter being published, the telephone started ringing and continued virtually non-stop for the next few days. As well as the calls, Stanley also received a huge volume of letters forwarded from the newspaper or addressed care of the local post office. Some doubted the veracity of Stanley's letter, denying that there had ever been any British servicemen in the camp or murdered. Several eminent historians were also dubious:

> "I advised them to read Professor M. R. D. Foot's epic *SOE in France* and Bruce Marshall's *The White Rabbit*. Various schools also contacted me requesting accounts of conditions in the camp such that they could pass them on to their senior modern history students. I also received several sad requests from hopeful relatives, seeking any possible knowledge of a lost loved one who had gone 'missing' and may have strayed into the camp. Letters also arrived from sick people seeking gruesome details of SS atrocities and excesses."

Among the letters was one from a retired senior British army officer who had been on General Eisenhower's staff in 1945 and was dispatched to the camp to discover the fate of Yeo-Thomas. It amused Stanley to think that the intelligence services did not know that one of their own had already escaped from Buchenwald long before the officer had been sent on his mission!

Stanley's quest to see the murdered SOE agents properly recognised led to a full account of his return to Buchenwald and the commemoration service to be forwarded to the Commonwealth War Graves Commission in Maidenhead, Berkshire. He urged the CWGC to consider establishing a modest roll of honour on the site. The response was, to say the least, disappointing, stating that the CWGC was not in the business of setting up memorials in foreign lands.[226] A second letter was duly dispatched, listing all 37 members of the SOE and SIS who had been in the camp and annotating the 31 who had been murdered and the dates on which they had been hanged or shot. The response, on this occasion, was more sensitive and encouraging. The challenge was that the SOE and SIS comprised agents of many different nationalities, and not all of them members of the British Commonwealth. The letter did, however, suggest that Stanley contact the SOE advisor within the FCO, Mr C. M. Woods, and outline his case.

On this occasion, Stanley sent not only details of the nominal roll, but also photographs of the existing memorial in its neglected state. Woods was able to reassure Stanley that, of the 31, 24 were already commemorated on various British and Commonwealth war memorials, and their lives not forgotten.[227] He also said that the FCO would look into the possibility of 'improving' the Buchenwald memorial stone and consult with the British embassy in East Berlin.[228] Woods reassured Stanley again in a subsequent letter that his roll of honour proposal was still being considered, and that a party from BRIXMIS had attended a ceremony at Buchenwald on St George's Day, with the help of the Soviet commandant in Weimar.[229]

Behind the news of the BRIXMIS delegation is a much bigger story that demonstrates Stanley's 'dog-with-a-bone' character. Concurrent to engaging with the FCO, Stanley had decided to go right to the top, and had written to the prime minister, Margaret Thatcher. He drew her attention to the fact that RAF officers had been held captive in Buchenwald, and SOE and SIS officers murdered there. He described his own personal visit to the camp, and the regrettable absence of any Union Flag or suitable memorial.[230] The prime minister replied almost immediately, thanking Stanley for his "dignified gesture in laying a poppy wreath in memory of the Allied war dead". In a handwritten postscript she promised to "follow up in the question of why no Union Flag flies on the Road [sic] of Nations. We must show that our people are not forgotten."[231]

The prime minister was good to her word and the text of her follow-up letter is worth printing in full:

"The British Embassy to the German Democratic Republic have spoken to the GDR Committee of Anti-Fascist Resistance Fighters who were responsible for the arrangements. The committee did not invite any British

> *or French Government representatives, so Mrs Booker and you were in a real sense ambassadors for our country. The committee say that there was no wish on their part to overlook the British role, and that the Union Flag will fly on the road of nations on future commemorative occasions. So I am very glad that you raised this point. You will, I hope, be comforted to know that ten days after the ceremony you attended a British/Soviet military commemoration ceremony was conducted at Buchenwald. The Commander of the British Military Liaison Mission to the Group of Soviet Forces in Germany, Brigadier Frank Bevan, laid a wreath at the same memorial tablet graced by the poppy wreath which you and your wife had brought. Two Scottish pipers played at the ceremony and a second wreath was laid by a former prisoner of war, now a Chelsea pensioner, on behalf of his fallen comrades. I hope that this will reassure you that your courageous fellow prisoners from the Special Operations Executive and the Royal Air Force have not been forgotten. But in addition, I thought it right to ask HM Ambassador to the GDR to visit the camp soon, both to lay a wreath and himself to raise the Union Flag. He will do so within the next ten days."*

On May 31 1985, Tim Everard, the ambassador mentioned in the prime minister's letter, did indeed visit the camp and raise the Union Flag and lay a further wreath, this time on behalf of the British government. He also met with Herr Trostorff, the museum curator, and signed the visitors' book within the infamous Bell Tower. The British embassy was advised by the GDR Committee of Anti-Fascist Resistance Fighters that no slight had been intended by not flying the flag, but rather that the Avenue of Nations was reserved for the flags of countries that had been occupied by Nazi troops during the war, and that there was no wish on the part of the committee to overlook the British role.

Stanley was delighted with the "commendable sense of duty" shown by the prime minister and her direct involvement in helping to show his fallen comrades due respect. He took comfort also that the FCO appeared to be listening and would keep him updated of progress with regards to a new memorial, but it was in fact another five full years before he heard anything further, and only then because he asked. By then, Mr Woods, the SOE advisor, had been replaced by Gervase Cowell, who sympathised with Stanley's position, but "did not hold out much hope" that the problems his predecessor had encountered would not again conspire to defeat him now. His letter reads:

> *"... the problems which were raised in 1985 were the difficulty of assembling an accurate and complete list of names, the fact that not only British people were concerned, the fact that it was in the DDR, and finally who would pay ..."*[232]

Of the 31 murdered SOE officers, 24 had been acknowledged by the FCO, but with the remainder there were links to the intelligence services that appeared impossible to break. In Stanley's mind, and in the mind of Vera Atkins, a wartime SOE 'F' Section intelligence officer, they could only have been SIS/MI6, and as such no further details were forthcoming.

Stanley had won a battle: the British presence at Buchenwald was now recognised, and an annual wreath-laying ceremony arranged. For the 45th anniversary of the camp's liberation, HM Ambassador Patrick Eyers and his wife laid wreaths at the Bell Tower and at the memorial at the former site of Block 17 "since there was no British monument on the Street [sic] of the Nations".[233] And so the war went on.

On 14 May 1990, a preview event for a public exhibition entitled 'Buchenwald – 45 years after' was held at the House of Commons.[234] It was remarkable in many ways, not least since it had been organised by the Holocaust Educational Trust with the full co-operation of the East German authorities. The *Direktorin* of the *Nationalen Mahn- und Gedenkstätten Buchenwald*, Frau Dr Irmgard Seidel, accompanied by Frau Ilse Erck of the East German Ministry of Culture, flew especially to London to attend and to bring several exhibits to include in the display.

A political breakthrough in every sense (the Berlin Wall had only recently come down), the event was also honoured with the presence of the German ambassador, His Excellency Baron Hermann von Richthofen, together with the East German chargé d'affaires, Sigfried Reichel, and a host of other dignitaries from church and state. Stanley, who had been invited by the event sponsors Sir Bernard Braine and Llin Golding[235] at the suggestion of Major Jonny Walker of BRIXMIS, gave the speech of welcome in German: "It is important," he said, "that our children, and our children's children, take advantage of this event and through the exhibits better understand how appalling and painful it was."[236] He reminded those present of the words on the Buchenwald national memorial and how they related to the anniversary event: "To remind the living – to honour the dead."

The exhibition caused quite a stir and was widely reported. Llin Golding said that never before had she seen so much interest in an exhibition in the House and that she was deeply moved by Stanley's speech.[237] It later left the House of Commons for something of a UK-wide 'tour', drawing great crowds of visitors, young and old, some learning for the first time the full horrors of the concentration camps.

A few months after the exhibition, Stanley took advantage of the recent reunification of Germany[238] to return to Buchenwald for a third time, enjoying the true freedom of the road as he drove down from Hamburg to the Harz Mountains that spoke of another, more peaceful world. On this occasion he travelled not only with his own wife, but also Barbara Yeo-Thomas, wife of the late 'White Rabbit', and with whom he was now well acquainted.

> "Once again, we were warmly received by the camp authorities and given a personal conducted tour of the entire former camp. Very little had changed, with the exception of the inspiring exhibition of paintings and memorabilia in the former *Desinfektionsgebau*, and further improvements to the museum in the old *Effektenkammer* building."

Stanley was also allowed access to the area where the Little Camp had been, to which on his last visit he had been denied on the grounds of 'hygiene'. The area was no longer overgrown; it had been cleared completely and dozens of new saplings planted as a symbol of regeneration and rebirth. The reasons soon became clear. Since reunification, some of the truth of what had happened in the camp under Russian control was now emerging. Hundreds of human remains from its time as Sonderlager II had only recently been uncovered, and the young trees were an attempt to cover up the horrors which had continued long after the camp had been 'liberated'. Youngsters in the nearby district had once been threatened with being sent to 'the Russians on the hill' but only now was the camp's true post-war purpose being admitted. Even the museum's deputy director, Heinz Koch, accepted that they had not been "open about this period" when previously questioned.[239] Without being noticed, Stanley managed to procure one of the saplings and hide it away in his briefcase. He would later plant the sapling in his garden in Bracknell, where it still stands tall and proud today, the ultimate beacon of renewal.

The coming together of East and West and a definite thawing of the Cold War led to greater cross-nation communication which manifested itself in many ways. One was the establishment of a committee of historians, created by the Thuringian minister for science and the arts who was tasked with rethinking the Buchenwald memorial. The move was welcomed by the Allied airmen survivors, confident that their modest involvement might now be more formally recognised and commemorated in the camp's history. The official press release[240] declared that the committee would "include representatives of International and National Associations and Religious Denominations". Stanley and his colleagues in the KLB Club waited for an invitation that never came:

> *"It was a severe disappointment and caused no little embitterment to learn that the third and final meeting of the committee of historians had invited representatives from former Buchenwald veterans' organisations in Germany, France, Holland, Belgium and Denmark, but there had been no invited official British or US representation."*

Concern was heightened even further when news emerged that the committee had decided to preserve three of the existing memorials within a newly-defined 'Buchenwald Memorial' site, but that the memorial to the prisoners of Block 17 (which commemorated the murdered agents) was not only to be excluded but actually replaced.

> *"It was the natural view of the former airmen that had there been Allied representation at the vital final meeting that took place in Weimar in February 1992, then the unfortunate 'oversight' would have been avoided, and the final approved layout plans would have included the appropriate British/Canadian memorial in a similar form as the other three national sites."*

A letter was crafted to the minister with responsibility for the 'Buchenwald Memorial', Dr Ulrich Fickel. He had said previously that "in my view the way in which a nation deals with its past is certainly an essential element of its culture". The letter expressed deep concern at the absence of an appropriate Allied memorial in the new plans, and received an immediate reply from the good doctor. He wrote that the fate of all groups of victims should be properly commemorated and that "naturally the same attention will be paid to the British and Canadian prisoners".

By the time plans were being discussed to commemorate the 50th anniversary of the liberation of Buchenwald on 11 April 1995, it was still unclear what form the memorial to the Allied contingent would take, or the level of engagement from the British authorities in the event. It was not known, even, if they were to be invited.

Since the unification, and the recommendations of the committee of historians, the *Gedenkstätten Buchenwald*'s leadership had changed several times – partly, Stanley believed, as a result of the considerable influence being imposed by the dominant and politically motivated left-wing veterans' organisations.[241] Stanley described the post-unification administration of the memorial and museum as "a disaster and a serious embarrassment to the German authorities in Bonn". Staff were accused in the press of grossly distorting history, with exhibitions being shaped by "loyal communists" to suit political needs, and the glorification of German communists who died there.[242] Various directors were appointed and sacked, leaving in chaos plans for an ambitious new museum that accurately reflected both periods of the camp's former history.

What was also still an unknown was where that left any plans for a memorial both to the murdered SOE agents and the 168 Allied airmen. For a time, and unknown to Stanley, the RAF had continued to honour its airmen by attending an annual commemoration service. Officers and men from RAF Brüggen had taken over where the official BRIXMIS delegation had left off. The driving force behind keeping the flame alight while the RAF remained in Germany was Wing Commander Peter Donlan. When it seemed that budget cuts might make future commemorations too expensive, Donlan was quick to lend his support in any way "in convincing the RAF authorities that Buchenwald deserves an ongoing RAF presence in the future". Stanley wrote to the wing commander to thank him for his efforts, which "had gladdened my heart to realise that somehow one of our sister Germany-based RAF units has become involved in the commemoration of our lost compatriots."[243]

In the event, it was not until 15 October 2010 that the issue of a permanent memorial to the murdered agents was resolved, when two were finally installed in the anteroom to the camp crematorium.

Organised by Duncan Stuart of the Special Forces Club in London, five members of the Berlin branch of the Royal British Legion attended the event – which included the Reverend Max Homewood, who officiated. A musician from the Welsh Guards played the Last Post, Aux Morts and Reveille, and military attachés from several countries were present to pay their respects. An address was given by General Sir Michael Rose, while Duncan Stuart read out the names of all of those who were executed. Colonel J. H. Debrun spoke on behalf of the French contingent of SOE and the Free French intelligence service murdered in the camp, and there was also a speech from Stephane Hessel, one of the camp's few survivors and a former Free French intelligence officer. (Sadly, Stanley's earlier efforts to memorialise the murdered agents had been forgotten and he was not made aware of the ceremony.)

The wait for a memorial to the 168 took longer. On 13 April 2014 a memorial stone was unveiled thanks to the efforts and campaigning of the KLB Club. The plaque reads: "In memory of the Allied Airmen of American, British, Canadian, Australian, New Zealand and Jamaican nationalities incarcerated here from August 20 to November 28, 1944." It also specifically records the names of Levitt Beck Jr and Philip Hemmens, the two Allied airmen who did not survive.

CHAPTER THIRTEEN
PER ARDUA

FROM THE VERY BEGINNING OF his quest to prove that his time in Buchenwald had not been a figment of his terrified imagination, Stanley had attempted to engage with the French authorities, with little initial success. Whereas Madame Laroche at the Musée de la Résistance et de la Déportation had been unstinting in her support, the authorities seemed less inclined to help.

On two occasions, prior to his return to Buchenwald, written requests (in 1983 and early 1984), each with supporting documentation, brought the same apologetic response: no trace of Stanley's wartime sojourn in Fresnes could be found. Madame Christine Diatta, *le chef du bureau de la documentation* within the relevant department of the French Ministry of Defence wrote to Stanley on 20 March 1984:

> *"Il n'a pas été trouvé trace dans les archives en ma possession de votre passage à la dite prison."*

Concurrent to this disappointing news that there was no record of Stanley's incarceration in Paris, however, one of the French security departments had written to the Air Historical Branch at the UK MOD requesting Stanley's help. They wanted to know further details of Stanley's contact with the Resistance after he had been shot down, and in particular his association with an individual who they implied was possibly improperly seeking a state Resistance pension.

Stanley's full and detailed response to the French authorities won him several admirers, and – given their offer of assistance should he need it – Stanley determined to exploit his new-found friends:

> *"I took the opportunity to copy the earlier correspondence for their comments, and very shortly afterwards a detailed letter arrived which outlined the exact dates of my arrival in Fresnes and departure, my destination and date of arrival at Buchenwald and even my official camp registration number. It included a copy of my forged identity papers."*

This letter (26 June 1984) represented something of a breakthrough, not least as his 'passport' for his imminent return to the camp. Christine Diatta, who had previously been unable to find any evidence of Stanley's ordeal, was now able to attest to the dates of his internment, deportation to the camp and subsequent arrival at Sagan. Stanley believes their earlier reluctance to help may have been their suspicions that his request was a presage to his own possible claim for compensation from the French government.

Having made progress on specific times and dates, Stanley also began to make progress on how and by whom he had been betrayed. Gérard Renault, a gendarme in the area in which Stanley had been shot down, had both a professional and personal interest in the local Resistance and escape lines. He had compiled a list of 51 Allied evaders who had passed through the local Resistance leaders' *réseaux* in Eure et Loir (they included Major 'Bud' Mahurin – the noted USAAF 'ace'). He also had the names of all of those who had sheltered them prior to being handed over to the traitor Jean-Jacques Desoubrie. Fourteen of the 51 had been positively identified as being betrayed, in many cases recounting the same story that Desoubrie was accompanied by a "red-haired woman", his mistress, Marie-Antoinette Orsini (code name 'Colette').

From Renault's research, it was possible to identify which groups, and which individuals, had contact with Desoubrie. Among them was Madame Orial, who along with Madame le Fèvre and Madame Duval had sheltered Stanley throughout. Joseph Bergeron, the leader of the local communist-run Resistance group, one of the two 'strongly built men' who had originally arrived at the chateau of Madame le Fèvre to interrogate Stan, was also named.

For Stanley, this was a disturbing discovery, for it threw out the possibility that his saviours may have known Desoubrie for what he was:

> *"When I returned to Europe in late May 1946 all three ladies and the local Resistance leader (Bergeron) were alive and well and had not in any way been apprehended by the Gestapo who had been Desoubrie's direct masters."*

Stanley also recalls his unease at a luncheon held in his honour by Monsieur Bergeron when afterwards he was taken upstairs to see a large cache of well-oiled and maintained weapons – including Sten guns and pistols – which had been supplied to the Resistance by the British and which the communists still had in their possession 12 months after hostilities had ceased. He kept the discovery to himself.

The explanation remains unresolved, and unsatisfactory. The Gestapo, via Desoubrie, must have known of the old ladies' involvement, and the identity of the local Resistance leader. Also unsatisfactory, and adding to the mystery, is a little-known official French 'trial of the collaborators' recorded by former Resistance chief Jean Moreau with the co-operation of a French investigative journalist. They found not only an apparent deliberate lack of co-operation by some of the magistrates involved but also that many of the cases were heard in camera. There was similarly some confusion regarding when and how Desoubrie was finally executed. It surmised:

> *"Throughout its four-year duration the trial did not call for any of the former Allied Buchenwald survivors who had been witness to the betrayal by Desoubrie to give evidence. No evidence was produced as to how Desoubrie had acquired the details and exact locations of the Allied airmen and their Resistance sympathisers who had given them shelter."*

In analysing Gérard Renault's comprehensive list of the 51 airmen and their fates, it appears that politics may have played a part in who was/was not betrayed to the Gestapo. Of the 14 known to have been handed over to the Gestapo, all came from *réseaux* controlled by the communists. Airmen within non-communist groups were all delivered into safety. That is true of Stanley's own crew: the navigator (Stan), flight engineer (Jack) and rear gunner (Terry) ended up in Buchenwald; the mid-upper gunner (Cliff) – taken in by a non-communist network – was home within three months.

Why so many who must have known of Desoubrie's treachery were not more closely examined nor held to account after the war may never be known. How

Marie-Antoinette Orsini escaped the hangman's noose is also shrouded in mystery. It is true that in late 1943 she helped two airmen to escape to Spain,[244] but her subsequent nefarious activities, and her relationship with Desoubrie, eclipse any good she might otherwise have done. She was tried and acquitted of any wrongdoing in May 1946 (coincidentally when Stanley was in France), an acquittal that brought an angry response from Raymond Picourt who claimed that none of the information he had brought to the prosecutors had been used and nor had any witnesses for the prosecution been present. Witnesses for the defence, however, were there in large numbers, and Picourt was "very disappointed in view of all the harm she had done, that she should escape with so little".[245]

And there it must probably rest, for the truth is rarely simple, and after 80 years it is unlikely that more will be uncovered. At what stage an escape line was compromised is also difficult to state with any degree of confidence. Why did the *forces françaises de l'intérieur* write to Mrs Gould in September 1944 to enquire whether her son had made it home, when he was at that point languishing in Buchenwald? It suggests that they were aware at some point that he was safe, well, and in an escape line, but did not know that he had subsequently been betrayed.[246]

Stanley's suspicions regarding the three old ladies may also have been unfounded. They are certainly at odds with a letter he was sent by Madame Orial while he was still a prisoner of the Germans in December 1944. In it, she enquires "how you ended your risky adventure", suggesting she was totally oblivious to Stanley's later betrayal. She had assumed he had gone all the way down the line.[247]

There are also many mysteries surrounding the fate of those, like Desoubrie, who betrayed the other men who were ultimately sent to the camp. Historian Franck Signorile conducted a detailed investigation in 2017 and found that of the 168 men, 84 were betrayed by Desoubrie, 41 by 'Captain Jack', and 11 by André Cauchemez and Paul Villette. The remainder are unaccounted for, betrayed by local gendarmes or by person/persons unknown.

After Desoubrie, 'Captain Jack' was the most prolific traitor. He was in fact Guy de Marcheret d'Eu, a Russian-born black-marketeer and psychopath motivated by power and greed. He could speak four languages fluently and passed himself off as a classic Englishman with an Oxford accent. It was de Marcheret who was responsible for the capture of Phil Lamason.

André Cauchemez volunteered to work for Germany as a 19-year-old and was soon recruited into their ranks. Teaming up with a mechanic, Paul Villette, to capture Allied airmen on the run, they used a similar technique to Desoubrie, pretending to be detained at a German roadblock while the airmen were in the car. As well as the 11 airmen they betrayed, they were also responsible for the arrest and deportation of 16 patriots, of whom 10 never make it back from Germany.

After the war, 'Captain Jack' was discovered in Denmark and returned home to face trial. He was found guilty and executed on 20 April 1949, principally for his part in a Resistance ambush and massacre. Both Cauchemez and Villette were also caught, tried and sentenced to death. Neither, however, was executed and both were later set free. Why they should have been spared is difficult to see.

A mystery also surrounds Stanley's attempts to uncover who within the Nazi hierarchy had given the orders for the 168 men to be detained in Fresnes and tortured. Stanley only had parts of the story.

In the official Luftwaffe report[248] referring to the loss of Halifax MZ630, the Germans list the names of the entire crew and their subsequent fate. In the column 'Gef/verw/tot' – abbreviations for 'prisoner, wounded, dead' – four names are reported as prisoners: Stokes as a prisoner in Dulag Luft, and Gould, Osselton and Booker as prisoners in Stalag Luft III. The document is dated 12 July 1944. At some point, therefore, the original intention to send the three men to a prisoner-of-war camp was overruled.

Stanley knew that their transfer to Buchenwald had come by the orders of the BDS Paris – the *Befehlshaber der Sicherheitspolizei und der Sicherheitsdienstes Paris* (i.e. the commander of the security police and security services in Paris). He had learned this from the International Red Cross tracing service at Bad Arolsen. He had also learned that they had originally been classed as 'enemy' fliers (*Feindflieger*) – the standard classification for enemy aircrew – and subsequently re-designated 'terror' fliers, putting them in the clutches of the Gestapo. He knew also that it had been Horst Kopkow, an officer in the Reich's main security office in Berlin, who had authorised the execution of the SOE agents and Allied airmen in the camp. What he didn't know was on whose orders he had been in Fresnes in the first place, nor how they came to be known as 'police' (rather than 'political') prisoners or why.[249]

During the war, the Allies had managed to break the Germans' Enigma cipher codes without the Nazis being aware. Stanley hoped that declassified ULTRA intercepts would give him the answers he was looking for. (ULTRA was the codename given to the wartime signals intelligence that came from the breaking of the Enigma codes.) Several approaches to the Public Record Office (as it was at the time, now the UK National Archives) were received cordially and with some sympathy but resulted in little action. Even as recently as February 2000, Stanley's hopes were raised when he was contacted by a university lecturer who had taken an interest in his case. Sadly, that too came to nought.

Despite Stanley's appetite to leave no stone unturned in his search for the truth, age and health were not on his side. The physical suffering he had endured during the war now began to manifest itself in a myriad of different ways, none of which were pleasant. Always a fit man, despite his ordeal, he began to experience discomfort in his joints and his bladder, which over time reduced his confidence in his ability to travel overseas. While he maintained an active correspondence with his friends in Europe who had rendered such valuable assistance, he was not able to see them in person.

After retiring from the RAF, Stanley joined Southern Electricity as a local manager for the Bracknell New Town district office. Many of his team were ex-servicemen with whom he enjoyed an immediate rapport. The transition to civilian life, however, was far from easy:

> *"After some 34 years of being part of a vast, caring, highly professional team, giving and receiving loyal support, suddenly one feels very insecure in a cold, uncaring and sadly selfish world of industry and commerce. Loyalty and working on one's initiative and experience – as one was used to in the service – was positively discouraged."*

To those who had worked in the public sector all their lives, Stanley was an unwelcome newcomer who had robbed them of possible promotion. It took all his management skills to win them over. Bracknell was a new town in development, requiring careful negotiation with every part of the supply chain:

> *"The early weeks and months were not easy. I introduced a new concept of 'caring management', getting my sixty-odd staff involved with the customers and getting the workmen from the yard – who after all were the true backbone of the industry – to discuss their customer requirements with the office staff. They shared problems that never became problems because we sorted them out without having to call in the union rep. We carefully selected new staff, not so much for their paper qualifications, but for their human compatibility. Our administration team of often 'older ladies' was no*

longer a joke – it worked. They enjoyed coming to work and being involved, while the old hands in the yard loved a little chat about old times over a mug of tea in the foreman's office. Nobody abused the issue. It was part of belonging to the team process, and valuing everyone's contribution."

Such successes won him enemies as well as admirers, and his unconventional way of achieving results did not go unnoticed. His team was reorganised and transferred to a different office, 15 miles away:

> "Our happy team was broken up and absorbed in an unwelcoming and grossly overworked main district office. They ceased to be appreciated for their contribution as individuals. Morale fell. There was no team spirit, no customer contact, no cosy canteen chat with the much-treasured tea lady around her massive metal tea urn – a hangover from her wartime WVS days. All that was gone."

Although promoted twice, the joy had gone out of the job, and Stanley opted for early retirement, recognising that the situation 'lacked soul':

> "The garden became my new master, ever demanding, ever a challenge to become a little more ambitious, and the grass ever seemingly growing faster (with the invading moss), seeking ever more frequent attention. There never seemed to be enough hours in the day."

As the years passed, Stanley steadily became one of the last witnesses, and the last survivors, of Buchenwald. Airey Neave, who died in March 1979, was the victim of assassination, claimed by the Irish National Liberation Army (INLA). Barbara Yeo-Thomas, wife of the remarkable 'White Rabbit', died in September 1999 at the age of 83, and is commemorated along with her husband on a memorial stone in Brookwood Cemetery near Woking in Surrey. Jimmy James, the Great Escaper who had been incarcerated and escaped from Sachsenhausen concentration camp, died in January 2008. Stanley had enjoyed many conversations with Jimmy about their shared experiences, not only in the camps and in Berlin after the war, but also on their mutual quest for compensation for the misery they endured. Jimmy had to fight tooth and nail before eventually being awarded £1,192 in 1968 – the equivalent of only £25,000 today – for spending months under the threat of execution. After the publication of Jimmy's book, *Moonless Night*, in 1983, Stanley toyed with the idea of committing his own story to paper:

> *"When they [the publishers, William Kimber] learned that I too had been in another similar but far less exciting situation, they asked me to prepare my story for them to follow up. Somehow, I didn't think I had the story they wanted."*[250]

Stanley's story, therefore, did not find a publisher in Kimber. He did help, however, with two other books – *Destination Buchenwald* by Colin Burgess, with whom he held a series of enjoyable exchanges, and *168 Jump Into Hell*, for which he received equal billing with his long-time friend and fellow inmate Art Kinnis. He also, at his own expense, and with the help of the No. 1 AIDU (his old unit), published *The Royal Air Force in Buchenwald 1944* – a 300-page hard-backed 'dossier' designed as an historical record of his own and fellow inmates' experiences in the camp. Copies were presented to the CO of No. 1 AIDU and lodged with the Imperial War Museum, the RAF Museum Hendon, and the RAF Air Historical Branch. Dr Michael Fopp, Director of the RAF Museum, thanked Stanley for what he described as a deeply moving account: "I hope it will enable historians and researchers to document this infamous period of history well enough for the same mistakes not to happen again."[251]

Stanley was greatly pleased with the reaction to his book, and especially delighted to have his own copy signed by the former prime minister, Margaret Thatcher, who had been such an enthusiastic and encouraging supporter of his efforts to ensure the Allied prisoners in Buchenwald were properly remembered.

He was frustrated, however, when in 1994 the National Film Board in Canada broadcast a 50-minute documentary – The Lucky Ones: Allied Airmen and Buchenwald. It was billed as "moving testimony, interwoven with rare archive footage and photographs". Stanley was far from impressed; while he had been consulted in the early planning stages, he was not invited to Buchenwald to help liaise with the museum staff:

> *"It was a sorry episode, with emphasis being paid to the more dramatic events such as the shrunken heads and the tattooed skins made into lampshades, which we [were] never in a position to see. Perhaps even worse, from the harrowing bowels of the evil crematorium, being seen to make the grim*

eulogy of the hanging of the British agents from the wall hooks, [there was] no attempt to lay a few flowers on the nearby sad little memorial tablet to their memory, which didn't even appear in the film. [There was] plenty of ridiculous comment of the terror in the induction centre looking up at the ceiling to the water shower head, which we apparently 'dreaded was then going to spew out the deadly gas' when that was complete nonsense; nobody apart from a few senior intelligence chiefs knew anything about the dreaded gas chambers in the Polish camps – that was only revealed at the closing stages of the war after the Soviet forces had overrun them, long after we left. Buchenwald, like all the other Germany-located concentration camps, never had any gas chambers."[252]

Of his crew, Clifford Hallett died on 15 July 2013 peacefully at his home in Chard at the ripe old age of 90. After his repatriation, he had been posted from Bomber Command to air-sea rescue duties, which he wrote at the time "was much safer as regards fighters and flack [sic]".[253] Clifford returned to France with his second wife Dorothy in the spring of 1994 to retrace the route of his evasion and visit the house of Elie Thorossov where he had originally been given shelter. Elie celebrated his 100th birthday on 7 November 1987 and received a card from HM Queen Elizabeth II, thanks principally to the help provided to Clifford. Donations at Clifford's funeral were invited in support of the Escape Lines Memorial Society.

Terry Gould died at the desperately young age of 32 from heart failure and lung cancer. He had been hospitalised for some time after returning home, and later married and settled in Berkshire as a foreman butcher in a department store. He had been interviewed by his local paper in 1945 in which he claimed that when he was being looked after by the maquis, he joined them on one or two jobs, "doing bits of sabotage". He may well have done, or it could also have been – as Stanley suspected – a 'line shoot', but what did ring true was his memories of the camp: "The first three weeks was what they called quarantine. My opinion is that it was treatment to fetch out any weaknesses in us. We had no shelter at all. We slept in the open night and day. There were no bedding or blankets and no footwear. For punishment one was likely to be sent up to the 'museum' for a week. This was the laboratory where they treated human beings like Guinea pigs and inoculated them with loathsome diseases. People were dying all the time through lack of nourishment and typhus. The cremations of the dead took place every

Wednesday and Friday. We always knew the day because that day we had half rations of soup as they took our fuel for the crematorium."

Terry also told of one particular atrocity he witnessed: "One day a police officer who had collaborated with the Germans in Poland was brought into the camp. There were about 30 or 40 Poles there and they recognised and lynched him. He was soon dead."[254]

For several years, Stanley maintained a correspondence with Snooky Stokes. Snooky had endured months of treatment and years of pain for his smashed leg, and upon being repatriated had been sent immediately to the RAF hospital at Wroughton in Wiltshire. As well as top surgeons, Wroughton also had first-class psychiatric care, and Snooky often wrote to Stan about the impact their shared experience had had on his mental well-being. Snooky attempted to regain contact with Jack Osselton, but too much water had flowed under that particular bridge, and Snooky died in 1982 in Cornwall. As for Jack, he returned home to his parents and brothers and never spoke of his experiences, other than to his grandfather who had been in the trenches. Jack married Mary Phillips late in life and lived in Cambridge. He died in October 1999, shortly after he'd been reunited with his rescuer, Louis Godin, at the 50th anniversary celebrations for D-Day.

Stanley's only regret was that he never visited Sandy's mother and father after his return, neither did he contact the parents of 'Taffy' Williams. He suffered deeply from survivor's guilt but was always proud that he had returned to France in 1946 to find where the two men had been buried and been key in ensuring their burial site became an official Commonwealth war grave.

Death touched his own family in particularly tragic circumstances. In October 1999, his granddaughter Emma was diagnosed with a particularly aggressive type of cancer. Despite more than two years of treatment, some of it experimental chemo and radiotherapy, Emma died on 20 January 2002.

Stanley continued to keep himself busy. While he appreciated the efforts of those in the KLB Club, and became the de facto UK 'Mr Buchenwald', he was not well disposed to reunions. In the 1960s he had met up with one other survivor, Master Signaller Frank Peirson, while in Gibraltar, but they were two of only three out of the 48 Buchenwald RAF prisoners who had stayed in the service.[255] Ian Robb, a former 218 Squadron navigator shot down in August 1943, attempted a reunion, but there appeared little appetite from the British contingent: "They all had their personal reasons for not wanting to go back over those events," Stanley wrote.[256]

After being contacted by the oral histories department of the Imperial War Museum at the end of 2012, he gave more than 30 hours of interview to the researcher, Richard McDonough. The interviews were conducted over several months at his home in Bracknell. Stanley's wife would sit in the conservatory in tears while Stanley recounted his experiences. When a box of 32 CDs of the recordings arrived, Marjorie refused to have them in the house.

In deteriorating health, Marjorie wanted to move to a bungalow to be nearer to their eldest daughter, Pat, in Dorset, but Stanley refused to budge. He was not only attached to his garden, but also reluctant to leave the large pine that had grown from the sapling he had brought home from Buchenwald some 30 or so years earlier. Stanley would later come to regret that decision. Marjorie's health continued to fail, and she suffered a series of mini-strokes; with Stanley's reluctance to travel they became more reclusive and dependent on outside help. They took on a carer and a gardener and rarely left the house. Having been diagnosed with macular degeneration which required regular treatment, and with a fear of going blind, Stanley was forced to give up driving. Reading, writing and typing also became increasingly difficult, severing his contact with the outside world. Problems with his heart, compounded by high blood pressure, added to the challenge, softened only by the arrival of the first great-grandchild, Sennen, born to Pat's son Chris and his wife Jo in December 2007.

In the winter of 2014, Stanley lost his brother Leslie, and another link with the past. Les, ten years his junior, had been a constant support to his elder brother through the good times and the bad, and had been evacuated during the war to live with his aunt and uncle. It was only much later that the two men got to know one another better. Les had trained at RAF Halton as one of Trenchard's famous 'Brats' which gave them a common interest, and his passing brought a great sadness. The loss of his brother was followed soon after by the loss of his darling wife, Marjorie, who died on 18 November 2016, after succumbing to a major stroke.

Stan underwent bilateral knee replacements and remedial dental surgery, again all linked to his wartime troubles. Pat arranged for the newly formed veterans mental health team in Reading to pay Stan a visit, and after being assessed Stanley began to receive treatment for post-traumatic stress disorder – 75 years too late. It did, however, lead to an increase in payments for his wartime injuries, and it also provided Stanley with the first opportunity to properly reflect on his life and experiences – which had shaped not only his own life but also the lives of his children. As Pat wrote to Seb Cox, head of the Air Historical Branch of the RAF: "Children of the Buchenwald airmen are themselves traumatised by their fathers' experiences; the suppressed anger, PTSD and an obsessive search for the truth has impacted their lives."[257]

The arrival of twin great-granddaughters Ava and Isla in August 2018 to Pat's daughter Claire and her husband Kieran brought some light into the otherwise dark places to which his mind was still apt to travel. Meanwhile, Pat continued the fight for Stanley's compensation from the Ministry of Defence, writing to the then-Minister for Defence, People and Veterans, Johnny Mercer, in the summer of 2020. Her letter was passed to the defence people secretariat who advised that the MOD could "offer no remedy". Their response reads:

> *"You will appreciate that the alleged lack of credulity toward your father's story upon debrief, alleged lack of appropriate medical treatment and investigation, and any decision not to provide back pay for your father's period of being missing in action, are events which occurred some eight decades ago. It would not be appropriate with the benefit of hindsight to second guess the decisions taken contemporaneously with respect to your father. The rationale for this position is that those involved in an event are best able to judge the appropriateness or otherwise of the decisions and actions taken. I must advise that it would not be appropriate at this point to potentially second guess any determinations that were made at the time; there is a real risk of overriding decisions taken contemporaneously, by those who were in the best position to know all the facts and considerations involved."*

While the anonymous author of the letter from the defence people secretariat suggested that Stanley's loyal service to the RAF "remains appreciated by Her Majesty's Government and the nation", clearly there was a limit to how much appreciation they were willing to show![258]

When SSAFA, the armed forces charity, was preparing for the 75th anniversary of VE Day, a team came to visit, just before the Covid lockdown, and spent the whole day interviewing Stanley to capture his memories on film. With the lockdown came an upside in the guise of Gary Clarke, a former police officer, as Stanley's morning carer. Gary's knowledge of German helped Stanley in his continued quest to learn the truth about his captivity, and Gary, Stanley and Pat worked closely together on a special project – an online, virtual 75th anniversary of the liberation of Buchenwald.

Unwittingly, and perhaps more by dint of being a survivor, Stanley became something of a media celebrity in his later years, with features in the *Daily Mail* and *Sunday Express*, and regular contact with friends and families of aircrew whom Stanley had known during the war and not only in the camp. They included Suzanne Prescott, whose father had also been a navigator with the 'Shiny Ten', and Steve Williams, an enthusiastic amateur historian who became a regular visitor and friend. One of the most memorable visits came in April 2023, when Jean-Pierre Curato and his family came to Mudeford – where Stanley was now living in the Avon Reach Care Home (which he referred to as his 'hotel') – to help him celebrate his 101st birthday. Jean-Pierre had been instrumental in organising a permanent memorial to Stanley's crew in the village of Illiers-l'Évêque in October 2021, near to where Halifax MZ630 had crashed. He was a relative of Monsieur and Madame Porcher, the husband and wife who had sheltered Terry Gould. While Stanley was too unwell to attend in person, he was delighted to see representatives from the British, French and American military, among others, paying their respects. He was also honoured, two months later, to be awarded the *Chevalier de la Légion d'Honneur* by the government of France.

Stanley's achievements brought him to the attention of royalty. He had, of course, been to the Palace before to collect his MBE. In June 1989 he was a guest at a reception held at Clarence House at the request of Queen Elizabeth The Queen Mother to celebrate a visit by French members of *L'amicale de DORA* organised by the RAF Escaping Society.[259] In June 2022 he was disappointed to miss the opportunity of meeting Prince Charles at Windsor, having been admitted to hospital just a few days prior. He had bought a new suit and shoes for the occasion. He did, however, treasure the letter from Charles for his 100th birthday in which His Royal Highness said he was humbled to have learned of Stanley's suffering:

> *'It is a miracle that you survived such appalling conditions, and it can only be as a result of your astonishing courage and resilience that you have been able to endure, and to overcome, the kind of unspeakable difficulties that would have finished off most of us. During your lifetime you have set us all a shining example of fortitude and incredible bravery, which I admire profoundly, and which will never be forgotten by a most grateful nation.'*[260]

Charles also thanked Stanley for his positive reaction to a series of seven portraits the prince had commissioned in his capacity as patron of the Holocaust Memorial Day Trust. He said he was "touched" by Stanley's response and that he had commissioned the portraits "as a means of trying to ensure that their heartbreaking stories are never forgotten".[261]

The letter, along with a bottle of champagne from the Highgrove estate, were delivered in person by Major Jonny Thompson, the then-equerry to Charles and Camilla. It was one of the rare occasions where Stanley had allowed a small celebration to be organised for him, for such events were usually to be avoided.

Dozens of messages of congratulations and gifts were received from friends and well-wishers within the service, including a framed print of an Airbus Voyager from the officer commanding 10 Squadron, Wing Commander Tim Rushworth, and a similarly framed and signed print of a Lancaster from the Battle of Britain Memorial Flight. A note from the chief of the air staff, Sir Mike Wigston, said that Stanley's "courage and resilience" was an inspiration to all the men and women in the Royal Air Force.[262]

His centenary offered Stanley an opportunity to reflect on a full life, not quite fully lived. He thought of his three friends with whom he had shared so many adventures as a boy. All three had been killed in the war. He thought of their parents, and the pain and suffering that they endured and their resentment of him as the survivor. But mainly he thought of Buchenwald:

> *"I have experienced the best and worst of mankind; the generosity of a loving wife and family; the comradeship of fellow airmen during combat and imprisonment; the small kindnesses given by fellow prisoners incarcerated with me in the notorious Buchenwald concentration camp. I remember the bravery of members of the French Resistance who sheltered me after my Halifax bomber was shot down in June 1944 and the skills of my pilot and wireless operator, who were killed as they steadied the burning aircraft, enabling the rest of the crew to parachute to safety.*
>
> *"I was inspired by the leadership of Squadron Leader Phil Lamason RNZAF, who motivated 168 captured Allied airmen to find an inner strength to withstand the horrors and brutality of everyday life in KZ Buchenwald in 1944. He was a true hero and role model.*
>
> *"The bravery displayed by the SOE and other Allied special agents, who were murdered at Buchenwald in September and October 1944, has haunted*

me – it was a death sentence that I managed to escape by just two days. The discreet support by Captain Christopher Burney of F Section SOE during our incarceration, and his key role in our rescue by the Luftwaffe, enabled 166 Allied airmen to survive and be moved to Stalag Luft III.

"I have been betrayed by two double agents, the Belgian Jean-Jacques Desoubrie and the Cold War Soviet agent George Blake, whose treachery compromised our military intelligence work in Berlin.

"I have known fear, pain and abandonment during Gestapo interrogations and solitary confinement in Fresnes prison. This contrasts with my positive experiences during the Berlin airlift where the Allied air forces worked as a co-ordinated team to supply essential food and humanitarian aid to a starving German population.

"The Cold War provided interesting and dangerous challenges and when I was working in Gibraltar, the Cuba Crisis brought us to the brink of WW3. In 1965, I was honoured to be awarded an MBE by Her Majesty the Queen and in 2021, *Chevalier de la Légion d'Honneur* was bestowed on me by the government of France.

"In 1984, I returned with my wife to Buchenwald concentration camp to seek evidence which could prove that I had been a prisoner of the SS. The British government had denied that I had been in Fresnes prison and Buchenwald. Thanks to the archivist at the camp museum, the original Gestapo records were found which detailed the arrival of 168 Allied airmen on August 20 1944 and further documents provided the factual evidence that I had been seeking since 1945. We were invited to attend the 40th Anniversary of the liberation of Buchenwald which was very special.

"My life has been full of contrasts, and memories of family, friends and colleagues have sustained me over the years. I have been privileged to live a comfortable retirement where everyday things are valued: good food; clean sheets; warmth; my independence and the peace of my garden.

"These days I am supported by an excellent team of carers and medical staff, who enable me to live in my own home and I am enriched by memories of my late wife, Marjorie, whose love and affection provided comfort for 78 years.

"My belief and actions echo the words on the KZ Buchenwald memorial: 'It is the duty of the living, to honour the dead.'"[263]

Stanley's link with Buchenwald continued to feature right to the end. After becoming the oldest patient ever to have a pacemaker fitted, Stanley was imbued with a new sense of energy. He took great delight in making contact with Phil Lamason's family through the good auspices of his nephew Graham who was able to visit Phil's son and family in New Zealand. He was delighted to receive a visit from Martin Phelps, whose father had been with Stanley in the camp. He was also invited by Paul McCue to become an honorary veteran life friend of the Secret World War Two Learning Network. The network is an educational charity, of which Paul is an executive trustee, focused on creating greater public awareness of the contributions and experiences of those who took part in special operations, intelligence gathering and resistance.

On his 101st birthday, Stanley was especially pleased to receive a letter from Pierre Haché, a retired colonel in the Canadian Armed Forces. Pierre had met Graham at the memorial ceremony at Illiers-l'Évêque which he had attended in his official capacity as the defence attaché assigned to the Canadian embassy in Paris. Pierre wrote movingly about Stanley's endurance and incredible courage:

> *"You sir, represent the memory of all those whom you recall in your stories, all those you encountered, and most especially those who helped you, or whom you helped, whose suffering and bravery only you can claw back from historical obscurity. That sharing that you have done countless times ever since has helped perpetuate the memory of horrible events and acts that future generations must never forget. In spite of what is going on in the world today, you have moved the needle ever so slightly towards the horizon of peace."*[264]

He also received congratulations from his friends in France. These included letters from the Illiers-l'Évêque chapter of the *Amicales des Anciens Combattants* remembering the memorial day as being one of "happiness, smiles and special memories"[265] and a note from the village mayor, Joel Cloménil, honouring men, like Stanley, who had contributed so much to their liberation.[266]

Despite failing health, Stanley's memory seldom faltered, and he continued to enjoy listening to classical music and keeping abreast of current affairs. He maintained a satellite TV subscription that enabled him to watch German programmes and news channels, and he continued to maintain the highest standards in his appearance and in his generosity to friends and family.[267]

Stanley died on 26 January 2025, and a celebration of his life was held on 28 February at the Hinton Park Woodland Burial Ground. The moving service included eulogies from Kieran, Paul McCue, Steve Williams, his nephew Graham, and the author, and the reading of a poem ('He knows not Freedom') by his granddaughter Claire. The service was livestreamed and included a contribution from Jean-Pierre Curato from France. Keith Vinycomb, Stanley's son-in-law, read the dedication to the fallen and there was a haunting tribute to the death camps – Bach's Air on the G String played by Laura Heathcote – which ended suddenly and dramatically, mid-section, to symbolise the sudden and dramatic loss of life.

As much as being a time of sadness and reflection, the funeral was also one of celebration and even humour. One story recounted was of Stanley's meeting straight after the war with his former German-language teacher from school. When the teacher asked how Stanley had survived, Stanley simply replied "Abcochen". The teacher, whose family had been wiped out in the concentration camps, understood. With tears in his eyes, he nodded and added: "Booker – your German subjunctives were always poor, and nothing has changed."

On 28 March 2025, Pat received a letter of condolence from the former Prince – and now King – Charles. In it, His Royal Highness wrote:

> *"There is no doubt whatsoever that your father was an extraordinary man – one of remarkable courage and resilience – to whom we are all eternally indebted. My recent visit to Poland in January, to mark the 80th anniversary of the liberation of Auschwitz, served as a stark reminder of the unimaginable suffering endured by so many during the Second World War. It further reinforced my deepest admiration for those like your father whose immense bravery and resilience triumphed in the face of the most brutal dictatorship. I can only say that it is very much the end of a special era with his departure, and I very much hope you can find some comfort and solace in the incredible life he lived and the countless lives he touched. Your father's strength, sacrifice and heroism will never be forgotten."*

The author, in his eulogy, reflected on Stanley's remarkable ability to survive, echoing those thoughts later expressed by His Majesty. In a generation that produced some truly remarkable men and women, there were perhaps few, if any, more remarkable than Stanley Booker – airman, prisoner, saviour, spy.

APPENDIX A

THE 'TERRORFLIEGER' ORDER

The exact details regarding the infamous 'Terrorflieger' order are difficult to discern. The Bundesarchiv[268] refers to a talk given by Göring, the Luftwaffe chief, in Hitler's presence, probably on 20 May 1944, in which the Führer decided the following:

> *"Enemy airmen who are shot down shall be shot dead without court martial in the following cases:*
> 1. *If they have fired at our (German) airmen who have been shot down and are descending by parachute*
> 2. *If they have made an airborne attack on German aircraft which have made emergency landings and whose crew members are in the immediate vicinity*
> 3. *If they have attacked public transport trains*
> 4. *If they have made a low flying attack on individual civilians (farmers, workers, personal vehicles etc)".*

Airmen who are guilty of the above offences were thereafter referred to as Terrorfliegers. According to the written exchange of ideas between the relevant authorities, such airmen should be subject to popular lynch law or else receive 'special treatment' at the hands of the security service (i.e. be shot dead).

The German Foreign Office, however, was against the shooting of prisoners of war as it was contrary to international law and instead suggested, by letter of

20 June 1944, that enemy airmen suspected of such offences should not even be given the legal status of prisoners of war. As a result, such airmen were informed on capture that they were not regarded as prisoners of war but as criminals, and would thereafter not be handed over to the authorities responsible for prisoners of war but to the authorities responsible for prosecution.

If it later emerged, in the course of interrogation, that this special procedure was not applicable in an individual case the airman in question could then be given the legal status of prisoner of war by transferring him to the reception camp for airmen at Oberursel.

APPENDIX B

A GRANDFATHER REMEMBERED

IN YOUR DARKEST DAYS YOU never lost hope of tomorrow and family life – who would have thought that, from all that, we are all here now and blessed with your wisdom and kindness.

Grandad, you taught us to think bigger than ourselves, and to lead rather than follow. You showed us how strength can always be found, even when you have seen the worst of humanity. You taught us to be humble, to understand and accept we all make mistakes; we are all just trying to do our best.

You taught us there is beauty in the world to be enjoyed, especially in creating and sharing your peaceful garden. You taught us the importance of family gathering, that sharing of time and a meal are precious. You taught us to enjoy the simple things in life, like a good cup of tea. But, sometimes to indulge too in a tasty crab sandwich, real cream in your coffee and an extra-large slice of Granny's ever-so-boozy Christmas cake!

You loved the colour yellow, especially wearing it with a bow tie to bring light into your day. You shared joy and happiness through your tenderness to 'the bairns' – your great-grandchildren, Sennen, Ava and Isla. You taught us it is never too late to talk about your problems and how the road to solace is a journey, not a destination.

You taught us that tomorrow is always another day, and that by trusting yourself, and not to worry about the small things in life, great deeds can be accomplished.

Your kind and generous brother Les taught us: "one more thing today is one less thing tomorrow".

Your beautiful wife Marjorie taught us to see the best in people, and to love and care for your family. A wonderful woman, a heroine in her own right, never giving up on Stanley missing in Europe without any contact even after the war ended, rewarded with Stanley knocking on her family front door six weeks after VE Day. You showed us how we can all put others first, and not to forget those who are not with us today. Grandad, we are all so lucky to have had you in our lives – your strength, determination and kindness is an example to us all.

Heroes are in short supply these days, but you will forever be our James Bond, cherished in our hearts and your legacy.

By Claire and Kieran Vinycomb-Brown
(Stanley's granddaughter and Kieran, her husband).

NOTES

Unless specifically stated, all of Stanley's quotations are derived from recorded conversations with the author and/or Stanley's family, and previously published autobiographical material.

CHAPTER ONE

1 Eric Williams, Michael Codner and Oliver Philpot used a vaulting horse as cover to tunnel out of the camp.

2 This was not an exact science: a tour was based on a number of operational hours which typically equated to 30 operations and was often at the discretion of the squadron commander.

3 Stanley's service number was 591702. Of the two men either side of him, 701 (David Bond) was discharged from the RAF as a warrant officer in 1945, and 703 (Frederick Bray) became a pilot, and was shot down and killed on 24 August 1944. He was flying Wellingtons with 221 Squadron out of Malta.

4 Of the four boys, all went on to join the RAF, with all becoming aircrew. Only Stanley survived the war.

5 613 Squadron appendices in the NRA (AIR27/2118).

6 Among those flying with the squadron at the time was Paddy Barthropp, later a famed fighter pilot. In his autobiography *Paddy: Life and Times of Wing Commander Patrick Barthropp* (Howard Baker, 1986), he recalled a well-documented attack by six Hectors on German positions on 26 May 1940: "With two 120 lb bombs and machine gun firing through the propeller we approached France with devastating ferocity! One aircraft was lost, one was shot down by our own Navy, another force-landed on a golf course and the remainder returned to Hawkinge, holed and shaken but unharmed."

7 John Stephenson had been at Halton prior to pilot training and rising through the ranks. He had assumed command of 613 Squadron in July 1940. He retired as an air vice-marshal.

8 This appears little known, and yet there are several references within the 613 Squadron ORB to "gas spraying troops".

9 The two heroes were LAC Richard Farley and AC1 Thomas Coop.

10 Letter in Booker family archive.

11 The first three Tomahawks arrived on 24 August 1941 along with three Harvard training aircraft to help convert the pilots from the Lysander.

12 Stanley notes in his logbook that, before arriving at AOS, he had flown 25 hours of bombing and gunnery, and a further 375 hours as an air gunner, all in Lysanders.

13 See L. Ray Silver, *Last of the Gladiators: A World War II Bomber Navigator's Story* (Airlife, 1995), p. 91.

14 Ogilvie had won the DFC with 58 Squadron in August 1941 and added the Air Force Cross for his work in Training Command. He ended the war as commanding officer of 90 Squadron as Acting Wing Commander A. J. Ogilvie DSO, DFC, AFC.

15 The airfield at Riccall had been built in 1942 and opened at the end of the year as a satellite to RAF Marston Moor. Although officially open for business in December 1942, the Halifax conversion units of 76 and 78 Squadrons had moved in three months prior in September. The following month they formally merged to form 1658 Heavy Conversion Unit and soon after they were joined by 10 Conversion Flight from Melbourne, 102 Conversion Flight from Pocklington, and 158 Conversion Flight from Rufforth, bringing the establishment up to 32 Halifax aircraft. The officer commanding was Henry (Harry) Drummond AFC, DFM. Drummond, a former NCO, was an early exponent of the Halifax, winning the DFM in 1941 with 76 Squadron.

16 John Neville Osselton was born on 12 May 1923 and was one of four boys.

17 Now Zimbabwe.

18 In recounting this story on the website www.evasioncomete.be, Clifford says he was facing a panel of wing commanders who believed he was trying to mess them around: "They said they had a good mind to bung me in the army who were waiting outside for the LMF boys. [It was] a very near miss."

19 As remembered by Humphrey Phillips DFC in an interview with Sean Feast for Humphrey's book *A Thousand and One* (Mention the War, 2017).

20 Ibid. Humphrey Phillips had considerable experience of both types in operations and as an instructor.

21 Radford would later add the DSO to his medal tally and retired with the rank of air commodore. For four years between 1953 and 1957 he was ADC to HM Queen Elizabeth II. He died in 1984.

22 As it happens, 10 Squadron escaped quite lightly that night, with the loss of only a single aircraft.

23 Sandy flew his 'second dickie' with Flight Lieutenant E. Burgess on 9/10 April to the marshalling yards at Lille.

24 Maw was shortly after posted to command 640 Squadron. He was later killed in action. Jack Trobe ended the war with the DSO and DFC, the latter for bringing his heavily damaged bomber back from Düsseldorf after being attacked by four fighters. He died in 1986.

25 Martin Livesey was later lost with all of his crew on the night of 28/29 June 1944 on operations to Blainville.

26 Later DFC.

27 AIR50/180/223. The gunnery leader (in AIR50/298/151) observes that the pilot made a mistake by corkscrewing to port as he effectively turned away from the Dornier, thus making the shot much easier. In 4 Group, for the month of April 1944, 57 combats took place, of which 32 developed into attacks. Four enemy fighters were claimed as destroyed, two were probably destroyed, and two more were damaged.

28 AIR50/180/222. According to an intelligence report at the time, the Germans were using single-engine Focke-Wulfs and Messerschmitt Bf 109s, as well as twin-engined Bf 110s, Junkers 88s, Me 410s, and Dornier 217s.

29 The crew of Pilot Officer George Lassey. The second pilot in question was Kenneth Priske RCAF.

30 One of those attacked, Canadian John Hewitt, went on to win the DFC.

31 A 156 Squadron crew captained by Flight Lieutenant Henry Churchill DFC & Bar and a 405 Squadron Lancaster with Pilot Officer Robert Borrowes DFC at the controls. Churchill's crew included four other men who were decorated. Borrowes, a Canadian, had completed at least 44 trips.

32 Letter from Stanley to Marjorie dated 1 June 1944 in Booker family archive.

33 Letter from Stanley to Marjorie dated 2 June 1944 in Booker family archive.

CHAPTER TWO

34 MZ630 had only recently arrived on the squadron and was one of a batch of Halifaxes delivered between 24 April and 11 May 1944.

35 The official report suggests that damage was severe and widespread. At least 22 hits were scored on the electrified lines from Paris to Chartres, with six on a train of box wagons. More hits were also recorded on the sidings and coal bunkers, with anything up to 100 wagons destroyed: "Rolling stock was everywhere devastated". In terms of the scorecard, 16 aircraft of the attacking force were lost, most in the first 50 miles of the return route, while RAF bombers claimed nine enemy aircraft destroyed.

36 Fifteen bombers were shot down in the space of just 27 minutes, according to Theo Boyten's *Nachtjagd War Diaries* (Red Kite, 2008), p.62.

37 Referred to as Le Château de Saint-Georges-Motel.

38 The dog was called Flux.

39 Bergeron and 'Mr Dublin' (actually Dablin) were frequent visitors to Madame le Fèvre and Madame Orial. Both Francis and Maurice Dablin were notable Resistance fighters and both father and son have a street named after them in Dreux.

40 Airmen were issued with passport-sized photographs sewn into their battledress blouses for just such an eventuality.

41 Interestingly, his false identity papers gave his actual date of birth, presumably to avoid a simple slip up if challenged.

42 Jack's intelligence interview is in WO 208/3337. In it, he identifies the Resistance leader as 'Monsieur Dublin'. He also identifies Louis Gaudin [*sic*] and the family of Henri Hervé as giving him shelter.

43 Snooky remained in hospital for ten months, eventually being transferred to Stalag Luft I at Barth on 2 April 1945, from which he was liberated by the Russians the following month.

44 An official Luftwaffe report (KE: 8815) submitted to Luftwaffe HQ at Dreux on 3 June records the loss as being a Halifax from "10 Bomber Squadron", part of 4 Group, based at Melbourne, and coded 'S'. The names of all of the crew members are also listed.

45 Kumar's aircraft fell victim to a night fighter and all but the wireless operator were killed.

46 Letter from Gordon Culverhouse to his granddaughter dated 14 April 1999 via Gordon's son, Rob. Gordon had flown a different 'S' Sugar – Halifax LW716 – before she was damaged in an attack on Düsseldorf and replaced by MZ630. LW716 was repaired but finally lost on 4 November 1944.

47 Letter from Bessie Hall to Marjorie dated 4 June 1944 in Booker family archive.

48 Leslie Perfect MA joined the chaplain branch of the RAF in 1943 with the relative rank of squadron leader.

49 Letter dated 13 June 1944 in Booker family archive.

50 Pierre Juillet was later a leading French politician.

51 Letter from Stanley to Lieutenant Colonel Cocteau dated 16 April 1984 in Booker family archive. Lilly was often seen with 'Mr Dublin'.

52 A letter in the Booker family archive dated 3 March 1984 from Leslie Atkinson of the Air Forces Escape and Evasion Society asks Stanley to confirm the support given to him by Jean Gaspard. Gaspard's daughter was the socialist mayor of Dreux who lost her office in 1983 to a conservative alliance, and the letter hints at some skulduggery afoot, possibly to blacken the Gaspard family name.

53 Other names mentioned in Stanley and Jack's repatriation reports include Palmyra Martin and Marcelle Segui, though it is not completely clear what role they played.

54 As recounted in *The Longest Years: The Memoirs of Francis Dablin* (independently published, 2019).

55 The package is described as being 40 cm x 25 cm in an article entitled 'The Odyssey of Halifax MZ630S' by Jean-Pierre Curato.

56 The two Americans were Jim Hastin and George Scott – the former a P-51 Mustang pilot and the latter a gunner on an A-20 Havoc. Jim had not been brought down by flak but rather had strafed a pair of armoured cars which had exploded in front of him.

CHAPTER THREE

57 This information was all subsequently passed on to the German interrogators at Dulag Luft and used to convince captured aircrew that the Germans knew more about their lives than they did!

58 Blades were carried as part of aircrew escape gear, usually tucked into the top of their flying boots.

59 Stanley's possessions, such as they were, were listed as: dog tags; watch; fountain pen; rotary pen; briefcase; five francs; lighter; two books and a shaving kit. (Source: Gestapo receipt for personal effects on capture in the Booker family archive). In November 1989, Stanley wrote to the Embassy of the Federal Republic of Germany and the Ministry of Foreign Affairs citing the official 'restitution' policy and his right to claim compensation for "objects confiscated by the Third Reich". He was informed, however, that the window for compensation had long since been closed.

60 E. K. 'Peter' Phelps was the flight engineer in a 207 Squadron Lancaster. The squadron lost five of its aircraft that night. His comments are taken, via Martin Phelps, from a speech entitled 'A Youthful Experience'.

61 See www.historyhit.com.

62 There is some ambiguity regarding where Stanley was taken for interrogation. In one letter (10 April 1964) he claims it was in the Palais de Justice at the Gestapo HQ. This is not correct. The Gestapo HQ was at 11 rue des Saussaies, while 84 avenue Foch was the home of the SD – the SS counter-intelligence service. The rue des Saussaies location did have a courtyard as described by Stanley, the avenue Foch premises did not. The brutality of his treatment also suggests that it was the Gestapo at rue des Saussaies, rather than the SD, who interrogated and tortured Stanley. The sequence of Stanley's interrogations is also difficult to discern with 100 per cent accuracy, though it is known that he was tortured and assaulted on at least three separate occasions. It is believed his interrogators included *SS-Untersturmführer* Christian Schnell and *Oberleutnant* Kraus Brandstetter, the latter on the staff of Ic 3rd Luftlotte, Paris.

63 Many in the Gestapo were in uniform by then.

64 Press cutting in Booker family archive dated 4 June 1944.

CHAPTER FOUR

65 In his letter to Marjorie in the Booker family archive, Clifford thinks the airman in hospital must be Terry Gould, when in fact it is 'Snooky' Stokes.

66 This version of Clifford's escape was included in a letter from the Air Ministry to Marjorie dated 15 November 1944 in the Booker family archive. Stanley was never happy with Clifford's version of events, and in Stanley's opinion Clifford had jumped without checking on the rest of the crew. Hallett's evader's report in WO208/3337, however, says Clifford was told to jump by the flight engineer.

67 Research by Gerard Renault in the Booker family archive. Thorossov has also been spelled 'Thorrosov' and 'Thoroson' in various official documents and reports. One of Thorossov's three daughters was called Sirane, a name that Hallett would later give to one of his own children.

68 Parodi later became France's first ambassador to the United Nations (Source: *New York Times*, 16 May 1946).

69 Nordling continued in his attempts to stop the train as it continued on its journey, but once the convoy passed the German frontier all hopes of a reprieve were lost.

70 Other authors – including Oliver Clutton-Brock in his immense study *Footprints on the Sands of Time* (Grub Street, 2003) – believe this to have been Flying Officer Spierenburg. If so, the prisoners had no reason to be suspicious; Splinter Spierenburg was a highly accomplished Pathfinder pilot, flying with 582 Squadron. For more on Spierenburg, the reader is directed to the author's *Master Bombers* (Grub Street, 2008).

71 Flight Lieutenant Thomas Blackham, a Scot, was a pilot with 50 Squadron, shot down on the night of 3/4 May 1944 over Mailly-le-Camp. It was a bad night for Bomber Command and a bad night for 50 Squadron, which lost four aircraft in a single operation. Blackham had been awarded the DFC.

Mailly-le-Camp was his 26th operation. He stayed in the RAF after the war and retired as an air commodore.

72 E. K. 'Peter' Phelps, op. cit.

73 According to post-war records, a total of 2,453 prisoners, both male and female, were evacuated that morning from Fresnes prison; the remaining 532 were released three days later.

74 After the war it was learned that the evacuation had been hampered by a national rail strike which had given the German authorities problems obtaining a locomotive to take the assembled train on its passage to Germany.

75 Among those sharing Stanley's carriage were Art Kinnis and Tommy Blackham.

76 Stevenson was an American, shot down on the night of 4/5 July 1944 while flying with 419 Squadron. He arrived back in England on 4 September 1944.

77 From the wartime log of Flying Officer James Stewart. Stewart was a former Hawker Typhoon pilot, shot down by flak on 13 May 1944.

78 As recounted in *168 Jump Into Hell* (eds. Arthur G. Kinnis and Stanley Booker, privately published, 1999), p. 88.

79 Sergeant Andrew Rowe and Canadian air gunner Leon (Leo) Grenon. Rowe had been part of a crew shot down on the night of 7/8 June 1944. He gave a sworn affidavit as to the death of the young Frenchmen and his subsequent treatment on his return to Cosford. Grenon, an air gunner with 433 Squadron, had been shot down a few days earlier. There are multiple accounts of the shooting, some suggesting the boy was shot four times, and one – by an American sergeant – that claimed the body was buried by two Belgians. Tommy Blackham recalls the boy being shot in the back and twice in the head. Cyril Nuttall, a navigator with 158 Squadron, remembers the boy being shot and then shot again as he tried to crawl away. Harry Bastable of 640 Squadron says his request for aid for the boy was met with the guards "filling him full of lead". For the sake of this narrative, and given Andrew Rowe's obvious proximity to the event, I have taken his account as the benchmark.

80 Andrew Rowe's affidavit was sworn on 5 July 1945.

81 Phil Lamason was an extremely experienced Bomber Command pilot with 45 operations to his name. He had flown with both 218 and 15 Squadrons, and had been awarded the DFC and Bar.

82 E. K. 'Peter' Phelps, op. cit.

83 Not everyone remembers it this way. Cyril Nuttall recalls (in WO311/933) the glee with which some of the guards relieved him of his gold engagement ring and necklace.

84 From an article entitled 'The Odyssey of Halifax MZ630S' by Jean-Pierre Curato.

85 The 21-year-old daughter of Maurice and Fernande remembers him being taken away in a horse-drawn cart. Gould's escape-and-evasion report, however, suggests a bike was used (WO208/3340).

86 WO 208/3340.

87 As described in the liberation report of Wing Commander Yeo-Thomas.

88 Pister was executed on 28 September 1948. Ilse Koch escaped the hangman but was imprisoned for life, and later hanged herself on 1 September 1967 while in Aichach women's prison.

89 Letter to Colin Burgess dated 10 June 1986 in Booker family archive.

90 Hoffman was tried after the war by a general military court and, while cleared of the more serious offences, was jailed for five years. Source: document in the Jewish Virtual Library dated 18 November 1947, deputy judge advocate's office.

91 The real Kenneth Dodkin had been awarded the DFC while flying with 138 (Special Duties) Squadron in 1943.

92 Warren Barton interview with Phil Lamason, April 1999.

93 This story is recounted in Bruce Marshall's biography of Yeo-Thomas, *The White Rabbit* (Evans Brothers, 1952). In it, Marshall asserts that Yeo-Thomas and Phil Lamason immediately hit it off; Lamason's interview with Warren Barton suggests otherwise.

94 E. K. 'Peter' Phelps, op. cit.

95 Warren Barton interview with Phil Lamason, April 1999.

CHAPTER FIVE

96 The wartime log of Flying Officer James Stewart.

97 He was later convicted of war crimes and executed in May 1947.

98 Report number 6626 from His Majesty's Stationery Office.

99 It was of course known to the intelligence officers. In the interpretation report SA 2613 of 25 August 1944, Buchenwald concentration camp is clearly mentioned as being closely adjoined to the works.

100 The 14th flew reconnaissance missions in Europe from 12 August 1943 to 25 April 1945.

101 E. K. 'Peter' Phelps, op. cit.

102 Letter to Colin Burgess dated 5 May 1987 in Booker family archive.

103 The Channel Islanders in the camp at that time and recorded in Albert Kadler's official report (24 November 1944) were Gerald Bird, Alfred Baker, James Quick, Emil Dubois and S. G. Green.

104 The wartime log of Flying Officer James Stewart.

105 WO311/933, detailing ill-treatment of British nationals, given to the judge advocate general by Flying Officer Cyril Nuttall.

106 The camp's own prisoner record cards clearly give the date of death (*Verstorben*) of 12 September 1944. They also confirm the call to the tower on 9th.

107 Bruce Marshall, op. cit., p.196.

108 Some sources suggest the deaths had been ordered for 24 October, others 26 October. After the war, on 16 July 1945, Hermann Pister gave an account of the process regarding the execution of prisoners: "The Gestapo made an application for a death sentence enclosing a report of the facts addressed to the *Reichssicherheitshauptamt*, chief of Amt IV, who refused or approved it. It is unknown whether the chief of Amt IV had to ask for a decision of the chief of the *SS-Reichssicherheitshauptamt*, *SS-Obergruppenführer* and general of police, Dr Kaltenbrunner, or the *Reichsführer-SS* (Himmler). The concentration camps were merely the instrument of executions."

109 Warren Barton interview. A full account of Yeo-Thomas' activity before, during and after Buchenwald is given in *The White Rabbit* and a more recent (and more accurate) biography by respected historian Mark Seaman entitled *Bravest of the Brave* (Michael O'Mara Books, 1997).

110 Some documents seem to indicate that the Luftwaffe knew of the prisoners' existence while in Fresnes.

111 *168 Jump Into Hell* (eds. Arthur G. Kinnis and Stanley Booker), op. cit., p.92.

112 The wartime log of Flying Officer James Stewart.

113 In Frederic Martini's *Betrayed* (Rugged Land, 2017), he asserts that Trautloft was one of two high-ranking Luftwaffe officers seen in the camp, one of who was "tall and almost regal in his bearing", his grey uniform "adorned with countless ribbons and medals". He also "wore an Iron Cross at his throat". Substitute small details (the Iron Cross being the Knight's Cross of the Iron Cross for example), and Trautloft is almost perfectly described. Martini suggests a conversation was held in German, not English, by Sergeant Bernie Scharf. Other sources, most notably Colin Heaton in *The German Aces Speak Volume II*, suggest Trautloft had been on an authorised two-week inspection tour of facilities crucial to Luftwaffe supply in the area and had effectively stumbled across the camp *by chance*. This account is repeated in later books, and through repetition has become established as fact. It is known and documented that officers of the Luftwaffe appeared in the camp sometime in the middle of October, but no single source can agree a date. It is believed that Trautloft told Adolf Galland, his immediate boss, what he had found, and this was escalated to Galland's superior, Erhard Milch, and that Milch made good on a promise that he would do something about it. Trautloft then sent one of his officers to Buchenwald to oversee their transfer to a POW camp. While this is most likely true, the story itself was told to Colin Heaton second hand by Johannes Steinhoff, a fellow fighter pilot and close friend of Trautloft, rather than by Trautloft himself. The story was also in part confirmed by Trautloft's widow long after the war, but again repeating something she had been told rather than had witnessed for herself. A very full account of the Trautloft rescue mystery is given by Bernd Schmidt and the late Traugott Vitz in their book *The 168 Buchenwald Airmen and their Rescue* (privately published, 2025).

114 The British and Commonwealth airmen who had to be left behind for being too ill with pneumonia or pleurisy to travel were: H. D. Bastable RCAF J88378; J. R. Sonshine RCAF R14864; E. Carter-Edwards RCAF R1861108; and T. A. Malcolm RAAF AUS418755. They would later be taken by bus to Stalag Luft III, arriving on 28 November 1944.

115 Special Report given by Philip Lamason to Albert Kadler of the protecting power on 24 November 1944. The other airman to die was Levitt Beck, a P-47 Thunderbolt pilot.

116 Letter to Colin Burgess, 10 June 1986, in Booker family archive.

CHAPTER SIX

117 Testimony of First Lieutenant Ivan E. Moody. War Crimes Office, USA, 18 July 1945.

118 E. K. 'Peter' Phelps, op. cit.

119 Robert Key, *A Crowd is not Company* (Eyre & Spottiswoode, 1947). There were no gas chambers in Buchenwald, of course.

120 Ken Chapman's Kriegie diary.

121 Dean and Dawson was a famous travel agency.

122 *Kriegsgefangenenpost*, Christmas Day 1944, in Booker family archive.

123 It was reliably reported later that well over 20,000 intact Red Cross food parcels and millions of cigarettes had to be abandoned to the German servicemen following closely behind.

124 The American occupied compound had commenced their evacuation several hours earlier which included the 81 USAAF survivors of the original party.

125 Ken Chapman's Kriegie diary.

126 Sean Feast, *An Alien Sky* (Grub Street, 2015), p.75.

127 Ibid. p.75.

CHAPTER SEVEN

128 Wing Commander Alan Dowden. He'd won the DFC with 78 Squadron.

129 This aircraft can be seen, in its 'recovered' state, at the RAF Museum in Hendon.

130 Air Ministry correspondence, 14 June 1946, in Booker family archive.

131 Audio recording in Booker family archive.

132 Michael Wainwright flew with 64 Squadron throughout the Battle of Britain and was later awarded the AFC. He died in March 2015.

133 Peters signed Stanley's logbook.

134 Douglas 'Sammy' Hoare, formerly of 74 Squadron, shot down and captured in May 1940.

135 Stanley was posted from 62 Squadron to Dishforth on 25 May 1948 (AIR27/2427-11).

136 Keith Milton Davey was awarded the DFC for his service with 44 Squadron.

137 Squadron Leader P. J. S. Shaughnessy had been awarded the DFC while flying with 50 Squadron in 1940.

138 Friends of RAF Skellingthorpe website: www.no-50-and-no-61-squadrons-association.co.uk

139 See the US Office of the Historian, *History of the Berlin Airlift 1948–49*.

140 Ibid.

141 Vincent Orange, *Ensor's Endeavour* (Grub Street, 1994), p.129.

142 RAFHS seminar, 1989.

143 Mike Ensor was an exceptional pilot in Coastal Command who held the DSO & Bar, DFC & Bar and the AFC, and was credited with sinking two U-boats.

144 The Washington was the British name given to the Boeing B-29 Superfortress which entered service in the RAF in 1950 under the American military aid programme for Europe initiated as a result of the Cold War. It proved a worthy stopgap prior to the arrival of the V-bomber force.

145 Stanley went up in a Hastings (TG606) for the first time on 20 September 1949. The aircraft enjoyed a long and distinguished career, latterly with 24 Squadron.

146 Stanley had three commanding officers in his time on 99 Squadron: Squadron Leader S. E. 'Pat' Pattinson (a former bomber pilot with 207 Squadron); Squadron Leader William James AFC (who was posthumously awarded a King's Commendation for Valuable Service in the Air following his actions regarding an air crash in Benina in May 1951); and Wing Commander Brian Bennett. Bennett was the last to sign Stanley's logbook prior to his move into intelligence.

147 Nenes were sold to the Soviet Union on the naive understanding that they were not to be used for military purposes. Soviet engineers were also trained to repair and maintain the engines at the Rolls-Royce facility in Derby. It should come as little surprise to any student of Soviet history that the Russians reneged on the deal.

148 The receipt was signed by Stanley on 4 October 4 1951.

149 Pat Vinycomb in conversation with the author, October 2025.

CHAPTER EIGHT

150 Graham Booker remembers Prince receiving an electric shock on more than one occasion when rubbing his wet nose too close to the toy track!

151 Pat Vinycomb in conversation with the author, October 2025.

152 *Daily Telegraph* obituary, 7 December 2011.

153 Tony Geraghty, *Beyond the Front Line* (Harper Collins, 1996).

154 The refugee centre is now a museum.

155 Pat Vinycomb in conversation with the author, October 2025.

156 Ibid.

157 In 2006, it was claimed in the *Mail on Sunday* (26 March 2006) that Crabb had in fact been murdered by his own side because he was about to defect. A body was discovered with its head and hands removed, which his diving partner, Sydney Knowles, under the instruction of MI5, falsely identified as Crabb.

158 Also known as Templin, Gross Doelln was, at the time, one of the most advanced in airfield design, with living quarters separated from the airfield operations. During its time in Soviet/Russian hands, it was the largest military airfield in Europe.

159 Bears are expected to remain operational in the Russian air force until 2040.

160 Note by the JIC dated 22 December 1954 in PREM 11/1012. Papers within the file show the increasing urgency with which the British government wished to know about the mysterious 'goings on' at Gross Doelln.

161 According to the 'Abandoned, Forgotten and Little Known Airfields in Europe' website (www.forgottenairfields.com), the Beagles arrived in April 1955 and departed in September. MiG-17s, 19s and 21s from the 787th Fighter Regiment arrived soon after.

162 Operation Gold was in fact known by several different names. The British referred to it as Operation Stopwatch. It was also known as PBJOINTLY – the 'P' and the 'B' being taken by the respective British and American heads of station, Peter Lunn and Bill Harvey.

163 Operation Silver (also known as Operation Conflict). Peter Lunn had been head of the MI6 station in Vienna prior to his posting to Berlin. When US Defense Secretary George Marshall declared that all he wanted was "24 hours' notice of a Soviet attack", it may have been Lunn who suggested they repeat the same tunnel trick again. Whereas failure is an orphan, success tends to have many fathers, and the Americans maintain that the idea came from Bill Harvey, and that the tunnel was known colloquially as 'Harvey's Hole'. A third name, that of German spymaster Reinhard Gehlen, is also

in the frame, though a senior CIA official at the time (William Hood) said "some of the things his biographers credit him with are nonsense".

164 'The Tunnel Time Forgot' (Richard Nixon Foundation, May 2008).

165 Bill Harvey was a hard-drinking, hard-living chief who always carried a gun and achieved legendary status in the ranks of the CIA. He is credited with being among the first to identify Kim Philby as a traitor.

166 Declassified CIA report 'The Berlin Tunnel Operation 1952–56', released in 2019.

167 Three tunnels were built concurrently in Stalag Luft III and named Tom, Dick and Harry. Tom was discovered, and it was from Harry that the mass breakout was eventually made.

168 Declassified CIA report 'The Berlin Tunnel Operation 1952–56'.

169 Ibid.

170 Zhukov was one of Russia's greatest generals who oversaw some of the Red Army's most decisive victories, including the Battle of Berlin. Later a member of the Russian presidium, he lost favour in the years before and after Stalin's death and was forced to retire in 1957. He died in 1974.

171 It has been suggested that the decision was taken unilaterally by the deputy commandant of the Soviet Berlin garrison, Colonel Ivan Kotsyuba, while his boss was absent from the city. It was taken without the benefit of advice from Moscow.

172 The U-2 incident involved the shooting down on 1 May 1960 of a U-2 spy plane over Soviet territory and the subsequent capture, trial and imprisonment of the pilot, Gary Powers.

173 Declassified CIA report 'The Berlin Tunnel Operation 1952–56'.

174 *Boston Post*, 4 May 1956.

CHAPTER NINE

175 Flight Lieutenant Roger Read quoted in the *RAF Year Book* (1990).

176 The Valiant, Victor and Vulcan were collectively referred to as 'V' bombers.

177 Pat remembers this time as being almost idyllic: "This was probably the most relaxed time since 1951 for my parents, until the demands of Berlin called again and we mysteriously disappeared for the next few years."

178 Later Air Commodore John Bazalgette.

179 Letter from the War Office to Stanley, 17 January 1961, recalling him for special duties. Booker family archive.

180 The receipt is dated 7 July 1958 and refers to the Model 37 automatic pistol 7278 which he had originally received on 4 October 1951.

181 Booker family archive. The pass was issued on 18 February 1961.

182 Booker family archive.

183 David Stafford, in his book *Spies Beneath Berlin* (Overlook PR, 2003), supports the view that the KGB chose to protect Blake at the expense of letting Operation Gold develop as a successful operation. To that end the Soviets did not attempt to misinform the British or Americans for risk of their scheme being exposed, but rather allowed 'normal' communication channels to be maintained. Bill Harvey, the CIA's Berlin chief, was never satisfied that the tunnel was discovered by chance, and felt vindicated after Blake was exposed.

184 Marienborn was a major border crossing point from East to West.

185 See 'Building the Berlin Wall' article (NATO website)

186 While Stanley and what remained of Field Station Berlin appeared to have no notice of the Wall being built, the intelligence services had known of the plan for some time, and had been given the precise date for when construction would start by a source in the Socialist Unity Party.

187 See the US Office of the Historian, *History of the Berlin Airlift 1948–49*.

188 Loosely translated as 'scavenging'.

189 Soviet ELINT vessels at this time were converted trawlers.

190 Letter to Hugh Skillen, 1 November 1995, in Booker family archive.

191 From 'Seapower as a political instrument: the Soviet Navy in the Mediterranean' – a 1974 dissertation by John Broderick Chomeau, as cited in Jesse Lewis' book *The Strategic Balance in the Mediterranean* (American Enterprise Inst., 1976).

192 The Lockheed P-2 Neptune was an outstanding maritime and ASW aircraft developed for the US Navy and used by RAF Coastal Command on loan.

193 Letter to Hugh Skillen, 1 November 1995, in Booker family archive.

194 Air Commodore W. I. C. Inness CB OBE had been commanding officer of 9 Squadron in 1942 and been an air staff officer at Bomber Command. Earlier in his career as a flight cadet corporal at Cranwell he was obliged to bale out of a Bristol Bulldog when it went into an uncontrollable spin.

195 Letter dated 1 January 1965 in Booker family archive.

196 Stavangar airfield during the ill-fated Norwegian campaign of spring 1940.

197 No. 343 PSO Course between 8 March and 20 March 1970.

198 Stanley assumed command of the unit on 17 July 1971, *vice* Squadron Leader Richard Leviseur.

CHAPTER TEN

199 Airey Neave, *Saturday at MI9* (Hodder and Stoughton, 1969), p.306.

200 'Memorandum on the Betrayal of American Evaders' written by Major John F. White Jr of 6801 Mis-X Detachment, Military Intelligence Service, 17 August 1945.

201 As reported within *Information* published by the Association of Jewish Refugees in Great Britain, May 1964.

202 Letter of 10 April 1964 in Booker family archive.

203 Letter from Neave to Stanley, 21 April 1964, in Booker family archive.

204 Form A for use of surviving victims of Nazi persecution dated 4 November 1964 in Booker family archive.

205 Ibid.

206 MI(9)/S/P.G/LIB/1273.

207 Named after Sir Arthur Tedder, the certificates recognised the help given by citizens of a foreign country to British service personnel in avoiding/escaping German captivity. The awards were vetted and sanctioned by MI9.

208 A letter to Stanley dated 24 August 1983 from Bad Arolsen states: "Please be advised that the British Authorities are already in possession of proof of your detention from August 20, 1944 to October 19, 1944 in Concentration Camp Buchenwald. You will see this from enclosed copy of the Excerpt from Documents dated May 20, 1964, addressed to the British Embassy in Bonn."

209 Letter from Airey Neave, 2 November 1965, in Booker family archive.

210 79th Congress; 1st Session, 16 April 1945. Committee requested by Eisenhower through his chief of staff, George C. Marshall, to the Congress of the United States.

211 Copy in Booker family archive.

212 Letter from Miss A. Windham in the claims department of the Foreign Office, in Booker family archive.

213 Letter from Mr C. C. Jones of the Foreign Office in Booker family archive.

214 Letter from Mr C. W. M. Wilson of the Foreign Office, 15 March 1965, in Booker family archive.

215 Letter from Mr V. W. B. Slater, DHSS controller in Blackpool, 20 November 1973, in Booker family archive.

216 May 1983 edition.

217 Effective 21 November 1983.

218 This was in response to the DHSS's medical division's claim that the trauma would have had to have been much closer in time.

CHAPTER ELEVEN

219 Buchenwald was Special Camp Number Two.

220 Special Camp Number Two held 28,494 inmates between 1945 and its closure in 1950, of whom 7,113 are known to have died.

221 Trostorff was a former Buchenwald inmate who was betrayed to the Gestapo for supposedly spouting anti-Nazi sentiment which amounted to "subversive activities and pro-Soviet attitudes". He died in 2015.

222 The covers were subsequently printed to include reference to having been "carried from Fresnes Prison, Paris, to Buchenwald Concentration Camp, Weimar by Squadron Leader S. A. Booker, the journey he was forced to make on August 14–18, 1944. Then together with 1,650 French resistance patriots and 78 fellow members of the RAF captured by the Gestapo whilst evading capture in northern France." Unfortunately, the contents of the inserts contained many errors regarding spellings and dates, much to Stanley's annoyance. He had not been given the chance to check them. "It was completely unnecessary and spoiled its value in my eyes," he later wrote.

223 Of the balance, 30 of the original 168 were known to have died, leaving a further 54 to be traced.

CHAPTER TWELVE

224 Letter to Colin Burgess, 5 May 1987, in Booker family archive.

225 Letter in the *Daily Telegraph*, Friday 19 April 1985. Stanley described engaging with the media at any level as being "quite out of character!"

226 Letter from the director general of the CWGC in Booker family archive.

227 Six British, three Canadian, twelve French and three Belgian.

228 Letter from FCO in Booker family archive.

229 Letter from FCO, 27 September 1985, in Booker family archive.

230 Letter to 10 Downing Street, 20 April 1985, in Booker family archive.

231 Letter from 10 Downing Street, 12 May 1985, in Booker family archive.

232 Letter from FCO, 31 January 1990, in Booker family archive.

233 Letter to Stanley from Patrick Eyers, 17 April 1990, in Booker family archive.

234 The preview was on 14 May 1990; the exhibition was opened on 11 June 1990 in the presence of Dr Rudolf Hoeppner, vice president of the People's Chamber, GDR.

235 Baroness Golding. Her father, Ness Edwards MP, had been one of the parliamentary delegation to Buchenwald after its liberation.

236 The event organiser, Philip Rubenstein, wrote to Stanley on 10 May 1990 (letter in Booker family archive). Llin Golding was the Labour MP for Newcastle-under-Lyme. Her father was part of a delegation sent to Buchenwald immediately after its liberation in 1945.

237 Letter to Stanley, 15 June 1990, in Booker family archive.

238 Reunification Day is officially 3 October 1990.

239 *The Times*, 7 March 1990, 'Dark secrets of Buchenwald kept by Russians on the hill'.

240 Press release dated 15 September 1991, a copy of which is in the Booker family archive.

241 Letter to Max Hastings, 30 January 1995, in Booker family archive.

242 Article in the *New York Times*, 20 March 1991.

243 Correspondence between Wing Commander Peter Donlan and Flight Lieutenant M. J. Hollingworth at RAF Brüggen (cc'd to SB), 19 September 1996, and Stanley's follow-up to Donlan, 12 November 1996 – both in Booker family archive.

CHAPTER THIRTEEN

244 An American, Leonard Fink, and Timothy Hay of the RAF.

245 Visit of Picourt to HMC, 24 May 1946. Orsini had introduced Desoubrie to Picourt.

246 Letter from Mrs Emily Gould to Mrs Booker in Booker family archive, 31 October 1944.

247 Letter from Madame Orial to Stanley, 6 December 1944, in Booker family archive.

248 *Meldung über den Abschuss eines britischen Flugzeuges* (KE 8815).

249 Stanley's *Häftlings-Personal-Karte* within the Arolsen Archive clearly refers to him as a *Polizeihäftling* (police prisoner) sent to Buchenwald through the BDS Paris.

250 Letter to Victor Gammon of the RAF ex-POW association, 16 March 1989, in Booker family archive.

251 Letter of 2 November 1993 in Booker family archive.

252 Letter from Stanley to Wing Commander Peter Donlan, 12 November 1996, in Booker family archive. The technical advisor to the programme was Air Commodore Tommy Blackham, with whom Stanley had once shared a cattle truck and in Stanley's opinion "should have known better". It should be pointed out, however, that Stanley's statement is not quite right. Ravensbrück had one built in early 1945 and it was used for 5–6,000 murders. Sachsenhausen had one which was used. Dachau had one, but it was not used.

253 Letter to Marjorie Booker, 25 January 1945, in Booker family archive.

254 The cutting is undated but is in the Booker family archive along with a photograph of Terry.

255 Frank Peirson of 76 Squadron had been shot down on the night of 15/16 July 1944. He was a wireless operator and one of only three survivors in the crew.

256 Letter to Victor Gammon of the RAF ex-POW association, 16 March 1989, in Booker family archive.

257 Email to Seb Cox, 2 March 2022.

258 Letter of 25 June 2020 in Booker family archive.

259 The visit included a service at the RAF memorial at Runnymede to remember the fallen with no known graves.

260 Letter from Clarence House, 10 April 2022, in Booker family archive.

261 Ibid. The portraits are now part of the Royal Collection.

262 Letter from Air Chief Marshal Sir Mike Wigston KCB CBE ADC, 25 April 2022, in Booker family archive.

263 See www.secret-ww2.net.

264 Letter from Pierre Haché, 26 March 2023, in Booker family archive.

265 Letter from the *Amicale des Anciens Combattants* (undated) in Booker family archive.

266 Letter dated 17 April 2023 in Booker family archive.

267 Pat Vinycomb in conversation with the author, October 2025.

268 RW 4/v.700.

INDEX